T0330137

Asian Monetary Integration

Coping with a New Monetary Order after the Global Crisis

Woosik Moon and Yeongseop Rhee

Seoul National University
South Korea

Edward Elgar
Cheltenham, UK • Northampton, MA, USA

Published by
Edward Elgar Publishing Limited
The Lypiatts
15 Lansdown Road
Cheltenham
Glos GL50 2JA
UK

Edward Elgar Publishing, Inc.
William Pratt House
9 Dewey Court
Northampton
Massachusetts 01060
USA

A catalogue record for this book
is available from the British Library

Library of Congress Control Number: 2012935282

ISBN 978 1 84980 742 5

Typeset by Servis Filmsetting Ltd, Stockport, Cheshire
Printed and bound by MPG Books Group, UK

Contents

Preface

Regional monetary and financial cooperation is today one of the most debated issues in East Asia. When starting to write this book over ten years ago, right after the Asian crisis, there were two important motivations behind it. One was of course the outbreak of the Asian crisis. Unlike countries in Latin America or Eastern Europe, Asian countries had maintained robust economies, but met the same fate as these countries when the 1997 international financial crisis struck. It became necessary to reflect on why Asia had to suffer from the crisis and be condemned as a region of 'Asian sins' despite its sound economies. The truth is that the underlying causes of the Asian crisis were external as well as internal. Thus, it became clear that besides internal reforms, Asian countries needed to create a zone of monetary and financial stability, insulated from the extraneous influences of unstable capital flows. The other motivation for this book was the successful launch of the euro in 2002, which inspired hope that a similar initiative could be started in Asia.

Unfortunately, however, the progress of regional monetary integration in East Asia was slow. Since the launch of the Chiang Mai Initiative in 2000, there has been practically no major progress on East Asian monetary arrangements. This has diminished interest in this matter somewhat. Two main events helped revive enthusiasm for the book. The first was the global financial crisis and the new challenges it presented. This time the crisis originated not in Asia but in the US. Despite its non-Asian origin, however, Asian countries had to suffer again from the global crisis. It had now become quite clear that unless the risk of volatile capital flows is resolved, emerging Asian countries can again be victims of international financial crises at any time, and that they should prepare regional arrangements to protect themselves against unstable capital movements.

The other event was the rise of China, particularly since the 1990s. Until then, China had not yet equalled Japan economically, but it was thought that the emergence of China would be momentous and would gradually and significantly change the landscape of the political economy in Asia and eventually in the world. As China's economic influence widened in the region, the rivalry between China and Japan intensified. The struggle between the two leading countries would cause serious monetary and financial instability and damage the regional economies. This worrisome outlook also awakened awareness to the fact that Asian countries should prepare a collective monetary arrangement through which they can cooperate and avoid the detrimental effects of regional conflicts. China's conspicuous surge to a G2 country will also increase the fear of monetary instability in the region. This time the instability is due not to regional rivalry but to global rivalry between the US and China. As conflicts between the US and China have intensified rather than ameliorated, some even fear potential currency wars. Past experiences show that it is the volatility of global currencies that contributed to, if not caused, the volatility of small regional currencies: whenever currencies become more volatile, they increase the risk of triggering intraregional conflicts. This would definitely be undesirable both for China and for other Asian countries. Thus, regional exchange rate coordination is required to relieve the stresses and curb the influences on the region of the global conflicts between China and the US.

The core message in this book is simple: no country can survive in isolation from other countries in its region. No matter how big they are, it is not good policy for countries to isolate themselves, for their own sake as well as for the sake of their region, and countries must find a way to cooperate. In light of this fact, the authors' hope for the future of Asia is simple: the dream of a monetary union is remote, but if East Asian countries can share a common dream, it will be much easier to derive many cooperative policies to stabilize the regional economies and make the countries prosperous. Even the lowest level of policy cooperation would be very beneficial to all countries in the region. Critical is the cooperation between China, Japan and Korea.

There are so many people to whom the authors are much indebted for their help in the writing of this book. First we benefited from discussions with many people in the region who directly or indirectly were engaged in policymaking talks or negotiations. We thank Deok Ryong Yoon, our longtime colleague with whom we shared so many ideas and much research. We also thank In-June Kim, who has been our mentor for many years on issues of international finance. Without their continuous encouragement and support, this book would not have been completed. We are also grateful to many people in the Korean Ministry of Finance and Economy. Whenever we had the chance to work with them, they provided us with invaluable information. Outside Korea, we also thank Masahiro Kawai, Takatoshi Ito, Eiji Ogawa and Yongding Yu. The discussions with them at many international conferences helped us to understand how Japanese and Chinese scholars think on these issues.

Secondly, we thank two experts on European monetary integration,

Barry Eichengreen and Paul De Grauwe. Barry Eichengreen, whose various studies we have referred to and whom we have met on many occasions, widened our horizons on the subject with various, constructively critical points of view. Paul De Grauwe's famous book on European monetary integration stimulated us to undertake research on the subject.

Help from our students was also important in the completion of this book. Jinsil Kim and Min-lee Shin at the Seoul National University collected data and prepared many tables and figures. The Seoul National University Institute for Research in Finance and Economics provided us with financial support, which was helpful when finalizing the draft. We certainly thank Frank O'Callaghan for his excellent skills in correcting our English, and Edward Elgar for transforming our rough draft into a legible book.

Last but not least, our special thanks should go to our families. A book which took long years in the making is in a way a testimony to the endurance of our families who gladly withstood hardship and encouraged us throughout the whole process. We can never thank them enough for their support.

1. Introduction

1.1 PURPOSE AND SCOPE OF THE BOOK

East Asian economies have been growing rapidly and are likely to lead the world economy as the new locomotives, replacing the US and EU, two regions which are still suffering from the fallout from the global financial crisis. Greater economic openness and globalization are the key factors in the rise of the East Asian economy as a pole of economic growth. Despite this remarkable performance, however, East Asian economies are not immune from economic turbulence caused by global and regional financial crises. This has led many East Asian countries to search for collective remedial solutions and to intensify regional economic cooperation. Along with globalization, there is increasing regionalization in East Asia. East Asian economies are currently facing three challenges.

The first challenge is to construct a zone of sustained economic growth, amid the long and gradual decline of the US economy. The US has been the main East Asian export market and has played a dominant role in the 'East Asian miracle', headed by Japan and followed by the Asian tigers (Korea, Taiwan, Singapore and Hong Kong), then by the ASEAN economies, Malaysia, Thailand, Indonesia, and the Philippines, and finally by China. Compared to the past when the US absorbed more than half of East Asian countries' exports, however, the influence of the US on the East Asian economy has been declining rapidly and it currently absorbs only 15 per cent of East Asian countries' exports. Considering the recurring huge trade imbalances of the US economy, it is clear that the US will no longer be a main engine for the growth of the East Asian economy. The East Asian region itself will be a new pole of economic growth and this will lead East Asian economies to strengthen their economic ties among themselves and, in particular, with China. Increasing regional economic integration in East Asia will inevitably contribute to a significant reshaping of the global economic and monetary order.

The second challenge is to prevent financial crises and ensure economic stability. East Asian economies have an inherent weakness of being overly exposed to external shocks, because their growth is based on an export-oriented strategy. This weakness was demonstrated by two recent

financial crises. When the Asian financial crisis occurred in 1997, East
Asian countries recorded negative economic growth and experienced
severe social problems. This painful memory is still vivid in the minds of
many East Asians. For them, the crisis was triggered by a sudden outflow
of volatile short-term capital and the consequences were compounded by
the large sums owed to creditors and the inappropriate rescue policies
of the international organizations such as the IMF. This led to the first
strong awareness of the need for regional monetary and financial cooperation. In 2008, when the America-born global financial crisis spread
throughout the world, the region was again very severely stricken by
the crisis, experiencing a big drop in growth rates. The global financial
crisis shows that East Asian countries can suffer from a financial crisis
regardless of its origin, and that unless the risk of volatile capital flows
is resolved, they can be victims of an international financial crisis at any
time. To protect themselves from these recurring financial crises, many
East Asian countries made strenuous attempts to acquire resilient and
high-performing economic structures. Individual efforts are insufficient,
however, because no matter how well East Asian countries are internally
prepared, they are not strong enough to be able to stand alone against
global shocks in the globally-integrated world. Many commentators were
led to conclude that East Asian governments should take steps to create a
zone of monetary stability to insulate them better from these extraneous
influences.

The third challenge is the necessity to share the fruit of economic
growth and prosperity. A pessimistic view seems to prevail to-date in
relation to the possibility of regional cooperation in East Asia (e.g.
Eichengreen, 2002). The reason given is that East Asian economies are
too diverse and different in their degrees of development and income
levels. The wide income divergences, for instance, can generate political tensions among East Asian countries, leading to the isolation of the
economically-depressed regions or countries from the prosperous ones.
This will thwart all attempts to further regional economic integration
and construct a zone of monetary stability. Thus, East Asian countries
will have to endeavour to reduce the regional economic and social disparities that exist among them and thereby nurture regional cohesion and
solidarity.

This book attempts to examine how East Asian economies could establish their own zone of monetary stability. It is clear, however, that monetary stability cannot be addressed separately from the issues of economic
growth and solidarity. Without economic growth and solidarity, there
would be no purpose in pursuing monetary integration. All three challenges should be simultaneously addressed. Against this backdrop, this

book tries to address the issues of East Asian monetary integration in the broad framework of economic growth and solidarity.

Many proposals of varying scope and ambition for monetary and financial cooperation have been put forward both inside and outside the region. In particular, as the issue of East Asian monetary cooperation became urgent after the 1997 currency crisis, there have been many studies conducted in this regard (for instance, by Park and Wyplocz, 2010; Ito, 2009; Henning, 2002; and de Brouwer, 1999). Despite such an increase in interest, however, these studies were fragmentary and incomplete. They are not comprehensive enough to address all aspects of Asian monetary integration covering its history and future outlook. This book thus tries to seek, from a broader historical perspective, a feasible way for East Asian monetary and financial integration to occur that would fit well with the present and future circumstances of the region. Specifically, this book examines past East Asian monetary integration experiences, analyses and reviews the current conditions and ongoing efforts for monetary integration, and proposes some ideas towards achieving eventual Asian monetary union.

The main arguments of this book are as follows. First, the book emphasizes that history is important. In fact, monetary integration in East Asia is not unprecedented. Historically, East Asian countries belonged to a large natural monetary union linked by silver currencies, in particular the Spanish and Mexican silver dollars. This proves that East Asian monetary integration is not too unrealistic a project. Monetary integration can be realized, once the necessary economic and political preconditions are met.

Second, this book focuses on the endogeneity of the monetary integration process. As Frankel and Rose (1998) argued, the conditions required for monetary integration do not always exist at the beginning of the integration process, but may subsequently come into existence; that is higher monetary integration may improve the integration conditions, and in turn make regional countries more suitable for monetary integration. Thus, although the conditions for monetary integration are relatively unfavourable in East Asia compared to the EU, it does not necessarily mean that East Asia is less suitable for collective monetary arrangements, because those criteria evolve over time with the process of monetary integration. It is likely that the integration process itself will turn the region into an optimum currency area. Of course, there are many barriers to East Asian monetary integration which still persist. However, they are barriers that could be reduced with East Asian economic integration, depending upon how East Asian countries react in relation to a regional arrangement. Thus, the important issue is not how monetary integration will fit in with the current conditions but how to make the process move forward.

Third, this book reviews current efforts at East Asian monetary and financial integration. Although progress is rather slow, there have been some remarkable achievements. In particular, the multilateralization of the Chiang Mai Initiative (CMI) currency swap facility is one important step toward the creation of an Asian Monetary Fund (AMF). To evaluate these achievements and proposals properly, it would be helpful to compare the similarities and differences between East Asia and Europe. Clearly there are many European achievements that East Asia can emulate. The replication of the successful European Monetary System can be one such goal. Of course, East Asia is not Europe, and many people think that East Asian monetary integration will be very difficult to achieve. For instance, while the process of European integration deepens because of the highly interdependent structure of European economies, the push for an East Asian monetary and financial arrangement is less likely to do so because of the relatively lower degree of intraregional transactions among East Asian countries. Furthermore, while the process of European integration was propelled forward through the creation of strong supranational institutions, there are no equivalent institutions in East Asia because East Asian governments are reluctant to delegate power to supranational bodies (Eichengreen, 2002; Yoon, 1999). However, East Asia is changing and 'East Asia may be on the brink of a historical evolution' in integrationist thought and policy, not unlike that of Europe half a century ago (Bergsten, 2000).

Finally, the book highlights some challenges to be overcome if East Asian countries are to realize monetary and financial integration. As pointed out, East Asian economies face three challenges: economic growth, monetary stability and regional solidarity. This book emphasizes that monetary integration cannot be achieved without strengthening the other two pillars of integration. Thus, to realize a zone of monetary stability in East Asia, East Asian economies should first of all deepen their institutional cooperation structures in order to further their real regionalization and economic growth. Second and more importantly, East Asian economies should pay attention to regional cohesion, because the eventual goal of East Asian monetary integration should be to share in the prosperity of the region through establishing a zone of economic growth and monetary stability. Indeed, this lack of solidarity explains why the Japanese attempt to integrate Asian economies under the auspices of the yen bloc before and during the Second World War was bound to fail. Last, but not least, this book ends up by highlighting the importance of political leaders having vision and will, and of the existence of a regional identity as essential ingredients in framing a successful East Asian monetary integration.

1.2 ORGANIZATION OF THE BOOK

This book is divided into four parts, even though the individual parts are not specifically numbered. The first part consists of two chapters and introduces the historical experience of currency blocs in East Asia. Chapter 2 shows that silver currencies circulated as the main media of exchange in all parts of Asia, and that thus there was already a natural currency zone in East Asia with the silver dollar as a unit of account even before the nineteenth century. In contrast, Chapter 3 gives a case study of the past experience of monetary integration in East Asia, implemented by Japan from 1937–45. This experience suggests that when a leading country acts in a predatory, self-interested manner, regional economies disintegrate and the integration moves against the endogeneity process.

The second part consists of three chapters and addresses the background to the issue of monetary integration in East Asia. Chapter 4 provides an overview of the East Asian economy since the 1980s and identifies key factors that have changed its landscape. A clear understanding of the development of the East Asian economy is important in order to figure out how it has been transformed along with its rapid expansion and its severe crises. In Chapter 5, the suitability of conditions for monetary integration in East Asia is evaluated, basically in terms of countries' economic prospects, and it shows that despite some barriers, there are good reasons for promoting East Asian monetary integration on economic grounds. Chapter 6 explains what forces drive the necessity for a regional collective monetary arrangement in East Asia. The chapter highlights that monetary cooperation is needed not only to cope with external challenges but also to resolve internal problems in East Asian countries and conflicts among them.

The third part critically evaluates existing proposals regarding East Asian monetary and financial integration. Chapter 7 examines the main features of these proposals and compares their strong and weak points. When proposals are evaluated, particular focus is placed on two aspects: whether they fit the current status of the East Asian economy, and also, whether they fit the future path of monetary integration by promoting endogeneity. Chapter 8 changes the focus of interest from the monetary side to the financial side, and demonstrates how financial cooperation can be utilized as an alternative strategy for circumventing deadlocks in monetary and exchange rate cooperation and thus facilitating continuing regional cooperation. Chapter 9 explores the idea of a regional currency unit (RCU), what form it should take and how it should be utilized to promote regional monetary and financial integration.

Finally, the last part discusses the prospects for East Asian monetary integration and the barriers that need to be overcome to realize it. Chapter 10 provides some lessons for East Asian monetary integration, relying on the European experience. Considering the many barriers remaining, it is essential for East Asian to have a buffer period of an Asian Monetary System before moving to a Monetary Union. Chapter 11 ends the book with a discussion of what East Asian countries should do to overcome the barriers and to achieve successful monetary arrangements in the region.

2.   Silver and the origin of Asian currencies

When we look at the history of East Asia, we can find two interesting experiences of currency blocs in the region. One was a currency bloc linked by silver currencies, which was naturally formed by economic forces before the twentieth century. The other one was the yen bloc, implemented by Japan during the period 1937–45. These experiences provide very contrasting cases of how the process of monetary integration can be propelled to move forward or how the process can disintegrate. This chapter first looks at a natural currency zone in East Asia with the silver dollar as a unit of account before the twentieth century.

Asia was part of a large monetary union linked by silver currencies even before the nineteenth century. The silver dollars were supplied largely from the Americas and therefore Spanish and Mexican dollars were the most common units of account, with their standardized form and weight. They soon replaced the Chinese tael as the unit of account in the East Asian monetary system, and were given the name 'yuan' (according to Chinese pronunciation), 'yen' (Japanese) and 'won' (Korean). They circulated as the main media of exchange in all other parts of Asia. Thus, East Asia had already formed a natural currency zone with the silver dollar as a unit of account. These silver dollars were commodity monies, the value of the coins being determined by their intrinsic metallic value.

As the value of silver declined compared to that of gold, the value of Asian silver dollars had to decrease in relation to the gold standard currencies. Some Asian countries decided to adopt the gold standard. The silver dollars, however, continued to circulate for trade among Asian countries. Furthermore, as the silver dollars flowed more or less freely from one country to another and from one region to another, newly established nation states or colonies in Asia were incapable of controlling the amount of currency in circulation. They needed a national monetary system through which the amount of currency could be managed within their national or territorial borders. This led many Asian countries to adopt a national monetary system and thereby to substitute Mexican dollars for their national currencies. The emergence of these national monetary systems meant the end of the commodity money system based on the silver dollar because the value of the silver dollar was no longer determined by its absolute weight; the state guaranteed the value of national currencies. The Philippine peso, Indonesian gulden, Straits dollar, Thai baht, as well as the Japanese yen and Korean won were all created in this manner. The Chinese yuan finally took the same path, albeit belatedly in 1935. The circulation of paper currencies further contributed to the nationalization of Asian currencies and broke down the linkage between silver and paper currencies. This phenomenon was more or less universal after the First World War.

2.1 SILVER DOLLAR AS A GLOBAL CURRENCY

Well before the use of gold, silver played a pivotal role in integrating the world economy. The first world economy emerged from the sixteenth century. For instance, Findlay (1996) considers the year 1500 to be a decisive landmark in the creation of world a world economy due to the Voyages of Discovery that helped to construct the first global networks of trade. In contrast, Flynn and Giráldez (1995) date the origin of the world economy to 1571, when the city of Manila was founded, linking the trade of Europe, Asia and America. Although there is no consensus on the exact date for the creation of a world economy, it is clear that Europe, Asia and the newly discovered America were closely interconnected through trade from the sixteenth century. Asia exported spices, silk, tea and cotton, while America exported silver. Europe imported Indonesian spices, Chinese porcelain, silk and teas, and Indian cotton; these imports were largely paid for by Spanish silver. It has been a common argument that this world trade was dominated by European hegemony. Recent works by Findlay (1996) and Frank (1998), however, argue that Asia was at the centre of this world trade. For example, trying to overcome the Eurocentric view of the world economy, Frank writes: 'From a global perspective, Asia and not Europe held center stage for most of early modern history' (Frank, 1998, p.xv).

The most immediate consequence of this world trade system was 'the injection of large amounts of silver into the circuit of world trade' (Findlay and O'Rourke (2001, p.5). In particular the silver dollar served as the first important international currency to generate a global trade system in Europe, America and Asia (Flynn and Giráldez, 2002).

America was the main supplier of silver. With the discovery of large silver mines in Mexico and Peru, especially the enormous silver mines at Potosi, in what is now Bolivia, silver was exported to Spain, and the Spanish silver dollars became the international medium of exchange.[1] The Spanish dollars were circulated widely around the world. First they

Table 2.1　　*Annual bullion flows to Asia, 1601–1800 (tons of silver equivalent per year)*

	American Production	Asian Imports		
		Total	From Europe	Direct from America
1601–25	340	75	58	17
1626–50	395	85	69	16
1651–75	445	76	70	6
1676–1700	500	118	103	15
1701–25	550	150	135	15
1726–50	650	166	151	15
1751–75	820	166	151	15
1776–1800	940	144	124	20

Source:　Findlay and O'Rourke (2001); Barrett (1990).

were used in Britain's North American colonies and became the American unit of currency. The Spanish dollar coins were also circulated in Asia, particularly in China.

China was the end market for the world's silver for several centuries (Flynn and Giráldez, 2002, p.393). Silver in America reached Asia and China in two ways. First, tens of thousands of tons of silver passed through Europe and reached China via long-distance maritime and over-land trade routes. 'The Portuguese were the first Europeans who worked their way down the West African coast, rounded the Cape of Good Hope, crossed the Indian Ocean and established themselves in the Spice Islands of Indonesia and on the shore of the South China Sea' (Boxer, 1969, p.17). Second, silver reached China directly via the Pacific Ocean after the found-ing of the Spanish city of Manila in 1571. As Table 2.1 shows, around 15 tons of silver crossed the Pacific Ocean each year for most of the seven-teenth and eighteenth centuries. However, compared to the indirect export of American silver through Europe, the direct export of American silver was relatively insignificant.

Over this period there was a unity among Asian currencies based on the hegemony of the Spanish and Mexican silver dollars and, as F. King (1957) said, 'they were circulating throughout two American continents, in the West Indies, in the Pacific Islands and Japan, and in Asia from Siberia to the tip of Malaya'. These silver dollars were at the origin of most contemporary Asian currencies including the Chinese yuan, Japanese yen and Korean won. However, the dollar's wide acceptability started to wane

after the 1870s when a long decline of the price of silver in relation to gold
began, and Asia's trade turned toward the gold standard countries of
Europe (Drake, 2004, p.93).

2.2   HISTORY OF THE CHINESE YUAN

From the mid-sixteenth century, silver came to be widely used as money
in China. With the development of commerce and industry in China,
there was a general increase in the demand for a medium of exchange,
especially silver. In particular, the Chinese government (Ming dynasty)
attempted to collect all taxes (both in kind and in labour service) in silver,
as a part of the so-called Single Whip tax reform. This attempt made the
Chinese economy shift from a paper–metal money system to an official
bimetallic silver–copper system, enabling the Chinese government both
to collect taxes and make expenditures in silver. Chinese silver production, however, was insufficient. The purchasing power of silver increased
together with the relative price rise of silver to gold. Figure 2.1 shows that
silver remained overvalued in China vis-à-vis other countries, providing

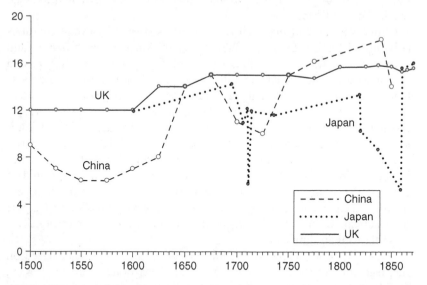

Sources: Data for China: Findlay and O'Rourke (2001); data for Japan: Shinjo (1962);
data for UK from 1700: officer and Williamson (2011).

*Figure 2.1   Gold–silver exchange ratios, 1500–1900 (units of silver per
                unit of gold)*

an opportunity for arbitrage profit to those who brought silver into China. In 1500, for instance, the price ratio of gold to silver was 9:1 in China, compared to 12:1 in Europe. It was not until 1650 that this ratio converged to the world ratio and that silver imports began to abate. By the beginning of the eighteenth century, however, another arbitrage phase emerged and this phase lasted until the mid-eighteenth century.

Silver flowed into China in a steady stream. In particular, the inflows of foreign silver and Western silver coins were officially made possible as the Chinese government abandoned its policy of banning foreign trade in the third quarter of the sixteenth century. Initially, Japan was China's main source of supply of foreign silver. After the late fifteenth century, silver production increased in Japan at a faster pace than in China. Hence, the purchasing power of silver dropped further in Japan than in China. As a consequence, the Japanese had an incentive to export silver to China in exchange for Chinese goods, sometimes by way of Korea, but more frequently directly from Japan. Once the Portuguese arrived, they became the most important intermediaries in this trade between Japan and China. The most important source of new silver in the long run was, however, the newly discovered America. American silver was first brought to China by the Portuguese in the early years of the sixteenth century. Then, in larger quantities than ever, it was brought in by the Spanish from Mexico and Peru by way of Manila from the latter part of the sixteenth century. Ultimately, large quantities of silver were brought in by the British and the Dutch. The British and the Dutch maintained a trade account surplus with Portugal and still more so with Spain; hence they obtained a great deal of silver from these countries, and could use it to buy large quantities of Chinese products such as tea, silk, wallpaper and porcelain.

In China, silver was circulated in Chinese-style ingots and broken piece forms whose weight was expressed in tael, referred to as 'liang' in Chinese. The tael's weight varied from place to place and thus the silver tael had to be weighed for each transaction and its purity assayed. Due to its inconvenience, the use of Chinese silver ingots became limited. In contrast, the imported foreign silver coins were standardized in form, weight and finesse, and were thus a convenient medium of exchange. In particular, Spanish and Mexican dollars were the most popular foreign silver coins used in China. The Spanish Carolus silver dollars, popularly known as the *peng-yang* (standard dollar) to the Chinese people, were introduced into China in the second half of the sixteenth century from the Philippine Islands. As China maintained a current account surplus vis-à-vis Europe, there was a massive influx of Carolus dollars throughout the country until the early nineteenth century. These dollars became the most popular unit of account in many coastal areas of China. For instance, these dollars were

Table 2.2   Forms and quantity of money in China, 1910 (unit: millions)

Forms of Money	Quantity	Value (in *yuan*)	Share (%)
Silver		1667	66.9
-Silver yuan coins	1320 yuan	1320	53.0
Chinese	240 yuan	240	
Foreign	1080 yuan	1080	
-Silver bullion	250 taels	347	13.9
Copper	700 000 pieces	522	21.0
Paper money		302	12.1
-Silver yuan notes	50 yuan	50	
-Silver tael notes	30 taels	42	
-Copper cash notes	134 strings	100	
-Foreign notes	110 yuan	110	
Total		2,491	100.0

Source: Hao (1986)

the standard coins in Canton until 1853 and in Shanghai until 1857. When the Spanish stopped minting these coins in the early 1840s, their monetary role was taken over by the Mexican dollar after the 1850s. Having become independent from Spain in 1821, Mexico started to mint silver dollars of its own from 1824. These were gradually known as the *ying-yang* (eagle dollars) and became the standard coin in Hong Kong as early as 1842 (Hao, 1986). These silver dollars were named 'yuan' and gradually established themselves as a unit of account in competition with the tael system.

From the nineteenth century, the yuan, the dollar unit of account, was in wider circulation. Foreign banks were established in China after the Opium War, and were issuing bank notes in yuan as well as in tael. Furthermore, public transactions such as tax collection were also denominated in yuan in some coastal areas. As a result, bank notes in yuan were issued first by various local government banks in the late nineteenth century and later by the Hubu Bank in 1906. However, paper money in China was relatively less popular.

The replacement of the tael by the yuan began in 1910. The imperial edict substituted the tael as the official unit of account, adopting the yuan coin of 0.72 *kuping liang* weight and 0.900 finesse as a standard silver currency. Table 2.2 shows the currency situation in China in 1910.

The tael, however, continued to be used throughout large parts of China. In particular, it remained as a unit of account for private transactions. It was only through the 1933 monetary reform that the tael was abolished completely and the Chinese currency was united on the basis of the yuan.

Finally China abandoned its historic silver standard in 1935, primarily because the American silver-buying policy drained away huge quantities of monetary reserves and caused severe deflation. This transition started with the creation of the Central Bank of China in 1928. Following the traditions of the Bank of England, this central bank had separate banking and issuing departments. Banknotes were to be backed by a reserve of 60 per cent in silver, gold coin or bullion, and 40 per cent in government bonds or commercial paper. These notes were in increasing circulation. However, this bank did not have a monopoly over the issuance of banknotes until 1937. The notes issued by the Central Bank of China along with those from other government banks were declared to be full legal tender notes, and as the use of silver as currency was forbidden, a managed currency system was adopted.

2.3 HISTORY OF THE JAPANESE YEN

Japan was the first country to set up its own monetary standard in Asia with the yen. At the beginning of the sixteenth century, a sharp increase in the production of silver in Japan allowed it to create a well-developed trade network with its neighbouring Asian countries. Silver production rose rapidly after 1530, causing a decline in the price of silver relative to gold and thereby leading to an outflow of silver from (and inflow of gold to) Japan. Japan exported large amounts of silver first to Korea around 1398 and then to China around 1490 (Kobata, 1965). After the arrival of Portuguese ships in Japan, the Portuguese acted as trade intermediaries between Japan and China. As shown in Figure 2.1, the Japanese gold–silver ratio remained far above that of China for about a century from the mid-sixteenth to the mid-seventeenth centuries. However, the technological limitations of the minting industry in Japan eventually led to a gradual decline in silver output from the mid-seventeenth century. Faced with the rising demand for money which accompanied rapid urbanization and commercialization, the Japanese economy had to adopt policies to restrain the export of silver. Japan adopted a seclusion policy (called the 'sakoku') in 1635 with a ban on foreign voyages, limiting its commercial relations with foreign countries to Korea, China and Holland only.

As silver production rose, silver came to be widely used in Japanese domestic circulation. The production of gold increased as well, and gold was used in the payment of tributes and taxes. Silver and gold coins were minted.[2] During the first period of the Tokugawa shogunate, this wide use of silver and gold coins led to the establishment of two authorized minting agents for gold and silver coins, Kinza and Ginza. While the eastern regions remained on the gold standard, the western regions, where virtually all foreign trade was conducted, shifted to the silver standard. With the spread of numerous silver and gold coins, there were different exchange rates between gold and silver, and numerous money changers. As these money changers were very keen on making a profit by manipulating the exchange rate between different coins; the debasement of coins and the changes in the relative price of gold and silver brought greater confusion and disorder to the monetary system in the later Tokugawa era.

Japan reopened its market in 1854 with the Treaty of Peace and Amity with the US. This treaty ended the long-maintained seclusion policy and led to the ratification of many other similar treaties with other Western powers. In such a situation, in 1858 the Tokugawa government permitted the export of Japanese gold and silver coins and the circulation of foreign currencies within Japanese territory. It also allowed for the exchange of foreign and Japanese coins in Japan.

Japan began its history as a modern, centralized nation when national rule was restored to the Japanese emperor from the shogun in the Meiji Restoration in 1868. One of the most important tasks facing the new Japanese government was to put the confusing monetary situation it inherited from the Tokugawa period in order. After the opening of trade with Western countries in particular, 'the fixing of a standard unit, silver or gold was a matter of urgency' (Shinjo, 1962). The Mexican dollar was by then the most important international money in East Asia. In February 1868, the Japanese government proclaimed the circulation of Mexican dollars throughout the country as lawful and fixed its exchange rate as equivalent to three Japanese silver coins (called 'bu-gin'). Then, in 1870, new coins denominated in yen, a new monetary unit with the same weight and purity as the Mexican dollar, were first minted. The value of the yen was only fixed to silver, in particular to the Mexican dollar, and was independent of the other gold or copper coins in existence.

In 1871, the New Coinage Act was enacted to change the monetary standard from silver to gold. It declared that the 1 yen gold coin should be the new standard money, while all silver coins were to be auxiliaries. The value of the new 1 yen gold coin contained 1.5 grams of fine gold. Although the new yen was defined on the basis of the gold standard, silver coins continued to be recognized as a standard because the silver 1 yen (known as the trade dollar) was circulated as a foreign trade currency. Finally after 1875, the government abandoned the single gold standard and allowed the unlimited circulation of the silver 1 yen coin. Thus, at this time the monetary system of Japan converted the bimetallic gold and silver standard.

Faced with increasing financial difficulties, the Meiji government also issued a large amount of government paper notes denominated in yen. Furthermore, with the adoption of the National Banking Law in 1872,

Table 2.3   Money in circulation in Japan, 1897

Forms of currency	Value ('000 yen)	Share (%)
Metallic currency	149 746	38.5
-Gold coins	79 990	
-1 yen silver coins	31 049	
-Auxiliary silver coins	29 356	
-Copper coins	9351	
Paper currency	238 706	61.5
-Government paper notes	7451	
-National banknotes	5025	
-Bank of Japan convertible notes	226 229	
Sum	388 452	100.0

Source: Shinjo (1962).

convertible national banknotes were newly introduced. But their convertibility could not be guaranteed due to the shortage of specie reserve. In 1882, the new Minister of Finance, Matsukata, was determined to resume specie payments in silver at the earliest opportunity. To carry out this plan, he adopted three measures: first, the gradual reduction of the paper currency and the accumulation of a sufficient reserve specie; second, the gradual diminution of national banknotes and the final abolition of all issuing power for these banks; third, the establishment of a central bank that was designed to gain control over the note issuance of the whole country. As a result, the Bank of Japan was established and its notes were issued. These notes were guaranteed to be payable in silver on demand, and the Bank of Japan had to hold a sufficient amount of silver for the notes issued.

Finally in 1897, following the example of major Western countries, Japan adopted the gold standard and enacted the Coinage Act in 1897, which stipulated that 1 yen was equal to 0.75g of gold. The Bank of Japan notes were re-established as convertible into gold instead of silver.[3] The banknotes issued by the Bank of Japan became the sole standard form of paper money when the circulation of all other government notes and national banknotes was banned two years later. By 1897, paper currency already accounted for 61 per cent of the currency in circulation in Japan (see Table 2.3).

2.4   HISTORY OF THE KOREAN WON

In 1876, Korea had a treaty of amity with Japan and gave up its centuries-long seclusion policy banning foreign trade. In the early days of opening up its ports, Korea's currency system was very confused. Until then, Korea had adopted the copper standard, and the Korean money in circulation was in the form of copper coins, similar in its shape to the Chinese ones. Most of these copper coins, however, were of no standard value and of poor quality. In addition, there was an excess coinage of copper coins, with old coins circulating alongside new ones. With increasing economic and trade relations, however, there emerged a strong need for silver money, because the copper coins could not be used directly as a medium of exchange for trade with foreign countries, especially with Japan.

To cope with this situation, the imperial Korean government decided to mint silver coins. In 1883, the first modern Government Mint was established, and in subsequent years it minted some silver coins, including a 1 dollar silver coin called the won (or hwan). However, shortly afterwards, it ceased mintage.

Finally, in 1894, the Imperial Korean government promulgated a Coinage Act, adopting silver as the standard currency. New coins in silver taels (called yang) were minted. In particular, the 5 yang silver coin was minted as the standard unit, together with the 1 yang silver coin. It is interesting to note that 'yang' in Korean was the same unit of account as 'liang' in Chinese and 'ryo' in Japanese. While the 1 yang coin was designed to circulate only in the domestic markets, the 5 yang coin was intended to be used for collecting tariffs and taxes from foreigners and thus facilitating trade. The 5 yang coin was equal in value to 1 silver yen or 1 Mexican dollar. Also, foreign coins equal in their quantity, quality and value to the 5 yang coin, such as the Japanese silver 1 yen and Mexican dollar, were legally allowed to be circulated within Korea.

Although the Coinage Act of 1894 was an important step in reforming the monetary system in Korea, its impact was by no means significant. The reason is that the silver coins were only issued in small amounts, as the real reserve assets such as gold and silver were in short supply and the expected seigniorage turned out to be far smaller. The shortage of standard currency 5 yang silver coin led to the inflow of foreign silver currencies into Korea. In particular, large amounts of Japanese and Mexican silver dollars were used as the chief medium of settlement in trade. There were also Russian roubles, but their circulation was limited to the Northern provinces. Soon, the Japanese silver yen drove out the Mexican dollar and remained dominant in the Korean economy.

From 1894 to 1900, the won started to be used in the public sector, though the yang still remained as the standard unit of account in private sector transactions. In 1901, the Korean government decided to shift to the gold standard from the silver standard.[4] The won became an official unit of account, with 1 won equal in value to 0.75g of pure gold.

BOX 2.1   OLD AND NEW CURRENCY SYSTEMS IN CHINA, JAPAN AND KOREA

In China, Japan and Korea, people used silver traditionally by weight expressed in tael, which was referred usually as 'liang' in Chinese, 'ryo' in Japanese and 'yang' in Korean. The word 'tael' is not Chinese, and derives from the Malayan 'tahil' or the Indian 'tola'. The chief form of tael silver was the ingot of about 50 taels. These were often called 'shoes' because they resembled the shoes of women with bound feet. The ingots were made by a few trustworthy private smelting firms and bore their chop mark certifying the content (see Young, 1971, p.183). The tael was a unit of account (often translated as a Chinese ounce of silver) and never really circulated as a coin, although there were some instances of tael coinage. The tael's weight varied from place to place, in the approximate range of 500 to 600 grains. Due to its inconvenience, however, the use of Chinese silver tael became limited. The imported foreign silver dollars became a convenient medium of exchange because they were standardized in their form, weight and finesse. Thus, the dollar replaced the tael as the unit of account in the Asian monetary system; it was given the name 'yuan' in Chinese, 'yen' in Japanese and 'won' in Korean, meaning 'circle' (see Table 2.4). In contrast to Western coins, traditional East Asian coins all had a rectangular hole in the centre.

Figure 2.2 shows the values of the Chinese yuan, Japanese yen and Korean won in terms of the US dollar. Because they were all based on the Mexican dollar, their values were almost identical. Some small divergence between the values of the yuan and the yen, however, became more frequent in the twentieth century, although the Korean won was always at par with the Japanese yen. Against this backdrop, a famous Korean general,

Table 2.4   Currency unit in three East Asian countries

	China	Japan	Korea
Traditional unit	Tael (liang)	Tael (ryo)	Tael (yang)
New unit	Dollar (yuan)	Dollar (yen)	Dollar (won, hwan)

Note: The word in parentheses indicates the pronunciation in each national language.

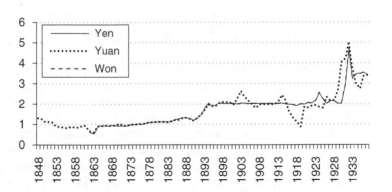

Note: The exchange rate of the yuan before 1862 was converted from the liang exchange rate.

Figure 2.2   Exchange rate trend of the yuan, yen and won vis-à-vis the US dollar

J.G. Ahn, argued for a common currency in Asia in his unfinished book *For Oriental Peace* (1905). According to him, China, Japan and Korea need a common currency, common bank and common army, to establish a permanent peace in Asia. It is also important to note that the yuan and the yen remained at par with the US dollar within a small margin of fluctuation until 1875 when the value of the US dollar was based on the value of silver. However, they started to deviate from each other thereafter. By 1900, for instance, Asian silver dollars fell to 50 cents in relation to the US dollar, as the US moved to a de facto gold standard after the Coinage Act in 1873.

Paper currencies also circulated in Korea. These were largely Chinese and Japanese paper currencies. In 1902, the Dai-Ichi Bank (The First National Bank of Japan), which handled the Korean government's custom duties, obtained permission from the imperial Korean government to issue banknotes, and issued three denominations of banknotes in yen (1, 5 and 10 yen), convertible with the Japanese currency, fixing the total amount of issue at 1.3 million yen. It is important to note that at that time the Korean won was at par with the Japanese yen. Finally, the Bank of Korea was established in 1909 as the central bank of Korea, taking over the issuing function of the Dai-Ichi Bank. It issued banknotes in won, heralding the era of the won in Korea.

2.5   MONETARY STANDARDS IN SOUTH-EAST ASIA

As in other parts of Asia, the silver dollar was common currency through-out South-East Asia. Until the emergence of national currencies in the late nineteenth or early twentieth century, there were a variety of silver dollars used in South-East Asia, including Spanish and Mexican silver dollars. Drake (2004) describes the history of South-East Asian currencies: 'These various silver dollars were "unified" by the practices of acceptance and con-versions by weight of silver. In particular, the Mexican dollar was numer-aire and other silver dollars were fixed against it with values according to their respective weight and known finesse of silver' (Drake, 2004, p.94).

In the Philippines, the Spanish and Mexican dollar remained as the main circulating medium from the early sixteenth century. With the estab-lishment of Manila in 1571, the silver dollar, commonly known across the Spanish empire as the peso, was first introduced to the Philippine Islands by the Spanish. After this, many other silver coins, including the Mexican dollar, were imported at different periods of time. The monetary situation in the Philippines, however, was chaotic because these coins differed in their purity and weight. An attempt was made to standardize the currency, with the firm establishment of the silver standard as the Philippines mon-etary system. The new coin, known as the Spanish–Philippine peso, was minted in 1897 and remained legal tender until 1904 when the US took control of the Philippines. Finally, the US passed the Philippine Coinage Act and minted the American Philippine peso again. Seeking to replace the Mexican dollar with the newly minted peso, the US fixed the value of the new peso at a value slightly inferior to that of the Mexican dollar: its value was defined at exactly half the gold content of the US dollar. The Mexican dollar was then demonetized.

Similarly, in Malaysia and Singapore, many different silver coins were in circulation (such as the East India Company dollars, British Trade dollars, American Trade dollars, Indian rupees and even Japanese yen, as well as Spanish and Mexican dollars) but the Spanish and Mexican dollars were the most common units of account. In 1835, the government of British India tried to make the Indian rupee the sole legal tender in the Straits Settlements because they were administratively part of India. However, faced with wide resistance from the public, the British Indian government soon had to resume the use of the Spanish and Mexican dollars in all transactions in the Straits Settlements. When the Straits Settlements became a British colony in 1867, Spanish and Mexican dollars gained exclusive legal tender status, and later other silver dollars such as the British Trade dollars, American Trade dollars and Japanese

yen were added to the list of legal tenders. The Straits Settlements and
Malaya States thus had a dollar unit of account and various legal tender
silver coins, with the Mexican silver dollar as the standard. However,
there was no standard silver dollar minted by the government of the
Straits Settlements. Furthermore, there was a perennial shortage of currency. For these reasons, the Straits Settlements' government established
the Currency Board and issued dollar notes in 1899. It is interesting to
note that until then, the dollar notes were relatively unimportant forms
of money in these regions. The result was the creation of the silver Straits
dollar coins in 1903, which replaced the Mexican dollar as a standard
unit of account for trade in the Straits Settlements and South-East Asia.
The Straits dollar was replaced by the Malayan dollar later in 1939.
Both the current Singapore dollar and the Malaysian ringgit emerged
from the Malayan dollar along with the independence of Singapore from
Malaysia.

In Indonesia, there was an expansion of trade during the sixteenth and
seventeenth centuries, which helped to greatly enlarge the circulation
of money throughout the archipelago. Silver and copper were in short
supply. From the sixteenth century, however, there was a large influx of
silver from Spanish America, transported by galleons heading for Manila
and Japan. Dutch money circulated as well, as Indonesia became the
Dutch East Indies in 1610. A variety of Dutch, Spanish and Asian coins
were in official and common usage. At the end of the eighteenth century,
the Dutch East Indies issued its silver guilder (or 'gulden' in Dutch), which
was at par with the Dutch guilder, and these coins, together with fractional
silver and copper coins, circulated until Indonesian independence in 1945.
Banknotes were also issued. In particular, De Javasche Bank was established in 1828 and issued its first banknotes in denominations of 25 to 1000
gulden, totalling 1.12 million gulden notes. During the period of 1951–53,
De Javasche Bank was nationalized and was renamed 'Bank Indonesia'.
Bank Indonesia issued rupiah notes in 1952, replacing the gulden notes.

In Thailand, 'baht' or 'tical'[5] refers to a unit of weight as well as the unit
of currency. During the latter part of the nineteenth century, Thailand was
on the silver standard. Initially, Thailand's currency consisted of bullet-
shaped lumps of silver known as baht, but due to the increase in foreign
trade, foreign silver coins circulated as well. In particular, silver dollars
circulated freely in the south of Thailand, while silver rupees circulated
in the north, reflecting trade with British Malaya and India respectively.
Soon they became legal tender and their exchange value was fixed at 5
bahts for 3 dollars, with the Mexican dollar being the most commonly
used silver dollar. This exchange rate remained unchanged throughout
the nineteenth century. Foreign banks were also established primarily to

finance increasing foreign trade and to deal with foreign exchange. They were authorized to issue convertible banknotes but the circulation of such notes was very limited (Ingram, 1971, p.150). However, the continuing fall in the price of silver in relation to gold and the consequent depreciation of the Thai baht after 1870 disrupted the Thai economy, which led the Thai government to break the link with silver and to adopt the gold-exchange standard in 1902, pegging the baht to the British pound. During World War II, the baht was again fixed at par with the Japanese yen.

NOTES

1. The genesis of the silver dollar goes back to the minting of the silver thaler in Bohemia, which is now part of the Czech Republic. Then the name was applied to similar coins minted in Central Europe. Its name was soon extended to the Spanish and Portuguese coins because these silver coins were identical in weight and finesse to the thaler (Davis, 2002, p.720).
2. There were three types of gold coins minted (keicho-oban-kin, keicho-koban-kin and ichibu-ban-kin), and two types of silver coins (cho-gin and mameita-gin) (see Shinjo, 1962).
3. It is noteworthy that the gold reserve required for the convertibility of Bank of Japan notes was replenished by the Reparation Fund (equalling 230 million taels), paid in gold by the Chinese government after its defeat in the first Sino-Japanese War of 1894–5.
4. This reform was carried out with the strong support of Russia, which started to increase its influence over Korea, defying Japan, and as a result included a measure to prevent the circulation of the Japanese silver yen which played the role of the standard currency in Korean trade.
5. The Thai currency was originally known as 'tical', the name being used in English texts until 1925, while the word 'baht' for Thai currency was established by the nineteenth century.

3. Destined to fail? The history of the yen bloc before the Second World War

For closer monetary and financial cooperation to occur, leading countries need to assume corresponding responsibilities because the viability of a monetary union depends on their responsible actions to boost regional solidarity and cohesion. The past experience of the yen bloc shows that Imperial Japan's absence of such responsibilities was the main cause for the failure of the so-called 'Asian Co-prosperity Sphere'. Indeed, unlike the experience of the silver currency bloc in the nineteenth century, the formation of the yen bloc by Japan did not result in the economic and monetary integration of East Asian economies. Rather, it led to the increasing disintegration of the East Asian economy, refuting the endogeneity of the optimum currency area criteria. This is demonstrated by the fact that the gap in the inflation rate and income level between Japan and other East Asian countries widened during the Japanese occupation period. This experience was frustrating for Asian countries, for it meant that the regionalization which centred on the Japanese yen was for the prosperity of Japan only, and not for the co-prosperity of the Asian region as a whole. The yen bloc era is still deeply relevant. Its memory still haunts East Asian countries to this day, nourishing their distrust of Japan, and throws a shadow on the monetary and trade cooperation movements in East Asia. This explains why ideas about regional monetary cooperation were rarely heard of until the eruption of the Asian currency crises.

3.1 THE FORMATION OF THE YEN BLOC

The yen bloc's[1] origins lie in the worldwide trend of regionalization during the Great Depression. As a response to the regionalization, Japan intended to create its own autarkic bloc devoid of Western influence. This idea gained momentum with the start of the Sino-Japanese War in 1937. As the war soon escalated into the Pacific War, Japan proposed the so-called 'Greater East Asia Co-prosperity Sphere', with the yen bloc as the basic principle regarding money and finance in East Asia. More precisely, the Japanese attempted

> to divide the occupied regions into a number of appropriate districts in con-
> formity with the administrative systems, and to let each district have its own
> system of note issuing central banks, the currencies issued by such institution
> being the only legal tenders of the respective districts and their value standards
> based on the Japanese yen. (*The Oriental Economist*, 1942)

What Japan tried to accomplish through the yen bloc was the imposition of its own political and economic order on the other East Asian countries. Naturally, the formation of the yen bloc was a result of the Japanese military occupation in Asian countries.

3.1.1 The First Step

Japan was the first nation to modernize and successfully resist Western political and economic encroachments. Thus, Japan could have served as a model and object of aspiration for anti-colonial movements throughout Asia. However, Japan itself soon became a colonial power; Japan emulated the Western imperialist states and followed the global trend of territorial expansion and colonialism. In the early twentieth century, Japan acquired its first colonial territories in Korea and Manchuria.

The idea for the yen bloc started even before the colonization of these territories. The first Japanese bank to open in Korea was the First Bank, in 1873. Following the deepening Japanese political and economic influence on Korea, First Bank rapidly increased its activities in Korea, in particular to cope with the chaotic monetary situation characterized by the circulation of numerous coins of different weights and standards. First Bank was officially in charge of harmonizing different currency standards and was authorized to issue its own banknotes in Korea. To this end, the Japanese government allocated First Bank the maximum limit for the issuance of its notes, and at the same time, required it to back up its issue by government securities and commercial papers as fiduciary reserves, as well as gold, silver and Japanese yen as specie reserves. After the Russo-Japanese War in 1905, the note-issuing function of First Bank was transferred to the newly created central bank, the Bank of Chosun.[2] For both First Bank and the Bank of Chosun, reserve assets for issuing notes were mostly Japanese yen; notes issued by these banks were exchanged at par with the Japanese yen. Thus, Korea is considered the first country in East Asia to adopt the yen standard system, which would constitute the core principle of the 'Greater East Asia Co-Prosperity Sphere' in monetary affairs (Shimazaki, 1989).

3.1.2   The Second Step

After the annexation of Korea, China was the next target for Japanese expansionism because of its abundant resources and huge market potential. In 1931, Japan occupied Manchuria and established a new puppet government, Manchukuo. Japan soon started the unification of currencies in Manchuria. There was a heterogeneous mixture of coins, weights and paper money, with their values fluctuating widely with each other. There were, for instance, 15 different paper monies issued by provincial banks or currency bureaux. To achieve standardization, the Central Bank of Manchuria was established in 1935, and the Manchurian currency was linked to and exchangeable at par with the Japanese yen.

It is important to note that by monetarily and economically integrating Manchuria with Korea and Japan, Japan followed the worldwide trend of creating economic blocs and this act later developed into the idea of a 'Japan–Manchukuo–China economic bloc'. Given that the world had already seen the emergence of the sterling bloc centred on the UK and its Commonwealth countries, and a dollar bloc centred on the US, the Japanese idea implies that the world was entering into the era of closed and self-sufficient economic blocs, replacing the era of international cooperation represented by the Washington conference system (Shimazaki, 1989).

The Marco Polo Incident took place on 7 July 1937, triggering the second Sino-Japanese war. Its battle fronts extended over all China, from its border with Russia to its central and southern parts. Because the monetary management of the newly occupied areas was urgent, Japan established the Inner Mongolia Bank (located in Kalgan), the Chinese Federal Reserve Bank (located in Peking) and the Central Reserve Bank (located in Shanghai). Table 3.1 summarizes this movement.

The Inner Mongolia Bank, established on 1 December 1937, was authorized to issue banknotes, which were at par with the Japanese yen and the Manchukuo yuan, and to handle the fiscal business of the puppet government and the public funds of the various local public bodies.

On 10 March 1938, Japan established the Federal Reserve Bank in Peking as the central banking institution for North China. The banknotes of the Federal Reserve Bank of China were also at par with the Japanese yen and Manchukuo yuan. *De jure*, the issuance of its banknotes had to be backed by specie, but de facto the banknotes were inconvertible because there was no rule regarding the specie resumption.[3]

At this time, the Japanese yen was rapidly attaining a key currency status similar to that of the US dollar in the Western hemisphere. The Japanese yen was identified with the industrial and political strength of

Table 3.1   Yen bloc in occupied China

	Issuing bank	Authorizing government	Date of creation	Exchange rate	Circulation area
National yuan	Central Bank of Manchuria	Manchuria Government	1 July 1932	Par with yen	Manchukuo
Yuan note	Inner Mongolia Bank	Self-governing Mongolia Government	1 November 1937	Par with yen	Inner Mongolia
Yuan note	Federal Reserve Bank	North China Committee	10 March 1938	Par with yen	North China, Sandong, Sansu
Yuan note	Central Reserve Bank	Government at Nanking New Government	6 January 1941 6 May 1939	18 yen against 100 yuan	Central China
Military yen note	Hua Hsing Bank	Japanese Army	November 1937		

Source: Bae (1990).

Japan (Banyai, 1974), and the Japanese yen-linked currencies such as the notes of the Bank of Japan, Bank of Chosun and the Central Bank of Manchukuo circulated widely together with the yuan notes (called 'fapi'[4] in Chinese) issued by the Chinese National Government (Kuomintang government). The Japanese military forces in North China initially used these currencies, especially the notes of the Bank of Chosun, for their military expenditure. These notes suffered from devaluation as a result of over-printing, which raised concerns over the devaluation of the Japanese yen that was linked to them. Thus, Japan decided to replace these notes with those issued by the newly created Federal Reserve Bank of China, establishing its notes as the sole legal tender in North China. Japan at the same time prohibited the circulation of the yuan notes of the Chinese National Government. In North China, however, the yuan notes of the Chinese National Government, the fapi, remained firmly in circulation and the Federal Reserve Bank notes did not dominate the fapi. In fact, the fapi was a secure and readily accepted currency in which people had confidence, while the Federal Reserve Bank note was a relatively new currency which people were reluctant to accept. To protect the value of the Federal Reserve Bank notes, Japan could do nothing but rely on comprehensive measures of exchange controls.

Similar developments unfolded in Central China. As Central China fell under Japanese occupation, the Japanese government decided to establish the Central Reserve Bank of China as a central banking institution for Central and South China. It started business in January 1941, taking over the business of the Hua Hsing Bank. Unlike in North China, where the Japanese army used Bank of Chosun notes, the Japanese army initially used Bank of Japan notes for its military outlay in Central China. As the amount of the Japanese yen notes in circulation became larger, however, their value dropped, and the Japanese yen was traded at a discount to other currencies. Many of these yen notes flowed back to Japan and upset the monetary management of Japan. The Japanese government was concerned about the continuing devaluation of its currency. To prevent it, the Japanese government decided to withdraw Bank of Japan notes from circulation in Central China and to substitute them with military scripts or military notes. Although these military notes were denominated in yen and fixed at par with the Japanese yen, they were inconvertible to yen and were prevented from circulating in Japan and other areas. Almost all currencies linked to the Japanese yen, including the military notes, were neither convertible into foreign currencies nor into the Bank of Japan notes, due to exchange controls.

Finally, the Japanese government decided to replace the military notes by Central Reserve Bank notes. The value of the Central Reserve Bank yuan notes was fixed at the rate of 18 yen against 100 yuan. The Japanese government proclaimed Central Reserve Bank yuan notes as the sole legal tender in Central China, banning the circulation of all the fapi notes. The redemption of the fapi with the Central Reserve Bank yuan notes was made at the exchange rate of 2:1. However, keeping the exchange rate of the Central Reserve Bank notes stable turned out to be a heavy burden for the Japanese government. In order to maintain it, exchange controls had to be reinforced strictly until at last all trade and foreign exchange transactions became impossible.

3.1.3　Currency War between China and Japan

In the late 1920s, as a result of imperialist rivalries and nationalist movements, the Chinese National Government was able to bring nominal political unity to China after decades of war politics. In fact, the National Government was able to assume nationwide responsibility in 1928. It immediately recognized the urgency of economic and financial rehabilitation. Recognizing the need for a modern financial system, the new government created the Central Bank of China on 6 October 1928, which was to be reorganized as a true central bank. The bank was given the right to issue its own notes, to mint and circulate coins, to deal with foreign exchanges and to handle the issuance and service of public debts. Notes were to have a reserve of 60 per cent in silver or gold coin or bullion, and 40 per cent in government bonds or commercial paper.

Yet the monetary situation remained chaotic until currency reform in 1935. The currency consisted of an endless variety of monies, differing from place to place. The first step in monetary reform was coinage reform, which consisted of abolishing the tael as unit of account and introducing the standard silver dollar, the yuan. The second step was to nationalize silver and to declare the notes of the Central Bank of China, the Bank of China, and the Bank of Communications as full legal tender (fapi) for all transactions in terms of the silver dollar. The exchange rate of the fapi was fixed at 1 shilling 2 pence per 1 yuan. The reform also created a Currency Reserve Board to control note issue and to keep the note reserves in custody. Finally, the use of silver as currency was forbidden, and prices were in fapi, the sole legal tender, with a managed and stable foreign exchange standard (Young, 1971, p.166).

In 1937, when China and Japan were at war, the fapi and the currencies of Japanese sponsored banks competed with each other for acceptability. Because printed banknotes were a major source of financing government expenditure, especially military expenditure for both the Japanese army and the Chinese National Government, it was essential for each party to win the currency war. To stabilize the value of the fapi and to increase its acceptability, the Chinese National Government obtained support from the UK and US. The Japanese government tried to support the value of the banknotes issued by the two banks under its control, the Federal Reserve Bank and the Central Reserve Bank.

To maintain the value of the fapi, China set up an Anglo-Chinese Exchange Stabilization Fund in April 1939 with a capital of £10 million. Soon after its establishment, however, the Fund was faced with a serious challenge arising from the Japanese operation to sell the fapi and buy foreign exchange. With the establishment of the Federal Reserve Bank in North China, the Japanese withdrew the fapi notes from circulation, replacing them with the Federal Reserve Bank notes, and used them at the Shanghai foreign exchange market for the purchase of foreign exchange. This brought about serious depreciation pressure on the fapi. However, China managed to overcome this crisis with British financial support. In the spring of 1940, the fapi was again under pressure due to the establishment of the Central Reserve Bank in Central China by the Japanese government. To support the value of the fapi, the Chinese National Government had to rely on foreign support. This time, the support came from the US. The US Treasury agreed to grant US$50 million to the Chinese Stabilization Fund for the purpose of stabilizing the value of fapi in relation to the US dollar. At the same time, the British Treasury made a further contribution equivalent to £5 million to support the fapi and sterling pound exchange.

The maintenance of the free exchange market in Shanghai and the support of the Chinese currency by the Fund were to some extent fundamental for the stability of the fapi. Two reasons could be mentioned in this regard. In the first place, it was partly the very existence of a free market and the possibility of convertibility that made the population of the occupied areas reluctant to give up their Chinese currency in exchange for the inconvertible currencies introduced by the Japanese puppet governments. It was reported that even in North China large numbers of Chinese notes remained in circulation or in hiding in spite of the severe penalties and prohibitions decreed by the Japanese authorities. Secondly, the existence of a reasonably stable exchange market tended to support the whole system of internal government finance in free China. It helped the public to maintain a certain level of confidence in the currency and to check the flight into commodities.

Despite the currency war for stability, the currencies of both the Chinese National Government and the Japanese puppet governments circulated in parallel, and China was plagued by hyperinflation because the long-lasting Sino-Japanese War forced both governments to print enormous amounts of money (see table 3.4 below).

3.2 YEN BLOC UNDER THE GREATER EAST ASIA CO-PROSPERITY SPHERE

3.2.1 Establishment of the Greater East Asia Financial Sphere

Japan's continual expansion into China heightened political tension, especially between Japan and the US. To curb the military expansionism of Japan, the US prohibited US exports of aluminium and scrap iron to Japan, froze Japanese assets in America and imposed a total embargo on oil exports to Japan. However, these measures did not stop Japan from indulging in military expansionism into South-East Asia, paving the way towards the Pacific War, which finally broke out in 1941.

With its invasion of South-East Asia, Japan set up a more comprehensive regional order under the banner of 'Greater East Asia Co-Prosperity Sphere', which was to include not only Japan, China and Manchukuo but also the South-East Asian regions, including French Indo-China, Thailand, the Malay Peninsula, the Philippines and Dutch East Indies. In fact, this Japanese idea was nothing but an extension of the 'New Order in East Asia' announced by Foreign Minister Konoye on 3 November 1938, just after the outbreak of the Sino-Japanese War. The concept of this New Order entailed the establishment of political and economic interdependence and mutual aid between Japan, Manchukuo and China. The Japanese pointed out that such a union would allow Japan to stand side by side as equals with the Western powers' blocs, and thus resist their aggressive advances. Japan also hoped that this would end Japan's dependence on the Western powers for raw materials for its industries. 'Asia for Asians' was another catchword. South-East Asia was essential to Japan as a source of raw materials such as coal, rice, iron, rubber and tin, and in this respect, fitted in well with Japan's plan for a 'Greater East Asia Co-Prosperity Sphere'.

Immediately after the outbreak of the Pacific War in December 1941, Japan established military administrations in occupied South-East Asia (except in Indochina and Thailand). To cover the increasing military and administrative expenditure, these administrations used military notes denominated in local currencies. These military notes were a general means of payment and circulated together with the pre-occupation local currencies. By this time, Japanese military forces had already used a variety of military notes in yen issued in the occupied Central and South China. However, military notes in South-East Asia differed, because previous notes had been denominated in Japanese yen and exchanged at par with the Japanese yen. The military notes issued in South-East Asia were denominated in local currencies and the exchange rate between these military notes and the Japanese yen was not fixed until 1943, after which it was set to be at par. Japan also created the Southern Development Company in 1942 to handle its military funds and to finance the long-term development of and construction in occupied territories, filling the gap left by the closing of existing local banks controlled by former colonial states such as the UK, the Netherlands and the US. However, as military expenditure continued to increase and inflation in occupied areas accelerated, this company was allowed to issue its own notes and withdraw the military notes starting from March 1943, thereby becoming a de facto central bank of issue; in order to exploit local resources, the Japanese government had to eliminate the local currencies from circulation and substitute them with its own notes.

During the Pacific War, the financial goal of the Japanese plan in the occupied areas was to establish its own 'Financial Sphere of Greater East Asia' devoid of Western influence, and thereby to exploit the occupied areas. The main principle of the Japanese plan for the financial management of the Sphere was to use the Japanese yen to fix the external value of the Sphere's currencies, to maintain a managed currency system and to settle the foreign exchange transactions in the Sphere, and thereby to eliminate the old gold and silver standard and the exchange system based on the US dollar and UK sterling. Japan hoped to set up a financial sphere with Tokyo as its financial centre, making the yen the anchor, reserve and settlement currency for the Greater East Asia Sphere.

3.2.2 Features of the Great East Asia Financial Sphere

Yen as the anchor and the par link policy
To establish the yen as the regional anchor currency, the currencies of the occupied areas were linked at par with the Japanese yen. In the case of the Bank of Chosun and the Bank of Taiwan, it was stipulated in law that their notes be convertible into the Bank of Japan notes at par without any reservation. Between Japan, Korea and Taiwan, there was no restriction of any kind with regard to exchange, circulation and transactions. In the case of the Central Bank of Manchuria notes, the conversion was allowed only to travellers. As already explained, this step was taken to protect the value of the yen from depreciating as the volume of money in circulation and the inflation rate rose more rapidly in Manchukuo. In the case of the Bank of Inner Mongolia and the Federal Reserve Bank notes as well as in the case of the Central Reserve Bank notes, however, there were strict exchange controls. Although these notes could in principle be exchanged with the Japanese yen at par (for the Bank of Inner Mongolia and Federal Reserve Bank notes) and at a ratio of 18 Japanese yen to 100 yuan (for

the Central Reserve Bank notes) respectively, the conversion was in fact rarely allowed.

After the outbreak of the Pacific War in 1941, Japan abolished foreign exchange flotation in terms of US dollars and UK pounds. The exchange markets vanished and the Japanese monetary authorities had to decide directly on the conversion rate between the yen and other currencies based on the consideration of various elements such as productivity capacity, natural resources, standard of living, and so on. The conversion rate between the yen and the currencies of the South-East Asian countries was set up to be at par, except for French Indo-China and Thailand, where the pre-existing exchange rates were available. Exchange transactions with the US and UK were completely suspended; these were limited to Germany, Italy and the countries in the Greater East Asian Co-Prosperity Sphere.

The fact that the currencies of South-East Asian countries were at par with the Japanese yen meant that the value of these currencies underwent a twofold drop, thereby reducing Japan's import price by half compared with the level that prevailed in the pre-war period and brought about the internal circulation of goods in Japan's favour. Although the conversion at par between the yen and local currencies seemed unrealistic, this conversion rate actually happened because of trade and exchange controls by the Japanese government. However, as the exchange rate became function-less in correcting trade imbalances, the par link policy caused numerous distortions and inefficiencies. In particular, as the inflation differential between Japan and its occupied areas accelerated, Japanese imports from the occupied areas declined while the Japanese exports to these areas increased. As this turned into a serious hurdle in financing the necessary commodities for war, the Japanese government had to reinforce its trade and capital controls.

The Japanese government resorted to two policy measures: one was to use an export levy and import subsidy system, in which the Japanese government taxed the exporters the differential between export and domestic prices and subsidized the importers the differential between import and domestic prices. The other measure was to use a special conversion rate for Japanese imports. That is, the Japanese government adopted a special conversion rate between the yen and the currencies of the occupied areas for importers to compensate importers for their loss in imports.

Yen as a reserve currency

As mentioned, Japan established a central bank of issue or institutions with a similar role in one occupied area after another. These institutions in the occupied areas were subject to holding the yen reserves or the Bank of Japan notes. The Bank of Japan extended its monetary loans and credits to the various central banks of the Japanese-controlled governments,[5] and borrowing central banks used these loans as the reserves for their note issues. Even though the holdings of yen by the central banks of the East Asian countries were initially intended to raise the credit standings of the yen-linked currencies, Japan blocked the use of the yen balances held by East Asian countries so as to exploit the local economies and to increase its military expenditure. A typical example was the introduction of the so-called 'Mutual Deposit System (Balances)', which forced other East Asian countries to lend the Japanese government their own local currencies in return for holding the blocked Japanese yen. The Mutual Deposit System was first introduced between the Chosun Bank and the Yokohama Specie Bank. With the start of the Japanese occupation of China, the system extended between the Bank of Japan and the Federal Reserve Bank and the Central Reserve Bank.

Yen-based settlement system

During the Pacific War, Japan introduced a clearing system, with the international transactions among nations being settled via transfers to the accounts of the central banks of the contracting countries. In fact, this clearing system was modelled on the German Nazi system, in contrast to the then UK or US system that consisted of setting up an exchange stabilization fund and intervening in the exchange market to fix the exchange rate (Shimazaki, 1989). Japan concluded many bilateral clearing contracts with the governments of the occupied and satellite areas. The first of these clearing agreements was made in December 1940 between the Yokohama Specie Bank, a special foreign exchange bank which handled the Japanese government accounts overseas, and the Java Bank. After this, the Yokohama Specie Bank negotiated seven more contracts. The Bank of Chosun and the Bank of Japan also respectively concluded a contract. In 1942, the Japanese government decided to make the Bank of Japan the leading central bank and clearing institution in the yen bloc, and revised the Bank of Japan Act to implement the settlements between nations via transfers in the 'Special Yen Account' that central banks of the occupied areas maintained in the form of a deposit at the Bank of Japan (see Table 3.2). Despite these actions, however, the Bank of Japan could not succeed in replacing the Yokohama Specie Bank as the central clearing institution in the yen bloc area. Thus the settlement system remained fragmentary.

Table 3.2 *Settlement system in East Asia*

From \ To	Japan	Manchuria	Mongolia	North China	Central and South China	South-East Asia
Manchuria	Yen (direct exchange between its own notes and Japanese yen)		Central Bank of Inner Mongolia note	Federal Reserve Bank note	Special yen account	Special yen account
Inner Mongolia	Federal Reserve Bank note (indirect via the exchange of its own notes and the notes of the Federal Reserve Bank and then by the exchange of the latter with Japanese yen)	Central Bank of Manchukuo note		Federal Reserve Bank note	Special yen account	Special yen account
North China	Yen (direct exchange)	Central Bank of Manchukuo note			Note of Central Reserve Bank Special yen account	Special yen account
Central and South China	Yen (direct exchange)	Special yen account	Special yen account	Federal Reserve Bank note Special yen account	Special yen account	Special yen account
South-East Asia	Special yen account Yen (direct exchange of the notes of the Southern Development Corporation with yen)	Special yen account	Special yen account	Special yen account	Special yen account	

Source: Shimazaki (1989).

33

3.3   CONSEQUENCES OF THE YEN BLOC

Although Japanese propaganda proclaimed the success of the 'Greater East Asia Co-Prosperity Sphere', in reality there were widening economic disparities between Japan and its colonies and occupied areas: the inflation gap and the income gap.

3.3.1   Inflation Gap

Under Japanese occupation, high inflation plagued East Asia, with each area having its own system of note-issuing bank and currency. Compared to Japan and its close colonies, the regions further away from Japan such as Central and South China and South-East Asian countries recorded relatively higher inflation. For instance, Tokyo's inflation rate on the eve of Japan's defeat in 1945 was little higher than twice that in 1937, but China and South-East Asian inflation rates were several thousand or ten thousand times higher.

Table 3.3 shows that the further away the region in question was from Tokyo, the higher its inflation rate. Thus, there was a widening inflation differential between Japan and other East Asian countries.

This arose because the use of the yen-linked currencies was not voluntary but was imposed on the occupied regions by Japan. As the occupied regions' obligation to meet Japanese war expenses increased, local central banks, most of which were controlled by Japan, had to issue more and more money. Indeed, the further the regions were away from Japan, the higher was the increase in their money supply, in parallel with the inflation rate movement. Table 3.4 clearly illustrates this.

One important instrument that obliged the occupied East Asian countries to print money excessively was the 'Local Borrowing System' introduced in 1943. With the rapid rise of inflation in the occupied area, which was a result of the increase in military spending, Japan had to procure ever increasing amounts of the Japanese-sponsored currencies to cover its military expenditures. However, because exchange rates of Japanese-sponsored currencies were fixed at par with the Japanese yen, in theory the government would have had to issue more Japanese yen in parallel with other currencies. To avoid this, Japan decided to rely on different ways to borrow local currencies. As explained above, the Mutual Deposit System was used to procure Federal Reserve Bank and Central Reserve Bank notes. In addition to this, the government arranged direct borrowing agreements (for the Central Bank of Manchuria notes) or used the Special Yen Account for borrowing (for Thai baht and Indo-China Bank notes). In this way, the Japanese government could procure as many local

Table 3.3 Movements of Wholesale Price Index in East Asia

	Japan	Taiwan	Korea	Manchuria	China			Philippines	Java	Singapore	Myanmar
					North China	Central China	Free China				
	Tokyo	Taipei	Seoul	Shinking	Beijing	Shanghai	Chungking	Manila	Batavia	Singapore	Langoon
1937.12	100	100	100	100	100**	100	100				
1938.6	105		118	130		88	113				
1938.12	106	113	115	125		93	139				
1939.6	112		106	146		123	171				
1939.12	130	126	115	159	262	248	275				
1940.6	127		119	186	430	370	488				
1940.12	129	141	120	192	410	527	983				
1941.6	139		123	197	439	719	1365		100		
1941.12	146	147	125	208	518	1290	2322	100	140	100	100
1942.6	150	151	128	212	646	2161	4183		134		
1942.12	151	151	132	235	817	3976	6965	200	166	352	
1943.6	161	160	142	241	1184	5944	11044	247	227	807	900
1943.12	168	169	147	255	1382	14194	19826	1196	492	1201	1718
1944.6	181	179	159	282	2156	46452	40696	5154		4469	3635
1944.12	193		166	338	5901	202419	56348	14285		10766	8707
1945.6	250		181	454*	15348*	2404919	177565		2421		30629
1945.8	264					6967742	213913		3197		185648

Note: * Price in May, 1945; ** Price in 1936.

Source: Shimazaki (1989); Young (1965); Monthly Statistics of Chosun Bank, various issues.

35

Table 3.4 Note issues by different Japan rated banks and the Central Bank of China (million yen or yuan)

	Japan	Taiwan	Korea			China			Southern Development Company (a)				
	BOJ yen	BOT yuan	BOC won	Manchukuo	Mongol yuan	FRB yuan	CRB yuan	Free China yuan	Phil peso	Burma rupee	Malai dollar (b)	Gulden (c)	Total
1937	2305	112	279	307	13			1639					
1938.6	2074	105	254	275	18	59		1727					
1938.12	2754	140	321	426	36	162		2305					
1939.6	2522	146	285	388	32	264		2700					
1939.12	3679	171	443	624	60	458		4287					
1940.6	3597	176	437	632	57	599		6063					
1940.12	4777	199	462	947	93	715		7867					
1941.6	4247	197	509	811	66	691	60	11296					
1941.12	5978	252	741	1262	114	964	237	15133					
1942.06	5545	250	667	1106	83	937	1172	22975					
1942.12	7418	289	908	1670	143	1581	3477	34360		34			34
1943.06	7363	321	864	1800	176	1949	9152	49873	106	137	149	83	463
1943.12	10266	415	1466	3011	379	3762	19150	75379	229	327	244	145	945
1944.06	12323	519	1817	3512	416	5995	38359	122779	497	664	425	369	1955
1944.12	17745	796	3135	5877	1058	15841	139699	189461	1115	1544	752	803	4246
1945.6	26181	1207	4376		2799a	55390	738273	397773	4948	2774	1438	1464	10623
1945.8	42300	2285	7987	8800	3600	132603	2697231	556907		5656	5640	2792	19468

Notes:
(a) Issued in local currency units but linked at par with the Japanese yen.
(b) Issued for Malaysia, Singapore and Borneo.
(c) Issued for Java and Sumatra area.

Sources: Bank of Japan (1970); Young (1965).

36

currencies as it wished. For instance, the use of the Mutual Deposit System accounted for more than 70 per cent of the total money issued by the Central Reserve Bank and was a significant cause of inflation.

Under these conditions, the supply of banknotes in occupied China was dependent on the Japanese government's decision to meet the increasing demand for money caused by the Japanese imperialist war. This system brought more inflation in occupied China than in Japan and its close colonies such as Korea and Taiwan.[6] In turn, it touched off the notorious hyperinflationary spiral in the Free China area, as it forced the Chinese Nationalist Government to issue more currency to finance increasing war expenses.[7]

Moreover, in South-East Asian countries (except Thailand and Indo-China), Japanese military authorities themselves issued their own notes (military notes) in local units, although they soon had to be replaced by the notes of the Southern Development Company. Unlike central banking institutions in other occupied areas, however, the Southern Development Company had no maximum limit and no backing requirement for the note issue. Consequently, this region was forced to endure higher inflation.

3.3.2   Growth Gap

The gap between Japan and its neighbouring countries widened, not only in monetary matters but also in terms of real income. Maddison (1995) offers quite comprehensive data for the pre-war period national income in some selected East Asian countries. Although incomplete and sometimes very roughly estimated, it is the only available data that make the comparison of national income in the same unit between countries during the period of Japanese expansion. Thus, the study is useful for examining the changes in the per capita incomes of the East Asian countries.

Table 3.5 shows the trend of per capita GDP in different parts of East Asia relative to that of Japan during the period 1910–45. It suggests that the economic gap between Japan and its colonies and occupied areas (measured in per capita GDP) continued to widen. For instance, in the period 1913–29, the per capita incomes of Taiwan and Korea, Japan's colonies since 1895 and 1910 respectively, fell from 59 per cent and 71 per cent of Japanese per capita income to 56 per cent and 59 per cent respectively. This trend was temporarily suspended during the period 1929–38. During the war period 1938–45, however, the decline in per capita incomes of Korea and Taiwan relative to that of Japan resumed. This trend continued even after the end of World War II. As a result, for the period 1913–45, the relative per capita incomes of Korea and Taiwan dropped from 59 per cent and 71 per cent of Japanese income to 53 per cent and 58 per cent

Table 3.5   Per capita GDP relative to Japanese income (%)

Year	Japan	China	Korea	Taiwan	Indonesia	Philippines	Thailand	Burma
1910	100			76.40	67.30			
1911	100		68.87	67.64	67.71			43.10
1912	100		67.87	59.08	66.07			
1913	100	51.57	71.06	59.52	68.74	106.30	63.42	47.60
1914	100		78.06	62.54	71.24			
1915	100		81.16	58.47	66.33			
1916	100		71.43	60.14	58.67			48.60
1917	100		73.66	63.42	57.43			
1918	100		78.26	59.07	58.32			
1919	100		69.00	56.77	56.94			
1920	100		71.55	56.47	59.66			
1921	100		68.14	50.42	54.44			36.78
1922	100		66.74	53.92	55.85			
1923	100		68.41	55.26	56.81			
1924	100		67.06	58.52	58.46			
1925	100		64.77	57.39	58.16			
1926	100		66.57	56.80	60.97			41.87
1927	100		69.54	55.31	64.42			
1928	100		62.86	56.44	62.49			
1929	100	39.97	59.72	56.80	61.93	80.25	41.00	
1930	100	44.16	65.90	62.47	67.30			46.97
1931	100	44.57	64.31	60.63	63.12			
1932	100	42.77	61.74	64.28	57.02			
1933	100	39.23	64.20	54.31	51.37			
1934	100	36.01	63.15	57.50	50.72			
1935	100	38.33	69.61	63.24	50.69			
1936	100	38.30	69.38	59.89	49.84			35.99
1937	100	36.06	75.48	57.97	51.86			
1938	100	33.02	69.99	56.03	48.22	63.54	35.31	29.07
1939	100		53.89	52.01	41.49			
1940	100		58.52	49.37	42.93			
1941	100		59.66	52.75	44.36			
1942	100		59.02	56.14	35.15			
1943	100		59.21	37.25	29.59			
1944	100		58.01	27.09	23.81			
1945	100		53.05	57.76	39.69			

Source: Maddison (1995).

respectively. The trend of widening income gaps relative to that of Japan is more or less the same for other occupied areas such as China and South-East Asia, although the precise data for the income level during the war period is missing. For instance, China was not a colony, but its sovereignty was limited by Japan (and Western powers) until the defeat of Japan in

1945. Its per capita income declined from 51 per cent of the Japanese per capita income in 1913 to 33 per cent in 1938. The same trend was true for the South-East Asian countries. Given the fact that South-East Asian countries were not yet under Japanese control until the late 1930s, it seems that the rising economic gap between them and Japan might reflect a decaying colonial economic structure rather than the detrimental effect of Japanese occupation. Nonetheless, it is still true that the Japanese occupation of these countries did not bring about the co-prosperity promised by Japan. In fact, as some observers put it, 'the Japanese occupation caused economic havoc in the occupied territories. The entire economic life of these regions regressed to the level of subsistence production and barter trade, and the economic gulf had widened between developed Japan and underdeveloped South East Asia.'

Hence, even on purely economic grounds, the yen bloc was doomed to fail, because the unity of the bloc could not be maintained in the face of widening diversities. In fact, after the military defeat of Japan in World War II, most of the newly independent East Asian countries broke their link to the Japanese yen and adopted the dollar standard system, while former British colonies such as Hong Kong, Singapore and Malaysia returned to pegging their currencies to the British sterling pound until the breakdown of the Sterling Area in the early 1970s. No single country in the region wanted to remain in the yen bloc.

The exact reasons why these countries were relatively backward compared with Japan are very difficult to pinpoint because of the complexity of the period. Worldwide depression, colonialism, open war, and many other factors must all be considered. But the growth performance during and after this period sheds light on what might have happened in Asia if these countries had regained their sovereignty. In fact, Japan achieved growth far faster than any other Asian country through early nation-building and the westernizing of its institutions. Other countries were late in these efforts or at least were prevented from doing so by Japan. It was only after the defeat of Japan that other East Asian countries could take off and begin to catch up with Japan economically. The effect of the catch-up has been evident especially since the1970s.[8]

3.3.3 Assessment

The Japanese idea of the 'Greater East Asian Co-Prosperity Sphere' dates back to the integration of Korea and Manchuria into Japan. It was extended to the Japan–Manchukuo–China Economic Bloc, and later to the idea of the Greater East Asian Co-Prosperity Sphere. No matter how or where the idea developed, however, the underlying objective remained unchanged: to exploit the neighbouring economies as much as possible for the sole benefit of Japan. As we have seen, the economic and inflationary gap between Japan and other East Asian countries during the Japanese invasion and occupation period continued to widen. Japan made no effort to fill the gap or to foster the solidarity necessary for the maintenance of the bloc. Rather, the other East Asian countries had to sacrifice their interests to support Japanese military expansionism unilaterally. Japan attempted to establish hierarchical relations between those who dominated and those who were dominated. Thus, Japan pursued a strategy of regional dominance, not one of regional cooperation. Clearly this was not acceptable to East Asia unless imposed by military force. Moreover, all these ideas were based on Japanese nationalism, which included exclusiveness and the shunning of the other parts of the world. All these facts show that the so-called Co-Prosperity Sphere was without question nothing but Japanese propaganda.

The result was that after World War II, it took a long time for Japan to normalize its diplomatic relations with neighbouring Asian countries. Even after the coming into being of significant economic relations with Japan, these countries could not trust Japan, a fact that explains the reluctant attitude of East Asian governments toward Japan's leadership in regional monetary and trade cooperation issues. At the same time, the US emerged as the new and sole hegemonic power in the region. Under American leadership, the post-war East Asian economy became much more liberal, multilateral and interdependent. This new world order led to an unprecedented expansion of the East Asian and world economy, providing a good opportunity to bridge the economic gap that existed between East Asian countries and the US on the one hand and between themselves and Japan on the other hand. This is another good reason why Japan's initiatives on regional economic and monetary cooperation received only a lukewarm welcome in the region.

NOTES

1. See Kobayashi (1975) and Shimazaki (1989) for the history of the yen bloc.
2. 'Chosun' is the old name for Korea.
3. The specie requirement ratio of this bank was 40 per cent.
4. 'Fapi' in Chinese literally means 'legal tender'.
5. These included the Central Bank of Manchukuo, Bank of Inner Mongolia, Federal Reserve Bank of China, Central Reserve Bank of China, Banque de l'Indochine, Central Bank of Thailand, Central Bank of Burma and the proposed Central Bank of the Philippines.
6. In Free China, the National Government of China was also obliged to issue its own money to finance the war against Japan. For a detailed explanation, see Young (1965).

7. The currency war with Japan intensified the internal contradictions of the Nationalist Chinese Government regime, providing a political space for the Communists to operate in. Indeed, it led to the Communist revolution in 1949. In this sense, not only Japan but also China was a loser in the currency war.
8. For instance, the per capita incomes of Korea and Taiwan in 1970 were respectively 23.3 per cent and 24.4 per cent of the Japanese income but since then they rose to 48.3 per cent and 55.6 per cent in 1990 and in 2000. Similar trends are observed for other East Asian countries.

4. Globalization and regionalization of East Asian economies

For quite a long time after the Second World War, East Asian countries did not consider the need for a regional economic and monetary order. The emergence of the GATT and the Bretton Woods systems caused this silence; they helped to stabilize the world economy and to ensure a stable growth in the region. Of particular importance was the Bretton Woods system, which was put forward by John Maynard Keynes of the UK and Harry Dexter White of the US. It established a world economy system based on a fixed exchange rate system with gold and the US dollar as the anchor for other currencies. The pegging of currencies to the US dollar in East Asia was still an unshakable principle even after the breakdown of the Bretton Woods system in 1973.[1]

However, increasing economic interdependency among countries in East Asia initiated some movements towards regionalism. As Katzenstein (2000) stated: 'while the old regionalism emphasized autarchy and direct rule, the new one relies on interdependence and indirect rule.' The financial crisis in 1997 was crucial, and sharply increased awareness on regional actions. Before looking at the needs for and conditions required for regional monetary and financial integration, this chapter examines how the rapid growth and development of East Asian economies has deepened economic interdependency and how they have overcome crises and transformed economic structures in the region.

4.1 EXPANSION OF EAST ASIAN ECONOMIES

4.1.1 Economic Catch-up of Japan

Japan's role in East Asia, especially among ASEAN countries, has been growing since the mid-1960s. By that time Japan had recovered completely from the devastation left by World War II. Its flow of trade, aid, investment and technology transfer accounts for this recovery. Indeed, during the two decades preceding the Plaza Accord of 1985, Japan already accounted for up to half of the total aid and FDI in the region. As the economic relations with other Asian countries widened, a Japanese ideology on regionalism was slowly being formed. Its theoretical foundation was first provided by what is called the 'flying geese theory' of industrial growth and senescence (Korhonen, 1994; Katzenstein, 2000), developed by Akamatsu in the 1930s (see Box 4.1). Kojima elaborated on this theory further and sought to implement it in the 1960s by creating a regional system in the Pacific area that would support the process of a regional economic transformation through which Japan and its Asian neighbouring countries would be indelibly linked.

On the basis of the FG theory, Kojima proposed the creation of a Pacific Free Trade Area (PAFTA) in 1965, which would reflect Japan's inclination toward the Western world so as to encompass the US, Canada, Australia and New Zealand, and to contribute to regional trade expansion. This advanced group would place their gains into a fund and use this fund to assist and promote the economic growth of associate PAFTA members. Kojima's proposal for a PAFTA basically aimed at facilitating economic development in developing Asian countries by having them follow Japan – the lead goose in the FG. Thus, Japan would be connected to both the advanced US economy on whose markets its exports depended vitally, and backward South-East Asia, which was destined to absorb Japan's sunset industries (Katzenstein, 2000).

At the same time, Kojima (1970) proposed a Pacific Currency Area for monetary affairs to work in parallel with a PAFTA. The main idea was to pool international reserves so as to increase international liquidity. It had five main characteristics. First, a Pacific Currency Area, together with a PAFTA, would include five developed countries: the US, Canada, Japan, Australia and New Zealand, although other developing Asian countries would not be excluded from membership. Second, the pooling assets would be gold and foreign exchange reserves. Third, fixed exchange rates with regard to the US dollar would be maintained; in effect, a Pacific Currency Area would be a dollar area. Fourth, regarding the adjustments of the area's balance of payments vis-à-vis the rest of the world, the dollar's par value in terms of gold would be allowed to fluctuate within a narrow band, and exchange equalization operations would be undertaken in terms of gold to limit these exchange fluctuations. Fifth, the balance of payments among member countries could be adjusted through freer capital movement and changes in each country's credit with the reserve pool.

In a strict sense, however, it would be difficult to consider a Pacific Currency Area as a serious proposal for Asian monetary cooperation. Japan was interested in building a cooperative institution between Japan and the US – not between Japan and Asia. Also, the

BOX 4.1   FLYING GEESE MODEL

The 'flying geese pattern of development' (FG) model was originally developed by a Japanese economist, Kaname Akamatsu, in the 1930s, but was not known to world academia until it was translated into English in 1962. One of his students, Kojima, refined, expanded and popularized this model. The FG model was made more popular by Saburo Okita, who presented the FG model in 1985 to explain the regional transmission of Asian industrialization. The FG model attempts to explain the catching-up process of industrialization in latecomer economies, which consists of: (i) a basic pattern, i.e., a single industry grows tracing out the three successive curves of imports, production and exports; and (ii) a variant pattern in which industries are diversified and upgraded from consumer goods to capital goods (Kojima, 2000). Akamatsu discovered these two patterns, which looked like a flying geese formation, through statistical analysis of industrial development in pre-war Japan. Kojima then developed a theoretical model in which the accumulation of physical and human capital induces the economy to diversify first to more capital-intensive industries, and then to rationalize them so as to adopt more efficient production methods. This model was also applied to regional transmission of industrial development. Okita (1985) made the FG model very popular, focusing on the regional spread of the FG pattern of industrial development from Japan (a leader goose) to NIEs, ASEAN and China (follower geese). A typical example was, for example, the shifting of the labour-intensive textile industry from Japan to the Asian NIEs and then to the ASEAN countries and China. A similar pattern has been observed for the electrical and electronics industry. Since the 1990s, however, there have been changes. East Asia has begun to shift away from the flying geese pattern; 'leading' has been replaced by competition between countries in a whole range of industries, from textiles to high technology. In particular, China is in fierce competition not only with ASEAN countries but also with the NIEs and Japan in all ranges of industry. This new trend continues to be strong, suggesting that the East Asian countries are going to confront fierce competition among themselves now more than ever before.

increase in international liquidity from the pooled reserves would have been insufficient to cope with speculative attacks, given the enormous size of short-term capital flows. Kojima's PAFTA idea was later realized in the creation of APEC, with the support of Okita Saburo, who contributed to making the flying geese theory popular in the Western world. However, a Pacific Currency Area never became reality.

4.1.2   Catch-up of Developing Asian Countries

Following on the heels of Japan's rapid growth in the 1960s, Korea also grew at very rapid rates from the mid-1960s, with its per capita income rising to match those in a number of advanced economies in Western Europe. Korea was not the only country with a spectacular growth performance. Taiwan, Hong Kong and Singapore all grew very rapidly; the growth of all these economies has been termed a 'miracle' (World Bank, 1993).

These countries were followed in the 1980s by the South-East Asian economies, especially Indonesia, Malaysia and Thailand, which then also grew exceptionally fast. Finally China joined this 'growth club'. After opening its door first in 1978, the Chinese economy grew at double-digit rates starting in the 1980s.

All these countries experienced sustained economic growth at rates that exceeded those earlier thought achievable, with some attaining growth of 8–10 per cent a year for a decade. For East Asia in general, the growth performance is staggering. The high and lasting growth has expanded East Asia's economy from a mere US$1741 billion in 1980 to more than US$17705 billion in 2009, and the region's share of the world's GDP rose by more than 10 per cent, from 14.1 per cent to 24.4 per cent during the same period (see Figure 4.1).

Along with the expansion of the domestic economy, East Asian countries continued to expand in international transactions in goods and factors. Whereas total trade (= exports + imports) of East Asian countries was barely over US$626 billion in 1980, it is now more than US$7810 billion (Figure 4.2). East Asia's trade has grown by 7.3 per cent per annum in real terms, far faster than its economic growth, and its share of the world trade now reaches 24.9 per cent – an increase of 12.2 per cent from 12.7 per cent in 1980 (Figure 4.2).

The rapid growth of developing East Asian countries represented a catch-up process with the Japanese economy. This catch-up process also coincided with the economic decline of the Japanese economy. In fact, the Japanese growth rate slowed down, showing the signs

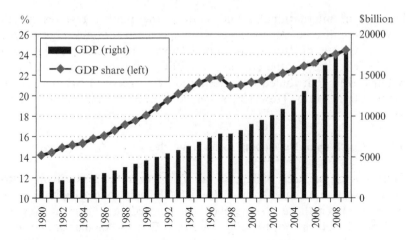

Sources: World Bank, *World Development Indicators*; IMF; IFS.

Figure 4.1   Trends in East Asian GDP

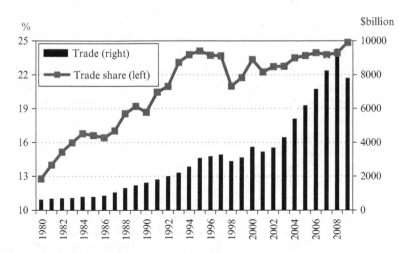

Source: World Bank, *World Development Indicators*.

Figure 4.2   Trade of East Asia

of a mature economy, beginning in the mid-1970s. However, Japan continued to outperform Western industrialized countries, including the US, until the end of the 1980s. The critical moment occurred after the bubble burst in 1990. Since then, the Japanese economy has experienced a prolonged depression and has still not recovered from this adversity.

There are many structural problems and policy mistakes that could explain the long Japanese depression, including the rapidly aging population and the failure of macroeconomic policy measures. What is undeniable is that the rapidly appreciated Japanese yen from the middle of the 1980s aggravated the boom–bust of the asset market cycle and prolonged the crisis. The Plaza Accord was particularly critical. After the Plaza Accord, the nominal dollar value of the yen, which had hovered at around 250 yen per dollar, suddenly moved upward to 120 yen per dollar. The appreciation of the yen was regarded as the worst of the many external shocks Japan had experienced since the war. Exports and manufacturing production declined drastically in 1986, and the Japanese government needed to boost the suffering economy by any means. But policy options scarcely existed. The trade dispute with the US made export expansion very difficult. Fiscal policy was barely available because of ballooning national debt. The only possible choice was a monetary solution – easy money plus consecutive cuts in the official discount rate – with the goal of boosting both the stock and property markets. Firms and individuals borrowed money without worrying about the interest cost. The banks, which had an excess of savings and a shortage of investment opportunities, lent money to new customers, including those involved in real estate. As a result, too much money flowed into the real estate industry and was lent as collateral loans, with real estate serving as collateral. Finally, the real estate bubble burst. Japan continued to experience difficult times because, no matter what the government did, monetary and fiscal policies were not effective.

The rise of developing Asian economies, along with the depression of the Japanese economy, was an opportunity to achieve an economic convergence between Asian economies. The economic convergence is especially evident in the case of the four newly industrialized economies called 'the Tigers' (Korea, Hong Kong, Singapore and Taiwan). These countries have had average annual growth rates of GDP per capita well in excess of 5 per cent over the last 50 years, while Japan had an annual growth rate of 3.6 per cent. In 1960, for instance, the per capita GDP in Korea was about 30 per cent of the Japanese per capita GDP. By 2009, it had increased to 78 per cent of the Japanese per capita GDP (see Figure 4.3).

A number of other Asian countries (for example, Indonesia, Malaysia, and Thailand) are also rapidly catching up, although their performance is less remarkable than that of the four newly industrializing economies. Since the 1980s, however, it is China that has achieved the most rapid catch-up with Japan.

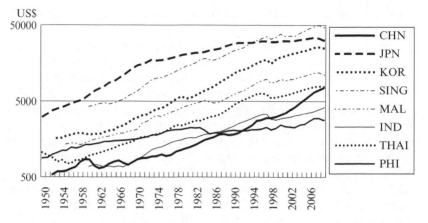

Source: Penn World Table 7.0 (2011).

Figure 4.3   Trends in per capita GDP

4.2   REAL REGIONALIZATION AND FINANCIAL GLOBALIZATION

4.2.1   Real Regionalization

East Asian economies have achieved remarkable growth over the past decades. This growth is largely attributable to market-driven expansion of trade in the region; intraregional trade in East Asia accounts for about one third of all East Asian trade. Figure 4.4 summarizes this trend over the period 1990–2008. Now, intraregional trade accounts for around 37 per cent of total trade in East Asia,[2] while it was a mere 29 per cent in 1990. Geographical proximity, common life styles and intercultural understanding all contribute to intensifying intraregional trade.

Similar trends are observed for exports and imports. When exports and imports of East Asian countries are considered separately, a notable trend is that East Asia's share has largely expanded in both exports and imports. This implies that East Asia has become more important not only as a region of resources or intermediate goods but also as a market for final goods for East Asian countries themselves. On the other hand, the importance of the US as a market for final goods has declined, while that of the EU market has stayed at a similar level over the two decades (see Figure 4.5).

The rise of China is an important factor in explaining increasing intra-regional trade because it accounts for one third of all intraregional trade.

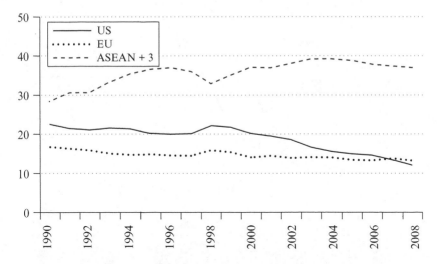

Source: IMF Direction of Trade Statistics; ADB, Asia Regional Integration Center.

Figure 4.4 Geographical distribution of trade in East Asia

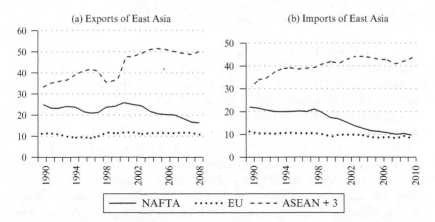

Source: IMF Direction of Trade Statistics.

Figure 4.5 Exports and imports in East Asia

For instance, after Korea started trade relations with China in 1992, its trade with China soared. Now China is the largest trade partner for Korea, far outpacing the US and the EU. As a result, East Asia accounts for 44 per cent of total world trade. The same pattern is observed for

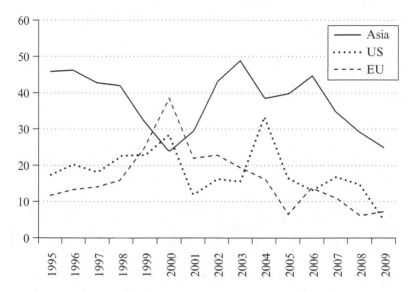

Sources: Authors' calculation from UNCTAD stat; OECD stat; Census and statistics department of Hong Kong; Department of Statistics Singapore; Mainland Affairs Council.

Figure 4.6   Geographical distribution of FDI flows in East Asia

Japan and the ASEAN countries. China–ASEAN merchandise trade has ballooned from US$6 billion in 1991 to US$202 billion in 2010. Figure 4.5 shows the geographical distribution of exports and imports for East Asia including Korea, Japan, China and the ASEAN 5.

The increase of FDI in East Asia is another important factor accelerating intraregional trade among East Asian countries. Global multinational companies and East Asian firms have formed international production networks and supply chains throughout East Asia through their FDI. According to Ando and Kimura (2003), these international production networks account for a significant share of trade flows of most countries in the region and are spreading over a large number of countries. The cross-border production and trade networks explain the rapid increase of both trade and FDI flows between Asian countries themselves (Ando and Kimura, 2003).

Figure 4.6 shows the trend of foreign direct investment in East Asia since 1995. Apart from the year 2000, intraregional FDI flows accounted for the largest share of East Asian FDI flows (sum of inflows and outflows).

If inbound and outbound FDI flows are considered separately, then the inbound FDI flows to the East Asian region from the US and EU are as great as those from East Asia, while the outbound FDI of the East Asian

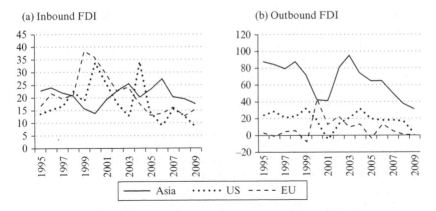

(a) Inbound FDI   (b) Outbound FDI

Asia ······ US ---- EU

Sources: Authors' calculation from UNCTAD stat; OECD stat; Census and statistics department of Hong Kong; Department of Statistics Singapore; Mainland Affairs Council.

Figure 4.7   Inbound and outbound FDI flows in East Asia

countries mostly go to other East Asian countries. Indeed, Japan and the NIEs are the major FDI investors in the East Asian region (see Figure 4.7).

Traditionally, Japan was the most important player regarding FDI outflows in East Asia. Japan's investment in East Asia started in the light industry sector, such as textiles, at the beginning of the 1970s, but it soon extended to the heavy and chemical industries. Since the mid-1980s, the NIEs have also become important players regarding FDI flows in East Asia. In the 1980s, especially after the exchange rate realignment following the Plaza Accord in 1985, Japan shifted its production to lower-cost East Asian countries even in the technology-intensive sectors such as electrical machinery and transport machinery. As the Chinese economy expanded, Japan's investment in China rose dramatically and it also shifted its investment in the NIEs to China.

While the NIEs have recorded huge current account surpluses, their domestic wages and production costs have risen sharply, generating booms in the service sector at the cost of declines in the export manufacturing sector, which could be seen as a kind of 'Dutch disease'. The NIEs started to move their production abroad and soon became the leading regional supplier of capital, replacing Japan and the US as the largest foreign investors in the ASEAN countries and China. Indeed, the NIEs invested more than half of their FDI in East Asia, mainly in the ASEAN countries and China.

This shift from Japan to the NIEs as the main actors regarding the FDI flow in East Asian developing countries is significant for the regional division of labour. It means that the spectrum of the intraregional division of labour has expanded substantially from inter-industry to intra-industry specialization. In particular, East Asian countries' FDI led to the rise of vertical intra-industry trade in parts, components, and semi-finished and finished manufactured products (Kawai and Urata, 1998; 2004). Furthermore, the rapid growth of a very large emerging market economy, China, was an important factor that contributed to closer economic linkages and increases in FDI between East Asian economies. China plays a major role in these production networks and supply chains, as its expanding export industry requires more imports of industrial materials, parts, components, and other intermediate products from its neighbouring economies. China has become a manufacturing assembly location for East Asian economies and has developed its comparative advantages in manufacturing industries.

Large intraregional FDI in East Asia supported increasing intraregional trade. It is, however, important to note that trade is interregional as well as intraregional. East Asian countries started their industrialization relying largely on the US and world markets, and therefore their economies were intimately integrated with the global economy, particularly with the US economy. Thus, although the intraregional market has grown steadily and has become dominant, the US and global markets still remain very important. The US and European markets are especially important for Asia's finished manufactured products. As ADB (2010) pointed out, the US and the EU absorb 46 per cent of emerging Asia's total exports as the destination place of final demand for Asian manufactured goods, while the emerging East Asian economies themselves absorb only 22.9 per cent of Asian exports. When it comes to final import demand, China's influence is still limited. For instance, the US final import demand for the world economy is three times greater than China's import demand (Capannelli et al., 2009). Furthermore, the US and the EU are the largest investors in East Asia, which means that the Asian trade structure reflects global as well as regional production sharing.

4.2.2 Financial Globalization

Financial globalization can be defined as the process of increasing financial transactions between different nations and currency areas. There exists a general consensus that financial market integration contributes to long-term economic growth. Financial market integration increases benefits for portfolio risk diversification and consumption smoothing across countries through borrowing and lending. At the same time, financial integration contributes indirectly to the economic welfare of countries. In addition to consumption smoothing and risk sharing, the positive impacts of capital

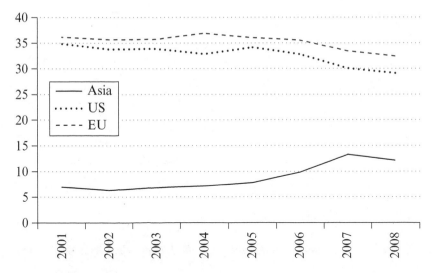

Source: IMF, International Financial Statistics.

Figure 4.8 *Geographical distribution of portfolio investment flows in East Asia (%)*

flows on domestic investment and growth, enhanced macroeconomic discipline, and increased efficiency and stability of the financial system are the main benefits of financial integration (Daiwa Institute of Research, 2005).

Following major industrialized economies, East Asian countries pursued financial globalization. From the late 1980s, they gradually removed many controls and restrictions on capital movements across borders. This process accelerated after the 1997 Asian currency crisis, leading to the deregulation of domestic financial systems, the opening of financial services markets, and the relaxation of capital and exchange rate controls. As a result, the degree of financial integration in East Asia has increased recently, but compared to real regionalization, financial integration in East Asia is far more global than regional.

Figure 4.8 shows the geographical distribution of the cross-border portfolio investment flows in East Asia. For East Asian countries, the US and the EU are two major portfolio investment partners. Although East Asia's share in the region's portfolio flows have tended to increase recently, the East Asia region is far behind the US and the EU as a portfolio investment recipient or destination.

Figure 4.9 shows the geographical distribution of inbound and outbound portfolio investment flows separately. The major source of portfolio

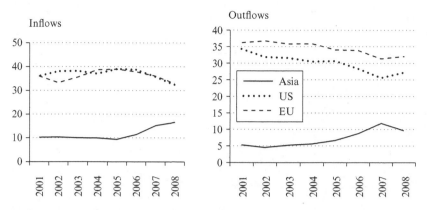

Source: IMF, International Financial Statistics.

Figure 4.9 Inbound and outbound portfolio flows in East Asia (%)

investment in East Asia comes from the US and the EU, which together account for around one third of portfolio investments in East Asia. In contrast, nine East Asian countries (China, Japan, Korea, Hong Kong and the ASEAN 5) receive only 10–16 per cent of the inbound portfolio flows. Similar patterns are observed for portfolio investment destination. As of 2008, the US and the EU constitute 27 per cent and 32 per cent, respectively, while East Asia represents only 9.6 per cent of the total of East Asian outbound portfolio investments (eight East Asian countries excluding China).

In conclusion, the East Asian financial markets are becoming increasingly integrated with global financial markets. More importantly, the increasing financial globalization in East Asia has led to financial regionalization through deepened linkages between Asian and global financial markets. For instance, East Asian countries have been increasing their capital investments in safe US Treasury bonds, while US financial firms reinvested these funds in rather risky Asian assets (García-Herrero et al., 2009).

4.3 EAST ASIAN FINANCIAL CRISIS

4.3.1 Development of the East Asian Crisis

The East Asian crisis began in Thailand. The bursting of the bubble in asset prices and the worsening of current accounts led the markets to

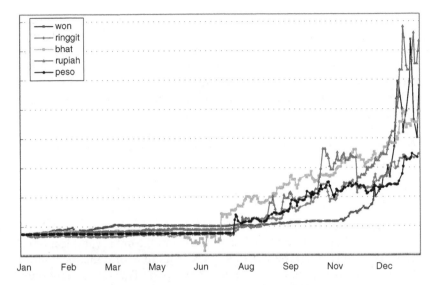

Note: The scale of exchange rates is adjusted to 1 January at 1.00.

Source: Datastream International.

Figure 4.10   Exchange rates of East Asian currencies, 1997

doubt the sustainability of Thailand's external position. After periods of speculative attacks, the Thai baht came under sustained pressure in May 1997. All the measures to defend the baht failed, and finally on 2 July, the Thai government yielded to the market forces and the baht was allowed to float (Figure 4.10). The effects of the fall of the Thai baht quickly spread to neighbouring ASEAN countries, leading to the fall of the Philippine peso and the Malaysian ringgit in mid-July 1997 and of the Indonesian rupiah in mid-August of the same year.

Contagion was not limited to South-East Asia. Initially, Taiwan tried to defend its currency. But as speculative pressure on the New Taiwanese (NT) dollar accumulated, Taiwan decided to float its currency on 17 October 1997. The fall of the NT dollar immediately shifted the pressure to Hong Kong, which had maintained a pegged system to the US dollar since 1983. Hong Kong's financial authorities had to raise interest rates sharply to defend the peg. This sharp increase in interest rates produced a precipitous decline in the Hong Kong stock market and had global reverberations.

The crisis spread to Korea at the end of October 1997. A growing number of bankruptcies of major chaebols fuelled concerns about the health of the Korean economy. After the fall of the ASEAN currencies, Korea lost market confidence and the Korean won was forced to devalue. Taiwan's devaluation of the NT dollar and the plunge of the Hong Kong stock market put further pressure on the Korean won. In 1997, Taiwan was running a huge current account surplus and its reserve of almost $100 billion was the third highest in the world, behind only Japan and China. Thus, Taiwan could maintain a competitive position. Meanwhile, Korea was in a weak position and was Taiwan's closest competitor. So when Taiwan let its currency fall, it was natural that markets expected Korea to let its currency fall.

4.3.2   The Causes of the East Asian Crisis

The underlying reasons for the East Asian crisis are multifaceted, but broadly speaking, the crisis can be attributed to the unfavourable international economic circumstances ('bad luck') and to poor domestic political judgements ('bad policy') (Hiwatari, 2003, p.1). The vast international capital movement generated a huge boom–bust cycle and internal problems such as moral hazard leading to the financial fragility aggravating the bust of the cycle. Furthermore, adverse shocks such as speculative attacks on East Asian currencies and foreign banks' refusal to roll-over short-term debts caused the bust to develop into a crisis.

Unlike the Latin American crisis in the 1980s, the East Asian crisis was not driven by severe macroeconomic imbalances. But in the 1990s, the reinforcing effects of high and rising investments, capital inflows and asset booms led to sharp increases in the aggregate demand. The main expressions of excess demand were large, and they widened current account deficits. By and large, these were not accompanied by a deterioration in countries' ability to service their foreign debts from export revenues. The widening of deficits, however, brought attention to the underlying factors that affected the sustainability of the excessive investment and the external imbalance, including the quality and risk of the investment being financed by external funds.

Despite these increasing imbalances, the chief external source of vulnerability arose not from major macroeconomic imbalances but from a sudden build-up of vulnerability in the financial and corporate sectors. In hindsight, the East Asian crisis highlighted the structural and institutional challenges posed by financial liberalization. Most countries in East Asia were ill-prepared for fast financial integration into the world because of their inefficient financial systems. Many companies overinvested with little scrutiny of investments, many of which were financed by short-term debt. Financial institutions did not consider the risks incorporated in lending, and much of the lending was directed to speculative investments in real estate and the stock market, leading to a volatile boom and bust.

However, the cause of vulnerability build-up was as attributable to external lenders as to internal borrowers. Both external and internal factors reinforced each other and cumulatively created growing macro and financial vulnerability. While much of the underlying process may have occurred without inflows of private capital, the growing financial integration and easy access to private capital flows contributed to the dynamics, increasing the speed and magnitude of the build-up in vulnerability and the potentiality of the crisis.

Following the structural reforms and liberalization of the late 1980s and the 1990s, improvements in growth performance and prospects led to expectations of higher permanent rates of return that would cover the risk in investments. This expectation provided validation of and added impetus for higher rates of investment, and inflow of foreign capital sharply increased in East Asia. Capital inflow brought about the appreciation of domestic currency while increasing domestic credit. With the increase in domestic credit came an excessive economic boom; as a result asset prices in real estate and stock markets took a leap, leading to a bubble economy. The asset price rises and increases in wealth sustained higher consumption, which, by adding to aggregate demand and output growth, reinforced the entire process of investment impetus, asset price rise and consumption growth, making the financial condition of banks and firms seem sounder than it was. In the meantime, governments implemented tight monetary policy and heavy sterilization, which sustained high interest rates and stabilized exchange rates by further providing impetus to capital inflow; this high interest rate policy only aggravated fragility in the corporate sector and therefore the financial sector.

The current account deteriorated rapidly following the rise in import demand and the appreciation of domestic currency due to the excessive boom. As the current account deficit accumulated, the disequilibrium in fundamental economic conditions worsened. Consequently capital flew out, the exchange rate became unstable, and the circular process went into reverse. As the economic boom came to an abrupt halt, non-performing loans increased with failing firms, and financial conditions sharply deteriorated. As a result, the international credit ratings of financial institutions fell, and they began to experience difficulty in financing foreign currencies, which eventually led to the currency crisis. The currency speculation of international investors only worsened the situation.

The process of financial liberalization, and the large capital inflows that accompanied it, worked as the main forces generating this cycle and made the East Asian financial sector fragile. In particular, favourable

Table 4.1   Capital flows in five Asian countries ($billion)

	1994	1995	1996	1997	1998
Capital flows, net	47.4	80.9	92.8	−9.7	−20.2
Private flows, net	40.4	77.4	93.0	−30.8	−45.4
Equity investment	12.1	15.5	19.1	15.4	7.7
Direct equity	4.7	4.9	7.0	12.4	11.8
Portfolio equity	7.5	10.6	12.1	3.0	−4.1
Private creditors	28.2	61.8	74.0	−46.2	−53.0

Note: The five Asian countries are South Korea, Indonesia, Malaysia, Thailand and the Philippines.

Source: IMF, International Financial Statistics.

international market conditions contributed to the surge in private capital inflows. Low interest rates in Japan and the United States encouraged international investors and lenders to expand their activities in East Asian markets in search of higher yields. The competitive upgrading of credit ratings of East Asian countries, reflecting credit rating companies' desire to expand their business scope, and the following declining spreads in both international bond and loan markets also seduced borrowers in East Asia to look abroad for lower-cost finance than was domestically available.[3]

The increase in private capital inflows provided the additional liquidity that allowed banks and non-bank financial intermediaries to increase lending. But according to the 'good times are bad times for learning' theory,[4] a lending boom following macroeconomic expansion tends to lead to a deterioration of portfolio quality and an increase in financial vulnerability. For example, in order to expand a loan portfolio very rapidly, bankers typically need not only to increase the size of their exposure to their existing clientele, but also to find new borrowers about whom the bankers have relatively little information. As the lending boom proceeds, therefore, the risks of the portfolio will rise and loans to non-creditworthy borrowers are likely to increase. Also, when credit is plentiful, borrowers can easily pass creditworthiness tests because they can find another lender who is willing to provide them with credit. Hence, credit booms are excessively rapid and associated with deteriorating loan portfolios.

Table 4.1 shows the trend in foreign capital flow in the five crisis-stricken East Asian countries around the crisis period. First of all, capital inflow increased by 95 per cent, from US$47.4 billion in 1994 to US$92.8 billion in 1996. Equity flows through direct investment or portfolio investment grew from US$12.1 billion in 1994 to US$19.1 billion in 1996. But a more striking increase was in borrowings from private lenders, including commercial banks and non-bank creditors, from US$28.2 billion in 1994 to US$74.0 billion in 1996. The inflow of capital to the East Asian region had increased greatly each year due to inflows generated by Japan's low interest rates and high returns in the emerging countries.

The increasing trend suddenly reversed, and the five Asian countries suffered a net private capital outflow amounting US$30.8 billion in 1997. The portfolio investment dropped significantly, from $12.1 billion in 1996 to US$3.0 billion in 1997. However, the sharpest decline occurred in the flows of borrowings of financial institutions. Borrowings of commercial banks reversed direction from a net inflow of US$55.5 billion in 1996 to a net outflow of US$22.9 billion and those of non-bank creditors from a net inflow of $18.4 to a net outflow of $23.3 billion for the five Asian countries in 1997.

A fundamental problem lies in the fact that the capital that had been flowing in rapidly just before the currency crisis, flowed out at an even greater speed in 1997. Although foreign lenders and investors withdrew their money following the currency crisis in this region, they had actually exacerbated the crisis by suddenly withdrawing international liquidity just before the crisis broke out. This view is also connected with the question of whether there was enough of a significant negative economic change in this region to reverse the direction of private capital flow amounting to US$123.8 billion, from an inflow of US$93.0 billion to an outflow of US$30.8 billion, within the course of one year. If they had excessively supplied capital despite having foreseen the currency crisis in East Asia, they were guilty of a moral hazard behaviour; if they had not foreseen it, then they should share a joint responsibility for triggering the crisis by suddenly withdrawing capital from the region.

Moreover, the inappropriate exchange rate policies implemented by many East Asian countries turned out disastrously. Indeed, a common feature of the East Asian countries affected by economic crisis was their explicit or implicit commitment to defend their existing exchange rate parities (ESCAP, 1998).

There was a fear that forsaking parity could cause a large devaluation which would unleash a massive surge of corporate insolvencies, given their large foreign-currency denominated borrowings. These insolvencies would have an adverse effect on the financial sector. Preserving bilateral parity with the United States dollar was taken to be a key element in avoiding those risks. It depended upon the availability of net foreign exchange reserves whether East Asian countries could defend exchange rate parities. Thus, while Indonesia, Korea and Thailand suffered large exchange rate depreciations as their short-term debts far exceeded their reserves, Hong

Kong, China and Singapore were able to stave off speculative pressure in this regard.

4.3.3   The Role of the IMF during the Currency Crisis

The IMF provided the crisis-hit Asian countries with a series of rescue packages, tying these packages to economic reforms that were intended to model the restored Asian currency, banking and financial systems to those in the United States and Europe as much as possible. In other words, the IMF's support was conditional on a series of drastic economic reforms incarnated in the so-called 'structural adjustment package'.

The main content of the structural adjustment package was cutting back on government spending in the crisis-hit countries to reduce deficits, aggressively raising interest rates, and accelerating financial liberalization, thereby eliminating any remaining restriction on capital flows. The reasoning was that these steps would restore confidence in the nations' fiscal solvency, protect currency values, and increase economic efficiency.

The IMF intervention was criticized for the following two reasons. First, the macroeconomic policy prescriptions imposed by the IMF conditionality were too contractionary and caused Asian economies to sink into unprecedentedly deep and enormously painful recessions rather than helping these economies. As Kawai (2009a) rightly pointed out,

> the fiscal policy prescribed in the early phase of the Asian financial crisis – in Thailand and Korea – was contractionary despite the fact that fiscal spending and budget deficits were not causes of the crisis and that the countries were severely affected by the sudden withdrawal of foreign capital and plunged into a major recession.

The monetary policy was also wrong because the high interest policy aggravated the crisis. Numerous companies had to go bankrupt. For instance, the Korean government raised its policy interest rate to almost 30 per cent a year – over double the pre-crisis rate, which was approximately 12 per cent. In retrospect, this tightened monetary policy only aggravated the currency crisis, causing it to grow into a generalized banking crisis. The goal of the high interest policy enforced by the IMF was to prevent the hoarding of the US dollar and the capital outflow. However, this policy turned out to be ineffective in holding foreign capital outflow or attracting foreign capital. Instead, it ended up hardening the business environment for domestic firms who were already in difficulties (see Ito, 1999).

Second, some IMF interventions were unjustified because they reached beyond its competency and responsibility. For instance, 'the Indonesian program had over 100 conditions including the reform of the rice distribution system and the dismantling of the clove monopoly, which had nothing to do with the country's capital account crisis' (Feldstein, 1998). In retrospect, it is undeniable that the 'IMF conditionality' was 'too harsh in the Korean crisis' (Siebert, 2008) and the IMF and US advanced 'their interests not at the point of a gun but at the tip of a check-signer's pen' (Rothkopf, 2008).

> Mutual trust between the IMF and country authorities is an important element in making IMF operations effective because it provides a healthy environment for frank discussion and exchanges of views. However, the IMF has a credibility problem in Asia. At the time of the Asian financial crisis, the IMF lost its credibility and trust among Asian policymakers and has not regained them yet. The IMF has been viewed as an outside institution that lectures and, at times of crisis, imposes tough 'conditionality' on emerging market economies with a 'top-down' analysis done in Washington without considering realities on the ground. (Kawai, 2009a, p.19)

4.4   THE GLOBAL FINANCIAL CRISIS AND THE IMF

The eruption of the global financial crisis in 2008 was a critical turning point for the IMF and IMF-recommended policy. The global financial crisis started with the collapse of Lehman Brothers in the third quarter of 2008. This collapse generated a ripple effect throughout the world economy, eventually evolving into a global financial and economic crisis. Most East Asian countries were severely hit by the crisis. For example, the real GDP in Korea, Taiwan, Singapore, Malaysia and Thailand fell by more than 10 per cent at an annualized rate and the financial markets also tumbled right after the onset of the crisis. China and Indonesia experienced somewhat lower growth rates in late 2008 than before.

The global financial crisis did not force any Asian country to go to the IMF for financial rescue, although several countries, such as Korea and Indonesia, faced a shock similar to the one they had experienced during the 1997 Asian financial crisis. For instance, in Korea exports shrank rapidly and the Korean currency depreciated heavily from 907 won per US dollar in October 2007 to 1483 won per US dollar in November 2008. Also, the Korean government lost an unusually large amount of foreign exchange reserves from March 2008, with its reserves declining from US$264 billion in March to just below US$200 billion in November. Korea almost experienced a recurrence of the currency crisis. Nevertheless, Korea did not rely on IMF liquidity assistance. Instead Korea, together with Brazil, Mexico and Singapore, concluded a currency swap arrangement of up to US$30 billion with the US Federal Reserve in October 2008. It also entered into currency swap arrangements with the central banks of Japan and China in December 2008. The foreign exchange market was soon stabilized.

The most critical factor preventing the Korean government from borrowing from the IMF was its harsh conditionality. Indeed, it is difficult to imagine that countries like Korea that had experienced the 1997 financial crisis would rely again on the IMF, as borrowing money from the IMF implicitly implies that their economic policies have failed (stigma effect). This would have had significant political repercussions throughout the country. In contrast, the 'currency swaps could be drawn without any policy conditionality and, in this sense, were arrangements that competed against IMF' (Kawai, 2009a).

Speaking on the difference between the 1997 Asian crisis and the 2008 global crisis, the IMF managing director, Strauss-Kahn (2008), said:

> What originated in Thailand and spread to Korea, Indonesia, and other countries was mainly a balance of payments problem. That was our core business. This crisis, even if it is a huge crisis, is different. This is a different kind of crisis, so the solution to be applied is not the same. The main actors today are the central banks and treasuries; the main actors in the Asian crisis were institutions like the IMF.

The global financial crisis also changed IMF's policy stance. As Kawai said:

> The IMF appears ready to move away from a 'one-size-fits-all' approach to stabilization without always relying on prescribing contractionary macroeconomic policy in the face of crises originating in the capital account. The IMF has also decided to streamline and limit its structural conditionality to a core set of essential features that are macro-relevant and within the IMF's core area of responsibility, with any broader approach requiring justification based upon the specific country situation. Hence, IMF conditionality now covers only macroeconomic policies and macro-critical structural reform policies. (Kawai, 2009a, p.17)

As East Asian countries did in the 1997 currency crisis, so they recovered very quickly from the fallout of the 2008 global crisis. Since the second half of 2009, these economies have bounced back to their usual high growth rates. There are several reasons why the global financial crisis had a limited effect in East Asia and why emerging East Asian countries bounced back rapidly.

One reason is that most East Asian countries have very aggressively mobilized fiscal and monetary stimulus packages. First of all, monetary policy was expansionary. During the period of the 2008 global financial

Table 4.2   Export and import intensities of East Asian countries

	Period	With the US	With the EU	With East Asia
Export Intensity	1990:I–1996:IV	0.225	0.155	0.471
	1999:I–2002:IV	0.218	0.147	0.494
	2003:I–2006:IV	0.170	0.128	0.537
Import Intensity	1990:I–1996:IV	0.161	0.134	0.502
	1999:I–2002:IV	0.145	0.109	0.540
	2003:I–2006:IV	0.110	0.095	0.558

Note: The period of the Asian crisis (1997:I–1998:IV) is omitted to avoid the extraordinary influence of the crisis.

Source: Partly extracted from Shin (2008).

crisis, for instance, the Korean government quickly proceeded to lower interest rates and pump necessary liquidity into the Korean economy. The policy interest rate was lowered to 2 per cent, less than half the pre-crisis rate of 5.25 per cent, in response to the recent crisis. There is no doubt that the monetary easing in 2008 was crucial in guarding the domestic economy from the external storm. Fiscal policy was also expansionary. Indeed, in the past few years East Asia has conducted the largest fiscal stimulus policy in the world. Since most East Asian countries had maintained sound government budgets, they had more room for fiscal expansion. Moreover, households in East Asian countries are much less in debt than those in the US and eurozone countries. Thus, when confronted with fiscal expansion, such as tax cuts, households in East Asia are more likely to spend than save, while households in Western countries are more likely to save than spend, because of debt worries.

The second reason is that East Asian countries have become more economically interdependent and their dependence on the US and external markets has been reduced. As we saw above, intra-Asian trade and investment have been trending upward for several decades. Although this trend was disrupted by the Asian crisis of 1997–8, it resumed and grew even stronger during the post-crisis recovery. This is also confirmed by export and import intensities in Table 4.2. East Asian countries have much higher export and import intensities among themselves than with the US and the EU. Furthermore, the intensities with East Asia have been increasing, while those with others have been declining. The high trade share inside East Asia implies that other external markets have become substantially less important. Thus, East Asian countries have been less affected by the global financial crisis.

Table 4.3   Feldstein–Horioka coefficient

Region	Coefficient	
	1990–1999	2000–2006
ASEAN+3	0.534	0.349
EU27	0.109	0.080

Source: Partly extracted from Takagi (2008).

The third reason is that financial markets in East Asian countries are less closely linked to the US than the eurozone is, and their financial systems had become relatively healthy after the Asian crisis in 1997. Table 4.3 shows that East Asian financial markets are still less open than those in the EU, and that East Asia was relatively less exposed to the risk of the sub-prime mortgage-driven crisis. In addition, although financial integration contributes to business cycle synchronization, the impact of financial integration on business cycles is much weaker than that of trade integration in East Asia. This was also helpful in enabling East Asia to decouple from the US in recovering from the current crisis.

NOTES

1. The experience of East Asia is again different from that of the Europe and US where the pre-war competitive devaluation was remembered by all as a very bitter experience.
2. If Taiwan and Hong Kong are included, then the share of intraregional trade reaches more than 50 per cent of the total trade in East Asia.
3. McKinnon (1999, p.14) argues that the yen-data (yen-increase) in the 1990s provided the root of the Asian crisis. 'The expectation of a higher yen caused by the upward drift in the beginning of the 1990s drove nominal interest rates on yen assets far below those prevailing on dollar assets. In the East Asian debtor economies, unusually low interest rates in Japan further tempted banks with moral hazard to over-borrow by accepting cheap deposits without covering the foreign exchange rate risk. Also, on the creditor side, Japanese banks were tempted to overland by purchasing foreign currency assets with higher nominal yields. Moreover, American and European hedge funds got involved in the so-called Asian carry trade: they borrowed cheaply in Japan at short term, and on-lent to East Asian debtor economies.'
4. For an example, see Gavin and Hausmann (1996).

5. Conditions for monetary integration in East Asia

With an increasing need for monetary integration in the region, there have been many studies on its feasibility. The general conclusion is that East Asian monetary integration would be very difficult to realize. Some studies even say that integration is not desirable. This is due to the fact that East Asia is neither economically self-contained nor an optimum currency area, and that East Asian governments have policy objectives that are too different from each other. However, this kind of argument is mostly based on past analyses. As we saw in Chapter 4, East Asia is rapidly changing and the region's readiness for a monetary arrangement has changed accordingly.

Now, economic interdependence among East Asian countries has become so deep that closer regional cooperation is essential. If economic integration merely means an absence of any barriers to the free flow of goods, capital and people, countries in East Asia might have already attained quite a significant degree of market-driven integration. Some groups of countries already satisfy the preconditions for a currency union. As Watanabe and Ogura (2006) pointed out, 'some Asian countries exhibit almost the same level of external openness, intra-regional trade and symmetry in macroeconomic shocks as their European counterparts did in the pre-euro period' (p.3). More importantly, if the endogeneity of the optimum currency area works, then East Asian countries may be suitable for a currency union, although those preconditions are not yet fulfilled and countries do not meet many of these conditions *ex ante*. In sum, on economic grounds there seem to be good reasons to promote East Asian monetary integration, in whatever form it may be.

5.1 SELF-CONTAINMENT

In order to discuss the possibility of a regional monetary and economic arrangement, it is necessary to ask whether East Asia is economically self-contained. One of the preconditions for economic self-containment is the sufficient economic size of the region.

Table 5.1   Economies of the three major blocs, 2009

	East Asia	Eurozone	NAFTA
Population (million)	2131	327	457
GDP (purchasing power parity) (US$ bn)	17710	11670	16860
Trade (US$ bn)	6599	8844	4822
Foreign Reserves (US$ bn)	4885	591	285

Note: East Asia includes ASEAN+5 (Korea, China, Japan, Taiwan, Hong Kong).
The eurozone includes the 16 euro members, and NAFTA includes the US, Canada and
Mexico.

Sources: IMF, International Financial Statistics; IMF, Direction of Trade Statistics; CIA,
World Factbook.

If East Asia considers having a separate monetary arrangement in the
region, its economy needs to be large enough to become a major pole of
world economic growth. According to Table 5.1, which compares the
economies of three major blocs, East Asia as a whole is already nearly as
large as the EU or North America. The population of East Asia is over
2 billion, which is almost seven times and five times that of the eurozone
and NAFTA, respectively. The total output of the 15 East Asian countries
is US$17710 billion in PPP terms, which is larger than that of Europe
(US$11670 billion) and North America (US$16860 billion) in 2009. Also,
its trade with the world (US$6599 billion) is not much smaller than that
of Europe (US$8844 billion) and much larger than that of North America
(US$4822 billion). Finally, foreign reserves held in East Asia at US$4855
billion, are far greater than those in Europe (US$591 billion) and North
America (US$285 billion).

5.2   OPTIMUM CURRENCY AREA CONDITIONS

It is one thing for a region to be self-contained, but it is quite another for
a region to have a separate regional monetary arrangement which is desirable and feasible. From an economic perspective, the most commonly
used arguments for examining the desirability and feasibility of monetary
integration is the optimum currency area (OCA) approach, pioneered by
Mundell (1961) and further developed by McKinnon (1963) and Kenen
(1969).[1] According to this theory, there is a trade-off between benefits
and costs of joining a monetary union. The main benefits are the reduction in transaction costs and exchange rate risks[2] and the introduction of

a credible nominal anchor for monetary policy. The main costs are the abandonment of independent monetary policy and the elimination of the less costly method of correcting current account imbalances through exchange rate changes.[3] The theory suggests several criteria for evaluating the economic conditions for monetary integration: openness and economic interdependence among member countries, symmetry of shocks, factor mobility, and inflation rate similarity. When a national economy is open and deeply integrated with other regional economies, the benefits from the reduction in transaction costs and exchange risks will be high. When shocks to the countries in the region are symmetrical, they can be offset with a collective monetary policy and the costs of giving up an independent monetary policy will be low. Also, although asymmetric shocks occur, if labour mobility and capital mobility are high among the countries in the region, it will be easy to redress macroeconomic imbalances arising from them and the costs of joining a monetary union will be small. Finally, divergent inflation rates, which are usually regarded as policy objective differences, will eventually cause the purchasing power of member countries to diverge, which will have to be corrected by a change in the exchange rate. Therefore, differences in inflation rates would be a big cost to monetary union.

In this section, the OCA conditions of East Asian countries are further analysed and compared with those of the EU and NAFTA countries.

5.2.1 Openness and Economic Interdependence

Openness
Figure 5.1 compares openness in East Asia with that in Europe and NAFTA. According to Figure 5.1, although East Asia (72.2 per cent) has a slightly lower degree of openness than the EU (79.5 per cent) as of 2008, it is rapidly catching up with the EU. Furthermore, its openness is much higher than NAFTA (36.2 per cent). Most East Asian countries have a high degree of openness. The ASEAN countries have particularly high openness ratios which exceed their GDP. Among East Asian countries, Japan has the lowest degree of openness at 35 per cent in 2008 (see Figure 5.2).

Trade interdependence
Economic interdependence in East Asia is also deepening through trade integration. Intra-Asian trade has been trending upward for several decades. Although this trend was disrupted by the Asian crisis of 1997–8, it resumed even more strongly after the post-crisis recovery (Figure 5.3). Now, intraregional trade accounts for around 40 per cent of East Asia's total trade. This figure is similar to the intraregional trade share

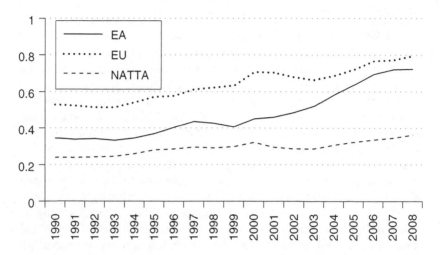

Note: Openness is the ratio of trade to GDP. The average is total regional trade divided by total regional GDP. East Asia refers to 9 Asian countries including China, Japan, Korea, Hong Kong and the original ASEAN 5 countries.

Sources: World Bank, World Development Indicators; IMF; IFS (for Singapore).

Figure 5.1 Degree of openness compared (%)

of NAFTA. The EU's intraregional trade share still remains the highest, although this has tended to decline over the period 1990–2008.

A simple comparison of the share of intraregional trade is not fully indicative of the economic force of regional interdependence, however, because such a comparison omits the special effects of many important factors. For example, geographical distances between countries, language differences between trading partners and many other factors affect trade. A more accurate assessment of deepening intraregional trade requires a model of bilateral trade, such as the gravity model, to set a benchmark. Table 5.2 reports the ratio of actual to predicted bilateral trade on the basis of the gravity model. If the number is greater than 1, it implies that the area is actually more integrated than predicted. If the number is less than 1, it implies the opposite. It seems that East Asia (4.15) is more integrated than was predicted, while the opposite is true for EU countries (0.87) and for NAFTA countries (0.58).[4] The increase in intraregional trade in East Asia has largely reflected the growing importance of the East Asian NIEs and China, and the potential benefit will increase with the growth of those economies.

Among individual East Asian countries and regions, ASEAN countries have the highest intraregional trade share, with more than 50 per cent of

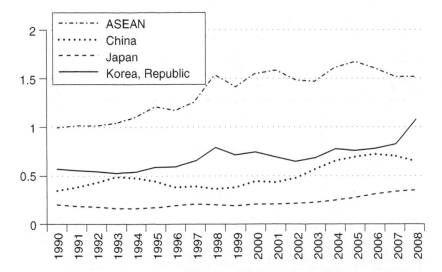

Note: ASEAN refers to the original ASEAN 5 countries (Indonesia, Malaysia, Philippines, Singapore and Thailand).

Sources: World Bank, World Development Indicators; IMF; IFS.

Figure 5.2 Openness of individual Asian countries and the region

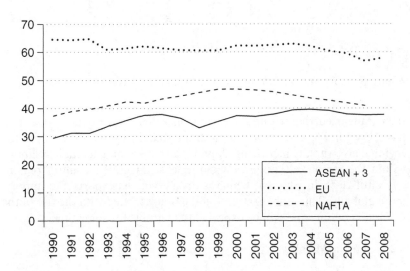

Sources: IMF, Direction of Trade and ADB; ARIC.

Figure 5.3 Intraregional trade share (%)

Table 5.2   Gravity ratio

	East Asia	EU	NAFTA
Average estimates	4.15	0.87	0.58
SD of estimates	1.60	0.34	0.20

Note: Gravity ratio is that of actual to predicted bilateral trade on the basis of the gravity model.

Source: Wyplosz (2001, p.7).

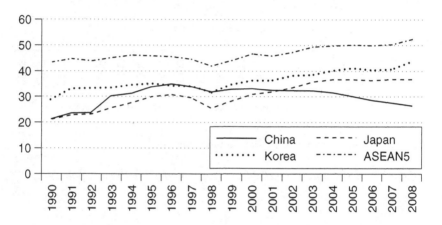

Sources: IMF, Direction of Trade and ADB; ARIC.

Figure 5.4   Regional trade share of individual East Asian countries (%)

their trade occurring within the region since 2005 (see Figure 5.4). Korea has the second largest intraregional trade share, with its trade within the regional area rapidly increasing. Japan is also deepening its trade relations within the region, although it was the least integrated country regionally until 2000. In contrast, China is diversifying its exports and imports more globally. This globalization trend has accelerated with the rise of the Chinese economy and will be expected to continue for some time.

5.2.2   Factor Mobility

Capital mobility
In addition to intraregional trade, factor mobility, such as the intraregional flow of people and capital, has also increased and deepened

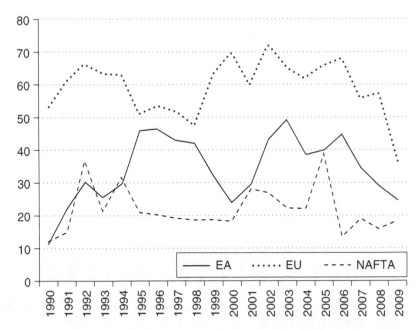

Sources: Authors' computation with data sourced from ADB; UNCTAD; ASEAN FDI Statistics Database; China's Ministry of Commerce; OECD; and EUROSTAT.

Figure 5.5 Intraregional FDI shares (%)

economic interdependence between East Asian countries. The share of intraregion FDI in East Asia increased rapidly in the 1990s and remained over 40 per cent in the 2000s before the recent decrease. This share has been higher than that in NAFTA but it has been somewhat lower than that in Europe (see Figure 5.5).

Figure 5.6 shows that among individual East Asian countries and regions, Korea and ASEAN countries have maintained the highest intraregional FDI share, with around 40 per cent of the intraregional trade share. The figure for China has stayed below 20 per cent, mainly because its outward FDI has been almost negligible while inward FDI has been large. Compared to intraregional trade share, intraregional FDI share shows much higher fluctuations.

Unlike FDI, the intraregional portfolio inflows appear to be not very large in East Asia compared to Europe. Figure 5.7 shows the intraregional portfolio flows in East Asia, the EU and NAFTA. The intraregional portfolio flows in the East Asian region account for only 12 per cent of the total cross-border portfolio flows (inflows and outflows) in 2008. The

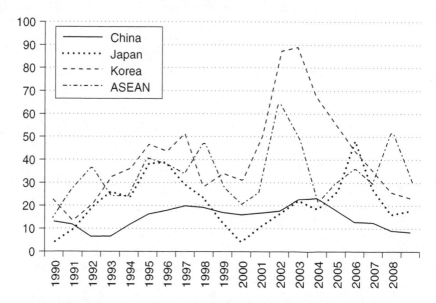

Sources: Authors' computation with data sourced from ADB; UNCTAD; ASEAN FDI
Statistics Database; China's Ministry of Commerce; OECD; and EUROSTAT.

Figure 5.6   Regional FDI shares of individual East Asian countries (%)

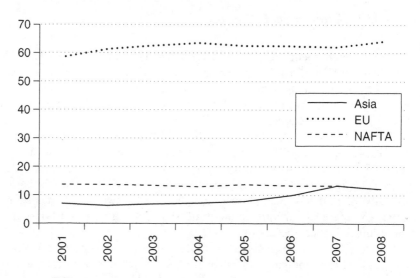

Source: IMF, Coordinated Portfolio Investment Survey.

Figure 5.7   Intraregional portfolio flow shares (%)

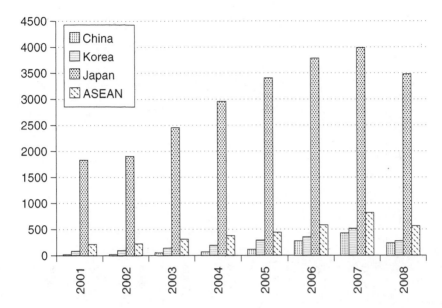

Source: IMF, Coordinated Portfolio Investment Survey.

Figure 5.8   East Asian countries' total FDI (billion US$)

numbers for intraregional portfolio flows in NAFTA are the same as those in East Asia. In contrast, the comparable figure for the EU is 64 per cent.

One reason for the lower intraregional portfolio share in East Asia is related to Japan's dominant role both as an international investor country and investment host country. Although Japan's financial dominance is declining, Japan still accounts for 70 per cent of all Asian portfolio investments abroad and 56 per cent of all portfolio investments in East Asia (see Figure 5.8). As its economy grows, China has increasingly hosted portfolio investments in East Asia. However, it hosts only 12 per cent of inbound portfolio investment and it has not yet begun to invest abroad due to its strict capital controls.

However, as Figure 5.9 shows, Japan has a very strong appetite for global portfolio investment in its assets. It also attracts portfolio investments from abroad, but these investments are mostly global investments coming from the US and the EU. In other countries, in particular China, the regional share is higher than in Japan. Considering Japan's dominance in portfolio investments, however, the overall figure shows that East Asian economies are far less financially integrated when compared to European economies.

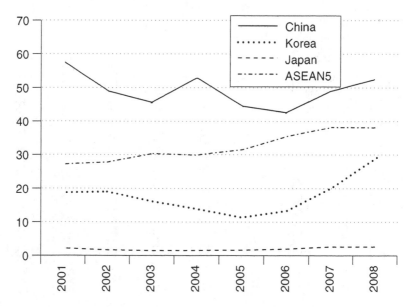

Source: IMF, Coordinated Portfolio Investment Survey.

Figure 5.9   Regional portfolio investment flows of individual East Asian countries (%)

Although the intraregional portfolio inflows do not appear to be very large, intraregional portfolio investment in East Asia is not far behind other regions once one controls for the standard gravity models (Kim et al., 2005; Eichengreen and Park, 2006). For example, Eichengreen and Park (2006) argue that if the low level of economic development could be controlled, the difference between the volume of intra-European and intra-East Asian flows is not large. In fact, financial and trade integrations are mutually reinforcing, so that more intraregional trade and FDI flows generate more intraregional capital flows and vice versa.

Labour mobility
In the past, labour mobility in East Asia was not as high as in Europe. But recently it has increased in East Asia while it has decreased in Europe, and the gap between two regions has narrowed. According to the intra-regional flows of people based on tourist data from the World Tourism Organization (see Figure 5.10), Asian groups have shares of intraregional flows of people in the mid-40 per cent range, while the share ranges are just below 50 per cent for Europe and below 40 per cent for NAFTA. The fact

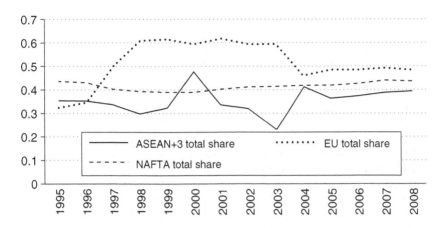

Source: Authors' calculations with data from the World Tourism Organization.

Figure 5.10 Intraregional share of tourists

that NAFTA's and EU's shares have been falling while Asian shares have been rising means that there is more regionalization in East Asia, whereas more interregional than intraregional movement of people is observed in the EU and NAFTA (Capannelli et al., 2009).[5]

It is important, however, to note that although there has been a deepening economic interdependence among East Asian countries, this regional integration is market-driven and, unlike the EU and other regions, there have been little formal and institutional regional arrangements.

5.2.3 Correlations in Macroeconomic Shocks

Empirical studies examining the symmetry of shocks on East Asian countries have usually focused on the movement of macroeconomic variables.[6] A simple exercise is to look at the correlation of output shocks among countries within regions. For the analysis of business cycle synchronization, we look at the correlation of cyclical components. To remove the trend component, we use the Hodrick–Prescott filter which is defined as follows:

$$\min \sum_{t=1}^{N} (y_t - g_t)^2 + \lambda \sum_{t=2}^{N-1} [(g_{t+1} - g_t) - (g_t - g_{t-1})]^2 \quad (5.1)$$

where y_t is the log of GDP and g_t is the trend of GDP. The difference between the two is the cyclical component $c_t = y_t - g_t$, and the correlation of business cycles between country i and country j is defined as:

Table 5.3   Correlations of output shocks, 1961–1998

	1990–1997			1998–2008		
	US	EU	EA	US	EU	EA
CHN	−0.02	−0.01	0.22	0.42	0.48	0.47
JAP	−0.26	0.5	0.53	0.82	0.84	0.72
KOR	−0.19	0.45	0.44	0.71	0.71	0.69
IDN	0.05	0.1	0.2	0.15	0.16	0.19
MAL	−0.02	0.24	0.45	0.66	0.57	0.79
PHIL	−0.34	0.21	0.29	0.22	0.25	0.29
SGP	−0.01	0.08	0.26	0.48	0.42	0.54
THAI	−0.2	−0.38	0.05	0.62	0.64	0.67
TWN	0.15	0.28	0.1	0.63	0.64	0.69
US	–	0.09	−0.23	–	0.71	0.83
EU	0.09	–	0.34	0.71	–	0.77

Source: Moon (2009b).

$$cor(c_t^i, c_t^j) = \frac{\mathrm{cov}(c_t^i, c_t^j)}{\sqrt{\mathrm{var}(c_t^i)}\sqrt{\mathrm{var}(c_t^j)}} \qquad (5.2)$$

Table 5.3 shows business cycle synchronizations of East Asian countries with other East Asian countries, with EU countries and the US. Two features are noteworthy. One is that business cycles among East Asian countries are closely connected, and that this interconnectedness increases over time. The other is that East Asian countries' business cycles are also well connected with the global economies.

However, the behaviour of macroeconomic variables may be sensitive to the choice of exchange rate regime. To avoid this problem, Baek and Song (2002) identify permanent components of output that rely upon the long-run characteristics of an economy such as economic, social and demographic structures, which are also less variant with the exchange rate regime. Table 5.4 presents the correlation coefficients of permanent components of output in East Asia and the EU. The number represents a correlation coefficient of a country with the rest of the countries in the region. On this measure, shocks appear to be at least as similar between East Asian countries as between EU countries. In East Asia, the average of correlation coefficients is 0.507 in the 1990s, which is very close to the average of 0.519 for EU countries. Moreover, the average of the correlation coefficients has sharply risen in East Asia from almost zero before the 1990s to 0.507 in the 1990s, while it has fallen in the EU from 0.564 to 0.519.

Table 5.4   Correlation coefficients of permanent components of output

	East Asia			Europe	
	1985–92	1993–2000		1981–90	1991–2000
China	−0.177	0.711	Austria	0.672	0.242
Hong Kong	−0.008	0.671	Belgium	0.754	0.712
Indonesia	−0.156	0.677	Finland	−0.597	0.495
Japan	0.029	0.654	France	0.737	0.723
Korea	0.022	0.662	Germany	0.652	−0.368
Malaysia	−0.117	0.706	Ireland	0.599	0.528
Philippines	−0.023	−0.045	Italy	0.494	0.691
Singapore	−0.092	0.700	Luxembourg	0.715	0.595
Taiwan	0.012	0.684	Netherlands	0.714	0.685
Thailand	−0.030	0.687	Portugal	0.737	0.702
			Spain	0.732	0.701
Average	−0.063	0.507	Average	0.564	0.519
SD	0.724	0.676	SD	0.393	0.327

Source: Baek and Song (2002).

The symmetry of shocks in a region can also be observed through correlations of financial market movements. According to Table 5.5, correlations between East Asian stock markets have increased since the 1990s. However, the table also shows that East Asian stock markets have increasingly become integrated with the US and global financial markets. The correlation of the East Asian stock market to the US one has increased over time since the 1990s, from 0.543 in the pre-crisis period to 0.645 in the post-crisis period.

This result again highlights an important change in the economic development pattern of East Asia: while the real sector is regionalized, the monetary and financial sectors are globalized. As East Asian countries started to liberalize and internationalize their financial sector, their financial markets became more and more connected to the world financial market. For instance, East Asian countries have been increasing their capital investments in safe US Treasury bills and notes, while the US financial firms reinvested these funds, thus acquiring rather risky Asian assets (García-Herrero et al., 2009). The result was a rising degree of convergence of interest rates and stock market returns among East Asian countries as well as between East Asian and global financial markets.

Table 5.5   Correlations of East Asian stock markets

	1991–1997.6		1999–2010	
	East Asia	US	East Asia	US
China	0.214	0.502	0.618	0.581
Hong Kong	0.619	0.898	0.789	0.736
Indonesia	0.621	0.854	0.731	0.503
Japan	−0.231	−0.170	0.113	0.598
Korea	0.469	0.255	0.774	0.604
Malaysia	0.664	0.790	0.779	0.615
Philippines	0.657	0.762	0.775	0.658
Singapore	0.665	0.754	0.803	0.817
Thailand	0.395	0.096	0.670	0.593
Taiwan	0.476	0.686	0.674	0.744
Average	0.459	0.543	0.673	0.645

Note: Correlations of stock price index. East Asia shows the average of an individual market's correlations with East Asian markets while the US market shows the correlation of an individual East Asian market and the US market.

Source: Datastream International.

5.2.4   Similarity of Export Structure

The focus is now on the correlation coefficients of economic structures rather than on the shocks themselves, because whether shocks are symmetrical or not reflects to a large extent the degree of similarity between the economic structures of two countries. Since the economic structure is well manifested in the trade structure, we compare the export similarities for 2-digit level of Standard International Trade Classification (SITC) Rev. 3 in each region. The export similarity index is measured by:

$$ES_{ij} = \sum_k [min(Export_i^k, Export_j^k) \times 100] \qquad (5.3)$$

where $Export_i$ and $Export_j$ are total exports of country i and j respectively and the superscript k denotes industry k. In Table 5.6, the number represents the mean of pair-wise export similarities with other countries within the region. The analysis with export similarities reveals that East Asian countries had shared a similar export structure with the EU countries until recently. Now, the export similarity index for East Asian countries has declined and is on average 48.9 per cent, which is a little smaller than the figure for European countries, which is at 59.7 per cent. When East Asian

Table 5.6   Export similarity (%)

	East Asia				Europe		
	1990	2000	2009		1990	2000	2009
China	46.1	56.4	56.4	Austria	53.6	59.6	65.2
Hong Kong	50.9	57.8	44.4	Denmark	35.2	57.3	63.0
Indonesia	32.6	43.0	38.8	Finland	45.0	45.9	54.4
Japan	40.3	49.3	48.2	France	56.1	63.3	65.3
Korea	54.2	58.4	49.8	Germany	39.9	63.7	66.2
Malaysia	46.8	59.2	55.8	Greece	38.0	44.9	55.4
Philippines	42.7	50.3	45.4	Ireland	41.0	39.7	39.0
Singapore	49.2	58.3	52.5	Italy	57.0	57.7	64.2
Thailand	47.9	54.4	48.9	Netherlands	52.7	54.5	56.0
				Portugal	45.2	53.8	59.5
				Sweden	51.3	60.0	63.6
				UK	58.6	62.6	65.1
Average	45.6	54.1	48.9	Average	47.8	55.2	59.7

Source: Authors' computation using data from UN Comtrade.

countries have similar economic structures to each other, shocks to the countries in the region are likely to be symmetrical, and they can be offset by a similar stance on monetary policy.

5.2.5   Similarity of Inflation Rates

Figure 5.11 shows the trend of inflation rates, which are considered a proxy for a long-term policy objective, in the three major economic blocs. Every country has maintained a low inflation rate. East Asian countries in general show higher inflation rates than the EU countries but they seem to outperform the NAFTA countries. Two things are noteworthy. First, inflation has been reduced to very low levels and has stabilized in all countries since 2000. In fact, as Figure 5.12 shows, there was quite a substantial convergence of inflation rates among East Asian countries. The inflation rate convergence between Korea and Japan is remarkable. However, there is a need to stabilize it further, especially for countries like China and the ASEAN members. Recently, their inflation rates have tended to diverge from Korea and Japan.

The second thing to note is the fact that inflation is dependent on the progress of monetary integration and would be an endogenous property. In fact, many European countries lowered their inflation rates so as to be

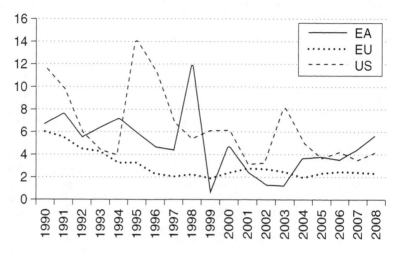

Note: Inflation rate is based on GDP deflator. The average is a simple mean of individual countries inflation rate.

Source: World Bank, World Development Indicators Database.

Figure 5.11   Average inflation rates

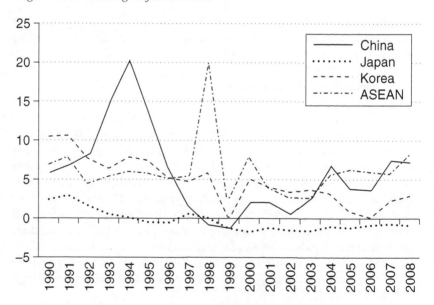

Source: World Bank, World Development Indicators Database.

Figure 5.12   Inflation rates for individual East Asian countries

Table 5.7   Political proximity

	1985–1990			2000–2005		
	US	Europe	East Asia10	US	Europe	East Asia10
China	0.150	0.487	0.852	0.106	0.532	0.819
Hong Kong	–	–	–	–	–	–
Indonesia	0.125	0.473	0.896	0.120	0.567	0.858
Japan	0.317	0.757	0.491	0.292	0.836	0.653
Korea, Rep.	–	–	–	0.278	0.805	0.597
Malaysia	0.143	0.495	0.920	0.121	0.571	0.863
Philippines	0.142	0.513	0.904	0.142	0.587	0.861
Singapore	0.154	0.524	0.888	0.137	0.593	0.849
Taiwan	–	–	–	–	–	–
Thailand	0.132	0.497	0.905	0.132	0.615	0.861
Average (East Asia10)	0.166	0.535	0.837	0.166	0.638	0.795
Average (Europe)	0.339	0.762	0.498	0.365	0.922	0.611
United States	–	0.339	0.141	–	0.367	0.148

Source: Modified using Yoon et al. (2005).

accepted in the monetary union because they had to meet the convergence criteria to join the union. Thus, as monetary integration proceeds, it is likely that inflations rates in East Asia will stabilize and converge further.

5.2.6   Other Non-economic Conditions

Besides the above economic conditions, non-economic conditions are also important for forming a monetary union. For instance, political proximity considers the possibility of military conflicts due to different political interests among member countries. Table 5.7 shows the political proximity among East Asian countries. The affinity of nations' index (Gartzke, 2000), is constructed by using UN voting data[7] as a proxy variable to measure the political proximity between two countries. The index ranges from −1 to 1. If the UN voting patterns of two nations are more alike, their political interests are more similar and the index will be close to 1. In contrast, if two countries show different voting patterns in the UN, it implies that their political interests would be very dissimilar and the index would be close to −1. According to Table 5.7, the political proximity among countries in East Asia (0.795) is lower than that in Europe (0.922) in the 2000s. Korea and Japan, which have maintained close security relations with the US, show particularly low proximity compared to other countries in the region. However, it is noteworthy that the current political proximity of East Asia (0.795) is higher than that of Europe in the 1990s (0.762), before its full monetary unification.

5.2.7   Assessment of the OCA Conditions

Countries in East Asia have achieved sustained economic growth through market-driven integration with global markets. Greater economic openness and globalization in East Asia has created a regional concentration of trade and FDI activities. Compared to this real regionalization, however, financial globalization is more recent and has not yet shown a sufficient level of regionalization in East Asia. East Asian countries are globally connected. Nevertheless, there seems increasing evidence that financial globalization in East Asia is leading to financial regionalization through the deepened linkages between Asian and global financial markets. The result is a rising degree of convergence of stock market returns among East Asian countries as well as between East Asian and global markets. The speed, scale and extent of the contagion of the financial crisis further confirm the growing financial market linkages among Asian countries. This result affirms the observation that the business cycles of East Asian economies are closely connected with global economies as well as other Asian economies. Thus, as Kuroda, President of the ADB, said, East Asia is 'regionally integrated yet globally connected' (Kuroda, 2010).

Now East Asian countries are rapidly catching up with the global trend of regionalization, intensifying the economic ties between themselves. Economic interdependence has been deepening, making closer regional cooperation essential. If economic integration means just an absence of any barriers to the free flow of goods, capital and people, countries in East Asia may already have attained quite a significant degree of market-driven integration. As Watanabe and Ogura (2006) pointed out, after surveying the empirical literature on the OCA conditions for East Asian countries, some groups of East Asian countries satisfy the preconditions for a currency union. In fact, Table 5.8 shows the groupings of the optimal currency area identified by these empirical studies. According to Table 5.8, all studies except for two take a positive view on the existence of optimal currency areas in subsets of East Asian countries. In particular, Singapore and Malaysia turn out to be an optimal currency area in all these studies.

Thus, Watanabe and Ogura conclude that 'some Asian countries exhibit almost the same level of external openness, intra-regional trade

Table 5.8   Optimal currency areas in East Asian region

	China	Hong Kong	Taiwan	Japan	South Korea	Singapore	Malaysia	Indonesia	Thailand	Philippines	Other ASEAN countries	Australia and NZ	India
Bayoumi et al. (2000)													
Loayza et al. (2001)													
Yuen (2001)													
Baek and Song (2002)													
Chow and Kim (2003)													
Lee et al. (2003)													
Kawai and Motonishi (2004)													
Kwak (2004)													
Zhang et al. (2004)													
Girardin (2005)													
Sánchez (2005)													
Tang (2006)													
Ogawa and Kawasaki (2006)													
Huang and Guo (2006)													

Notes: Shaded boxes indicate that countries are included in optimal currency areas identified in each paper. If several optimal currency areas are identified in a paper, the boxes corresponding to each area are surrounded by thick lines. The boxes marked with diagonal lines indicate that those countries are not covered by the respective studies.

Source: Watanabe and Ogura (2006).

and symmetry in macroeconomic shocks as their European counterparts did in the pre-euro period' (2006, p.3). Unlike the EU and other regions, however, East Asian countries remain behind in official cooperation and institutional arrangements.

5.3   ENDOGENEITY OF THE CONDITIONS

So far we have evaluated the conditions for monetary integration in East Asia assuming that various criteria are exogenous variables and are not affected by the integration process itself. However, as the EMU experience shows, and Frankel and Rose (1998) argue, those criteria evolve over time as monetary integration proceeds. Furthermore, the suitability of regional countries for collective monetary arrangements cannot be judged only on the basis of historical data.

Theoretically speaking, there are two possible ways in which the process of monetary integration is linked to the evolution of the integration conditions. One is the specialization scenario put forward by Kenen (1969) and Krugman (1993). If monetary integration proceeds in a region, exchange rate risk will be reduced and some obstacles to trade will also be removed. Intraregional trade expansion encourages economies of scale, which lead regional countries to specialize in the production of goods with comparative advantages. Countries under monetary integration will thus be less diversified and more likely to be exposed to asymmetric shocks. Consequently, their business cycles will be less synchronized. This specialization scenario suggests that higher integration will lead to an increase in specialization and decrease in diversification, and in turn will make regional countries less suitable for monetary integration.

In contrast, Frankel and Rose (1998) propose the endogeneity scenario, which postulates a positive link between the evolution of the criteria and the process of monetary integration. This positive link can be mainly due to the increasing intra-industry trade within the region. If the production chain deepens as monetary integration reduces trading costs and expands intra-industry trade in the region, shocks to a single country will immediately affect its regional trading partners. Correspondingly, their incomes will be more correlated with each other. Apart from the intra-industry effect, increased trade due to monetary integration will foster policy coordination. This discipline effect of common monetary or exchange rate arrangements will reduce the asymmetry of policy shocks and lead to synchronization of business cycles in the region. The endogeneity scenario suggests that higher integration will lead to higher output correlation.

The scenario the integration process will follow has an important

Table 5.9   Intra-industry trade in East Asia and the EU (%)

	1990	2000	2009		1990	2000	2009
China	26.3	36.3	32.5	Austria	41.3	42.8	46.5
Hong Kong	39.3	36.9	33.0	Denmark	37.9	42.9	44.9
Indonesia	20.6	26.5	30.8	Finland	30.5	28.1	31.8
Japan	21.1	35.4	34.0	France	46.3	47.1	48.9
Korea	28.2	41.6	37.9	Germany	50.7	51.2	49.9
Malaysia	28.4	47.5	41.2	Greece	17.3	19.0	24.6
Philippines	28.1	42.2	37.9	Ireland	27.7	28.4	26.6
Singapore	34.9	44.9	45.6	Italy	36.3	40.6	40.9
Thailand	27.8	46.6	41.4	Netherlands	41.0	43.8	43.2
				Portugal	22.2	32.0	32.1
				Sweden	41.6	44.7	43.0
				UK	49.3	52.0	47.8
Average	28.3	39.8	37.2	Average	36.9	39.4	40.0

Source: Authors' calculations based on data from Comtrade.

implication for the suitability for monetary integration. If countries become more specialized and their outputs become less correlated following the specialization scenario, this will increase the costs of monetary integration. In contrast, if the endogeneity scenario prevails and integration leads to higher output correlation, the costs of entering into monetary integration will decline and in turn regional countries will be more suitable for monetary integration.

A key element in determining the applicability of specialization scenario or endogeneity scenario is whether trade expansion from monetary integration is through inter-industry trade or through intra-industry trade. Table 5.9 compares the intra-industry trade index (IIT) between East Asia and the EU using the 3-digit level data of the SITC. The index is measured as:

$$IIT_k = 1 - \frac{\sum_i |Export_{ij}^k - Import_{ij}^k|}{\sum_i (Export_{ij}^k + Import_{ij}^k)} \tag{5.4}$$

where $Export_{ij}^k$ is total exports in industry k from country i to country j and $Import_{ij}^k$ is total imports in industry k from country j to country i. As intra-industry trade increases, the index will monotonically increase from 0 to 1.

The results in the table show that until the beginning of the 1990s, intra-industry trade in East Asia was not as high as that in the EU. The intra-industry trade index for East Asia was on average 28.3 per cent in 1990, which was far lower than the 36.9 per cent for the EU in the same year. However, the index has been increasing so fast in East Asia (37.2 per cent in 2009) that it has recently climbed almost as high as that in the EU (40.0 per cent). If this trend were to continue in East Asia, the endogeneity process of integration would prevail. Thus, East Asian countries would be likely to experience more symmetric shocks and they would become more suitable for monetary integration.

In sum, on economic grounds there seem to be good reasons for promoting East Asian monetary integration, in whatever form it may be. As pointed out above, according to self-containment and the OCA criteria,[8] East Asian countries seem to be as plausible candidates for regional collective monetary arrangement as the members of the EU are. Of course, many barriers to East Asian monetary integration still linger. For example, political interests are different from one another due to different political systems and political rivalries, especially between China and Japan. Economic disparity is wide and may cause conflicts around the sharing of benefits and costs from monetary integration. The legacy of history is also still strong enough to hamper regional cooperation among East Asian countries. But as cooperation efforts continue, these conditions are likely to improve along with economic expansion and the deepening of regional interdependence, enabling the endogeneity process to be realized. In that case, although those conditions are not yet fulfilled and countries do not meet many of the conditions *ex ante*, it is more likely that the integration itself will turn East Asian countries into an optimal currency area.[9]

NOTES

1. See also De Grauwe (1997) for its recent development.
2. Recently, Rose (2000) presented a powerful trade-enhancing effect of common currencies.
3. However, some literature (Calvo and Reinhart, 2002; Hausmann et al., 2001) argues that because of fear of floating, many countries with *de jure* floating regimes cannot pursue independent monetary policies and are de facto importing the monetary policies of major-currency countries, such as those with pegs. For empirical examination related to the issue, see Frankel et al. (2002).
4. Wyplosz (2001) found it striking that 'trade integration is deeper in Asia than it is in Europe, more than 40 years after the creation of the Common Market' (p.12).
5. Goto and Hamada (1994) also showed that migration, mostly from less-developed ASEAN countries to the more industrialized NIEs, was extensive and in some countries, the shares of the migrant labour force were larger than those in many European countries.
6. To test synchronization of disturbances, Eichengreen and Bayoumi (1999) use the structural VAR methodology and Goto and Hamada (1994) use the principal component analysis, while Taguchi (1994) simply calculates correlation coefficients for

macroeconomic variables. Although they use different methodologies, their results suggest similar implications.

7. The data are UN roll-call votes on resolutions in the United Nations General Assembly collected by Erik Voeten (http://www9.georgetown.edu/faculty/ev42/UNvoting.htm).

8. Besides these factors, national pride in using an independent currency is often considered as another important factor. For related references, see Cohen (2000); Barro (2001).

9. Frankel and Rose (1998) have stated: 'countries which join EMU, no matter what the motivation may be, may satisfy OCA properties ex-post even if they do not ex-ante!' See also Fukuda (2002) and Mongelli (2002).

6. Need for regional monetary and financial arrangements in East Asia

There have been long and recurring discussions regarding East Asian monetary cooperation. However, the idea of regional monetary integration in East Asia only recently gained momentum. There are several reasons behind this momentum. The first reason is East Asian countries' concern over their currency stability. It is undeniable that the rapid economic development and growth in East Asian countries was built on the stability of their exchange rates pegged to the US dollar. However, the dollar peg is no longer desirable. Furthermore, the dollar peg was also one important cause of the currency crisis East Asian countries experienced in 1997. There is an emerging need to stabilize intraregional exchanges rates between Asian countries, which reflects their increasing intraregional economic linkages. The second reason is East Asian countries' desire for protection against future financial crises. Capital flows are increasingly unstable and financial crises are more likely. Liquidity is the key to avoiding the recurrence of financial crises. Given that the financial assistance from existing international financial institutions is very limited, East Asian countries will have to either accumulate foreign reserves themselves or create their own regional financial institutions. The third reason is East Asian countries' continued interest in regionalism. In particular, the successful launch of the euro in 1999 demonstrated that a single currency could be introduced in East Asia and that East Asian monetary integration could better serve the interests of East Asian countries in the new international monetary and financial order.

6.1 EXCHANGE RATE STABILITY AND SUSTAINING THE EAST ASIAN MIRACLE

6.1.1 East Asian Exchange Rate Arrangements

First of all, East Asia needs regional monetary arrangements to promote regional trade and economic growth through stable exchange rates. The main benefit of regional monetary integration is the enhancement of micro-efficiency through the reduction in exchange rate uncertainty and transaction costs. The elimination of the foreign exchange risk through stable exchange rates will lead to a more efficient price mechanism in both the real and financial markets and thereby will boost overall welfare effects. This gain can be reaped as long as exchange rates are fixed. If one common currency is used in a monetary union, the benefits of eliminating transaction costs can be further reaped.[1] As long as national currencies remain in place, there will be a continual need to convert one currency into another and transaction costs will not be fully eliminated. But if countries switch to a common currency, the costs of exchanging one currency with another will disappear.

Another main benefit of regional monetary integration is increased macroeconomic stability. The adoption of an anti-inflationary anchor obliges member countries to commit to stable monetary policies. Specifically, if an inflation-prone country adopts the currency of a credible anchor, it eliminates the inflation-bias problem arising from the discretionary monetary policy that was emphasized by Barro and Gordon (1984). The adoption of another country's currency or the joining of a monetary union with a new form of currency provides a much better commitment device than alternative forms of fixed exchange rates. Once a common currency is used, the costs of turning back to using the old national currencies will be so high that the regime with a common currency is much more credible than customary promises to peg the exchange rate (Barro, 2001).

For the past decades East Asia as a whole has experienced the 'East Asian miracle', headed by Japan and followed by the four tigers (Korea, Taiwan, Singapore and Hong Kong), then by the four little dragons (Malaysia, Thailand, Indonesia and the Philippines) and China. A very important factor behind the rapid growth was stability in exchange rates in the region. Although East Asian countries have used a variety of exchange rate arrangements (Table 6.1), the dollar played a dominant role as a *de jure* and de facto anchor for East Asian countries except for Japan before the East Asian crisis. This is even true after the Asian crisis, although some crisis-stricken countries such as Korea, Indonesia, the Philippines and Thailand, have officially moved in the direction of greater exchange rate flexibility.

To examine the actual behaviour of the exchange rates and whether East Asia is still a de facto dollar bloc, a Frankel–Wei type of regression is carried out. Using the following regression equation, the change in the log exchange rate of each East Asian currency (Δe_t^i) is regressed on the changes in the log exchange rates of the US dollar ($\Delta e_t^\$$), the yen ($\Delta e_t^\yen$), and the euro ($\Delta e_t^\in$) (or the ECU before 1999). In all the exchange rates, the Swiss franc is used as a numeraire.

Table 6.1   Official exchange rate arrangements in East Asia

Country	Article VIII: date accepted	Pre-crisis and crisis periods: dates of change	Post-crisis period
Japan	1 Apr. 1964	Independently floating (Jul. 1982–present)	Independently floating
Korea	1 Nov. 1988	Managed floating (Jun. 1982–Nov.1997); Independently floating (Nov. 1997–present)	Independently floating
China	1 Dec. 1996	Managed floating (Oct. 1986–Sep. 1998); Conventional fixed peg to the dollar (Jan. 1999–present)	Conventional fixed peg to the dollar
Hong Kong	15 Feb. 1961	Currency board arrangement with a peg to the dollar (Oct. 1983–present)	Currency board arrangement with a peg to the dollar
Taiwan	–	Managed floating (Apr. 1989–present)	Managed floating
Indonesia	6 May 1988	Managed floating (Dec. 1983–Jul. 1997); Independently floating (Aug. 1997–Sep. 2001)	Managed floating with no preannounced path for exchange rate (Sep. 2001–present)
Malaysia	11 Nov. 1968	Peg to other currencies composite (Sep. 1975–Jun. 1993); Managed floating (Jun. 1993–Sep.1998); Peg to the dollar (Sep. 1998–present)	Conventional fixed peg to the dollar
Philippines	8 Sep. 1995	Independently floating (Nov. 1984–present)	Independently floating
Singapore	9 Nov. 1968	Managed floating (Dec. 1987–present)	Managed floating with no preannounced path for exchange rate (Sep. 2001–present)
Thailand	4 May 1990	Peg to other currencies composite (Nov. 1984–Jun. 1997); Independently floating (Jul. 1997–Sep. 2001)	Managed floating with no preannounced path for exchange rate (Sep. 2001–present)

Table 6.1 (continued)

Country	Article VIII: date accepted	Pre-crisis and crisis periods: dates of change	Post-crisis period
Brunei	10 Oct. 1995	Currency board arrangement system with a peg to the Singapore dollar (Mar. 1996–present)	Currency board arrangement system with a peg to the Singapore dollar
Cambodia	1 Jan. 2002	Managed floating (Jun. 1993–present)	Managed floating with no preannounced path for exchange rate
Laos	Article XIX	Managed floating (Mar. 1989–Sep. 1995); Independently floating (Sep. 1995–Jun. 1997); Managed floating (Jun. 1997–present)	Managed floating with no preannounced path for exchange rate
Myanmar	Article XIV	Peg to the SDR (Feb. 1975–Dec. 2001)	Managed floating with no preannounced path for exchange rate (Dec. 2001–present)
Vietnam	Article XIV	Peg to the dollar (Mar. 1989–Mar. 1990); Managed floating (Mar. 1993–Sep. 1998)	Pegged exchange rate within horizontal bands (Jan. 1999–Dec. 2001); Managed floating with no preannounced path for exchange rate (Dec. 2001–present)

Sources: IMF, International Financial Statistics (various issues); Annual Report on Exchange Rate Arrangements and Exchange Restrictions 2001; re-quoted from Kawai (2002, p.181, Table 5).

$$\Delta e_t^i = \beta_0 + \beta_1 \Delta e_t^\$ + \beta_2 \Delta e_t^¥ + \beta_3 \Delta e_t^€ + u_t \qquad (6.1)$$

In the regression, the coefficients β represent the weights that each East Asian country assigns to the corresponding currencies in their exchange rate policies. If an East Asian currency is closely fixed to one of the three major currencies appearing on the right-hand side of equation (6.1), the corresponding coefficient will be close to 1. If the currency has little exchange rate stabilization effect against a particular currency on the right-hand side, the coefficient will be close to zero. Consequently, the

Table 6.2   Exchange rate movements in East Asia, pre-crisis period

	Constant: β_0	Dollar: β_1	Yen: β_2	euro (ECU): β_3	adj. R^2
China	−0.00	1.00	0.00	−0.00	1.00
	(−4.79)	(748.19)	(0.65)		
Hong Kong	0.00	1.00	−0.00	0.00	1.00
	(0.39)	(928.66)	(−0.72)		
Indonesia	0.00	1.00	0.01	−0.00	0.94
	(2.71)	(117.60)	(0.63)		
Korea	0.00	1.01	0.01	−0.01	0.97
	(4.39)	(243.53)	(1.13)		
Malaysia	−0.00	0.96	0.05	−0.01	0.91
	(−1.03)	(91.03)	(3.67)		
Philippines	0.00	0.99	−0.02	0.03	0.78
	(0.85)	(80.47)	(−1.45)		
Singapore	−0.00	0.97	−0.01	0.04	0.92
	(−3.01)	(150.82)	(−1.16)		
Taiwan	0.00	1.01	0.03	−0.04	0.94
	(1.12)	(141.38)	(3.12)		
Thailand	0.00	1.02	0.02	−0.04	0.98
	(1.36)	(97.62)	(2.32)		

Note: The pre-crisis period is January 1990–June 1997.

Source: Authors' estimation using the data of Datastream International.

estimated standard error of regression residuals can be interpreted as a measure of exchange rate volatility.

Regressions were run over a sample period from January 1990 to June 2008, just before the global financial crisis. To examine the changes of the exchange rate practices over time, the whole sample was divided into three sub-periods, the pre-crisis period (January 1990 to June 1997), the Asian crisis period (July 1997 to December 1998), and the post-crisis period (January 1999 to June 2008).

Table 6.2 shows the regression results in the pre-crisis period. The coefficient estimate of the dollar (b_1) is statistically significant and close to unity and the adjusted R^2 is close to 1 for almost all economies. In the case of Singapore and Malaysia, the dollar coefficients are a little lower due to their formal or informal currency basket arrangements. In those economies with high dollar coefficients, the estimated standard error of regression is small, which suggests that exchange rates against the dollar were relatively stable. However, the coefficients for the yen and the ECU are small and close to zero. Even the largest weights assigned to the yen

Table 6.3   Exchange rate movements in East Asia, crisis period

	Constant: β_0	Dollar: β_1	Yen: β_2	euro (ECU): β_3	adj. R^2
China	−0.00	1.00	−0.00	0.00	1.00
	(−2.20)	(3890.46)	(−0.31)		
Hong Kong	−0.00	0.99	0.01	0.00	0.98
	(−0.00)	(135.15)	(1.07)		
Indonesia	0.00	0.89	0.76	−0.65	0.04
	(1.29)	(2.54)	(3.27)		
Korea	0.00	0.99	0.20	−0.19	0.09
	(0.60)	(5.11)	(1.54)		
Malaysia	0.00	0.83	0.23	−0.06	0.14
	(1.19)	(6.27)	(2.59)		
Philippines	0.00	0.96	0.18	−0.13	0.24
	(1.59)	(10.05)	(2.81)		
Singapore	0.00	0.92	0.15	−0.07	0.48
	(1.05)	(17.59)	(4.26)		
Taiwan	0.00	0.93	0.15	−0.09	0.57
	(1.28)	(21.38)	(5.26)		
Thailand	0.00	0.86	0.14	0.00	0.15
	(1.19)	(7.44)	(1.82)		

Note: The crisis period is July 1997–December 1998.

Source: Authors' estimation using the data of Datastream International.

and the ECU, appearing in the Philippines and Singapore respectively, are only 0.03 and 0.04. These results suggest that East Asia was a de facto dollar bloc before the Asian crisis. The other currencies, including the yen and the ECU, played a very limited role, if any, in East Asian exchange rate arrangements.

Table 6.3 shows that in the crisis period, there were significant declines in the dollar weights and in the adjusted R^2 for East Asian countries, with the exceptions of China and Hong Kong. The decline in the adjusted R^2 was particularly pronounced in the crisis-stricken countries, including Korea, Indonesia, Malaysia, the Philippines and Thailand. Together with the decline in the dollar coefficients, this implies a higher volatility in the exchange rate against the dollar. While the dollar coefficients declined in the crisis period, the yen coefficients rose from near zero to over 0.10 in most countries and to 0.76 in Indonesia. This suggests that the importance of the yen rose during the crisis in many East Asian countries. Still the role of the ECU was very limited.

In the post-crisis period, the exchange rates show different behaviour

Table 6.4   Exchange rate movements in East Asia, post-crisis period

	Constant: β_0	Dollar: β_1	Yen: β_2	euro (ECU): β_3	adj. R^2
China	−0.00	1.00	−0.00	0.00	0.99
	(−5.99)	(525.31)	(−1.63)		
Hong Kong	0.00	1.00	0.00	−0.00	1.00
	(0.46)	(1156.38)	(1.88)		
Indonesia	0.00	1.02	0.02	−0.04	0.36
	(0.30)	(36.95)	(0.79)		
Korea	−0.00	1.00	0.02	−0.02	0.74
	(−0.76)	(83.60)	(1.81)		
Malaysia	−0.00	1.00	−0.02	0.03	0.89
	(−1.29)	(144.90)	(−3.54)		
Philippines	0.00	0.99	0.02	−0.01	0.69
	(0.64)	(74.73)	(1.76)		
Singapore	−0.00	0.88	0.01	0.11	0.83
	(−1.23)	(111.97)	(1.57)		
Taiwan	−0.00	0.98	0.02	0.00	0.86
	(−0.44)	(125.85)	(2.14)		
Thailand	−0.00	0.99	0.04	−0.03	0.77
	(−0.55)	(92.69)	(4.43)		

Note: The post-crisis period is January 1999–June 2008.

Source: Authors' estimation using the data of Datastream International.

from that of the pre-crisis period (see Table 6.4). First, the dollar weights are again high. Only in Singapore is the dollar coefficient smaller than during the pre-crisis period. Second, the adjusted R^2 significantly declined, except in those countries that officially adopted a dollar-peg, including China, Hong Kong and Malaysia; in Indonesia, it was even below 0.36. This suggests that in the post-crisis period, exchange rate volatility increased in East Asia. Third, the euro coefficients are still very small, which is similar to the pre-crisis period. The result suggests that although 'dollar pegging has made a remarkable return' from the crisis period, as McKinnon and Schnabl (2003) said, its role is not as significant as before the crisis.

6.1.2   Problems of Dollar-pegged Arrangements

It is unquestionable that the rapid economic development and growth in East Asian countries was stimulated by their dollar exchange rate stabilization.[2] However, the de facto dollar-peg system was one of the underlying causes of the Asian crisis, and the fact that 'there are several problems associated with choosing the dollar as the sole nominal anchor currency in these economies' is equally unquestionable (Eichengreen, 1998).

First, East Asian countries now have diverse economic relationships not only with the US and the EU but also with intraregional countries through trade, FDI and other forms of capital flow. For East Asia, as shown in Chapter 4, the US is no longer the most dominant economic partner and the relative importance of East Asia itself is much greater than that of the US. Thus, the gap between real regionalization and monetary Americanization is likely to widen after countries choose the dollar as the anchor currency in East Asia.

Second, given the informal dollar-based arrangements in East Asia despite the high intraregional linkage, the yuan–dollar or yen–dollar exchange rate fluctuation would cause excessive movements in effective exchange rates of East Asian countries. For example, before the 1990s, if the yen depreciated vis-à-vis the dollar, East Asian economies' international price competitiveness deteriorated and direct investment from Japan decreased, and as a result real activity was dampened. Thus, 'as the yen–dollar exchange rate became volatile, dollar-based exchange rate regimes began to produce wide fluctuations of economic activity' (Kwan, 1998), severely limiting the benefits of intraregional exchange rate stability guaranteed by the informal dollar zone. Also, some argue that the devaluation of the Chinese yuan by about 40 per cent in early 1994 put tremendous competitive pressure on the rest of Asia, in particular on ASEAN countries, eroding their trade positions and eventually leading to the Asian crisis.[3] The reason for the close association between the yuan–dollar or yen–dollar exchange rate and the real economic activity in East Asia is that these countries not only trade with China or Japan, but also compete with them in third markets in certain products.

Together with the increase in intraregional economic linkages, this suggests that intraregional stability of exchange rates is necessary for the sustainability of regional growth. But East Asian countries still view each other as economic rivals more than potential partners, and they are always wary of competitive depreciation that is intended to gain their own price competitiveness over their neighbouring countries. Now that the WTO system has been established and several bilateral free trade agreements have materialized, other instruments to support export competitiveness, such as industrial policies, may not be readily accepted. Furthermore, there are concerns over the more frequent usage of exchange rate policy. The beggar-thy-neighbour policy of competitive depreciation will hurt regional economies and therefore should be avoided.

In a financially deregulated environment, however, uncoordinated

nominal pegs increase the risk of a contagious collapse, as the dollar-peg
system adopted by many East Asian countries before 1997 turned out
to be disastrous in the Asian crisis. To enlarge the economic potential
and sustain economic growth in the region, East Asian economies need
to coordinate exchange rate stability whereby they could avoid a self-
destroying, beggar-thy-neighbour policy and mitigate the negative transmission of exchange rate instability against outside currencies.

6.2   UNSTABLE CAPITAL FLOWS AND THE INTERNATIONAL FINANCIAL CRISES

It is almost impossible these days to start any discussion on monetary
cooperation in East Asia without a reference to international financial
crises such as the 1997 Asian crisis and the recent global financial crisis.
If the international financial crises had originated only from internal
problems,[4] remedies should have focused only on internal reforms backed
by the IMF during the Asian crisis with no specific need for regional
cooperation. However, if the underlying causes of the crises are diagnosed
to be not only internal but also external, regional and global responses
are needed as well, on top of internal reforms. Certainly, the underlying causes of those crises were externally caused as much as they were
internally. Western banks and other lenders created the East Asian crisis
by withdrawing their capital. Moreover, when East Asian countries were
temporarily short of liquidity, they could not depend on the IMF or other
international organizations as lenders of last resort.[5]

Thus, many concluded that in order to avoid the detrimental effects
of international financial crises due to unstable capital flows, East Asian
countries must protect themselves. Liquidity is the key to self-protection
(Feldstein, 1999). A country that has substantial international liquidity is less likely to be the object of a currency attack, can defend itself
better when attacked and can make more orderly adjustments when it is
attacked. However, no matter how much liquidity a country holds, this
amount is dwarfed by international capital flows and a country on its own
cannot protect itself against an attack by international capital. Past experience also shows that crises, once they occur, tend to spread quickly within
regions. Therefore, the self-protection of East Asian countries can only be
achieved by regional collective action.

Regarding the implementation of collective action for self-protection,
a fundamental question is whether there is a role for a regional financial
arrangement separate from a global one. At least three arguments can
be made to support the need for regional financial arrangements in East

Asia. The first is that international responses are not speedy enough to nip a crisis in the bud. The transaction costs of arranging a cooperative response may be lower at regional level because the number of participating governments is smaller and the countries involved are more cohesive (Eichengreen, 2001, p.40). When significant problems appear within a region, which are clustered because of intraregional interdependence, a regional institution could redirect its resources better than a truly global institution with its multitude of tasks (Kim, 2010).

Second, financial assistance from international financial institutions is inadequate, falling short of the amount that ought to be available. For example, the IMF is not only concerned about East Asia but must be concerned about other regions as well. Presently, although some additional provisions at IMF level have been made specifically by the G20 agreement,[6] the economic turbulence in Europe and doubts about the chronic implosion of Latin American economies would lead to a shortage of disposable funds at the IMF, as exemplified by the experience of many past crises.

Third, the response of the international financial institutions does not rest on regional peculiarities but on general rules. It is well known that the IMF conditionality imposed on the crisis-stricken East Asian countries during the Asian crisis was not appropriate, although it might have been proper for Latin American countries in the 1980s. The fact that East Asian countries share common problems does not justify the discarding of all regional peculiarities, as implied by the statement that 'The crisis, in short, was a punishment for Asian sins' (Krugman, 1998). As long as East Asian peculiarities matter, there is an obvious case for a regional arrangement.

Besides the need for collective action to handle a crisis, East Asian countries need monetary and financial cooperation to eradicate the possibility of a crisis. A fundamental question regarding this is why East Asian countries became so vulnerable to outside money. This problem concerns the effectiveness of financial intermediation in the region. Asian countries have very high savings rates, some as high as 30 to 50 per cent, and run huge current account surpluses (see Chapter 7). However, 'East Asian savings do not seem to have been adequately and effectively channelled into Asian investments in a manner more conducive to ensuring monetary and financial stability' (Yam, 1997, p.7).

Much of Asian savings are invested in assets in the US and European countries. Also, in the management of foreign reserves, they are invested largely in US Treasury bonds, which have lower risks and greater liquidity. At the same time, huge amounts of capital flow into East Asia from the US and European countries as foreign investment. It can be argued, therefore, that East Asia provides money to developed economies, particularly to the US to bridge its budget deficits, but simultaneously tries to attract money back into the region through foreign investment. The instability of these capital flows has been a major cause of disruption to the monetary and financial systems of the Asian economies. Some people even go as far as to say that 'the Asian economies are providing the funding to hedge funds in non-Asian centers to play havoc with their currencies and financial markets' (Yam, 1997, p.7).

This problem arises because of the inefficient financial systems in the region, which inhibit the flow of long-term savings into long-term investments. The underdevelopment of financial markets in the region has produced two unhappy consequences. One is the vulnerability to external factors due to the so-called 'original sin' hypothesis. According to Eichengreen and Hausmann (1999, p.3),

> [Original sin] is a situation in which the domestic currency cannot be used to borrow abroad or to borrow long-term, even domestically. In the presence of this incompleteness, financial fragility is unavoidable because all domestic investments will have either a currency mismatch (projects that generate pesos (local currencies) will be financed with dollars) or a maturity mismatch (long-term projects will be financed by short-term loans).
>
> Critically, these mismatches exist not because banks and firms lack the prudence to hedge their exposures. Rather, the problem is that a country whose external liabilities are necessarily denominated in foreign exchange is by definition unable to hedge. Assuming that there will be someone on the other side of the market for foreign currency hedge is equivalent to assuming that the country can borrow abroad in its own currency. Similarly, the problem is not that firms lack the foresight to match the maturity structure of their assets and liabilities; it is that they find it impossible to do so. The incompleteness of financial markets is thus at the root of financial fragility.

The other consequence is that many East Asian countries, in particular those that have experienced the currency crises, have taken resources to amass their foreign reserves to the level of a war chest (Bergsten and Park, 2002, p.17). This trend has been especially noticeable since the Asian crisis; now, the largest holders of foreign reserves in the world are mostly East Asian countries. For instance, China is ranked number one in foreign reserve holdings and Japan number two. Korea, Taiwan, Hong Kong and Singapore are also ranked within the largest 10 foreign reserve holders. As a result, as of March 2011, the region holds over two-thirds of the world's total foreign reserves (Table 6.5). Too many holdings of foreign reserves are costly because the forgone opportunities of foreign reserve holdings are higher than the returns from their holdings.

When financial markets are not developed, it is very difficult to establish private contingent lines of credit. Thus, without global or regional

Table 6.5   Foreign reserve holdings of East Asian countries (US$ billion)

	1993	1997	2001	2005	Mar. 2011
China	22.4	142.8	215.6	821.5	3044.7
Hong Kong	43.0	92.8	111.2	124.2	272.7
Indonesia	11.3	16.6	27.3	33.1	118.1
Japan	98.5	219.7	395.2	834.3	1091.5
Korea	20.2	20.4	102.8	210.3	307.2
Malaysia	27.3	20.8	29.5	69.9	132.8
Philippines	4.7	7.3	13.5	15.9	68.9
Singapore	48.4	71.4	75.7	116.2	239.9
Taiwan	83.6	83.5	122.2	253.3	390.7
Thailand	24.5	26.2	32.4	50.7	185.5
World	1026.9	1616.2	2049.7	4320.2	9694.5

Sources: IMF; IFS.

arrangements of credit lines for future crises, East Asian countries cannot but accumulate a large amount of foreign reserves to protect themselves.[7] If East Asian financial markets are well developed or East Asian countries can form an arrangement to pool and manage their reserves, a much smaller amount will be sufficient to provide a formidable line of defence against any speculative attacks.

Regarding the development of financial markets in the region, it can be argued that the integration of East Asian financial markets into the world market is the solution. This argument is partly but not entirely true. As shown in Chapter 4, East Asian economies have become increasingly interdependent on the real side, while their financial markets are more globalized and move together with the world and the US markets. With this disparity between the real regionalization and the financial globalization, financial markets' integration into the world market improves financial market efficiency only up to a point, because the real side and the financial side are not well connected.

Chai and Rhee (2005) compare East Asian financial integration with EU financial integration, with a focus on the role of global and regional factors in the process of regional stock market integration.[8] To compare and evaluate the relative importance of the regional factor with that of the global factor, they distinguish between the regional shocks originating in East Asia and global ones originating from the world financial centre, for which shocks from the US market are used as the proxy. Specifically, they estimate the following equation:

Table 6.6   Global versus regional factor in East Asia

	1991–2003.4		1991–1997.6		1997.7–1998		1999–2003.4	
	EA	US	EA	US	EA	US	EA	US
China	−0.049	0.054	−0.098	0.097	−0.114	0.085	0.024	0.012
Hong Kong	0.440	0.387	0.277	0.522	0.883	0.421	0.646	0.267
Indonesia	0.094	0.152	0.056	0.112	0.421	0.437	0.256	0.104
Japan	0.085	0.326	0.024	0.330	0.320	0.214	0.388	0.266
Korea	0.220	0.275	0.034	0.054	0.405	0.226	0.818	0.355
Malaysia	0.177	0.165	0.143	0.265	0.852	0.473	0.228	0.101
Philippines	0.153	0.247	0.030	0.301	0.523	0.334	0.254	0.138
Singapore	0.247	0.232	0.181	0.264	0.586	0.279	0.478	0.134
Taiwan	0.203	0.230	0.092	0.127	0.192	0.299	0.383	0.218
Thailand	0.274	0.170	0.211	0.280	0.693	0.138	0.441	0.092
Average	0.184	0.224	0.095	0.235	0.476	0.291	0.392	0.169

Note: EA and US represent β_{iR} and β_{iw} respectively.

$$r_{it} = \beta_{i0} + \beta_{iR}r_{Rt} + \beta_{iw}r_{wt} + \beta_{iX}X_t + \varepsilon_{it} \qquad (6.2)$$

where r_{it} is an individual market's index return, r_{Rt} the regional average of individual markets' returns and r_{wt} the world market return represented by the US market. In the equation, β_{iR} indicates the coefficient for regional influence and β_{iw} that for the global influence. The variable X is included to reflect other factors. To allow the ARCH effects of innovations and the possibility of volatility spillover effects as well, the GARCH model is formulated by adding the variance equation to mean equation (6.2).

$$\sigma_{it}^2 = \alpha_{i0} + \alpha_{i1}\sigma_{it-1}^2 + \alpha_{i2}\varepsilon_{it-1}^2 \qquad (6.3)$$

Tables 6.6 and 6.7 show the estimation results for East Asia and the EU respectively. Between two regions, there is a large difference in the relative importance of regional to global factor. In the movement of local stock market returns, the US is a very important force for the East Asian stock markets, but this is not true within the EU. In East Asia, the US market was the most important factor for almost all individual markets after the 1990s, except during the crisis period. During the Asian crisis, the regional factor was more important for an individual market's movement in East Asia. In contrast, the EU market has consistently become the dominant force for individual EU markets since the 1990s.[9]

The difference in the financial integration process between East Asia and Europe seems to be related to the fact that East Asian countries tried

Table 6.7   Global versus regional factor in Europe

	1992.8–2003.4		1992.8–1993.7		1993.8–1998		1999–2003.4	
	EU	US	EU	US	EU	US	EU	US
Austria	0.112	0.318	0.219	0.366	0.207	0.412	0.064	0.283
Belgium	0.562	0.106	0.419	0.131	0.489	0.153	0.510	0.069
Denmark	0.559	0.126	0.601	0.044	0.659	0.037	0.512	0.162
Finland	0.940	0.249	0.424	0.265	0.866	0.240	1.184	0.301
France	1.128	−0.005	1.597	−0.162	1.705	0.101	1.152	0.053
Germany	1.104	0.039	0.944	0.199	0.925	0.281	1.273	−0.121
Greece	0.316	0.238	0.225	0.054	0.132	0.119	0.322	0.176
Ireland	0.452	0.238	0.428	0.476	0.482	0.314	0.412	0.189
Italy	0.887	−0.057	0.020	−0.005	1.039	−0.090	0.838	0.063
Netherlands	1.099	0.044	0.902	0.008	0.035	0.008	1.144	0.067
Portugal	0.478	0.048	0.095	−0.031	0.573	0.057	0.444	0.037
Spain	0.882	−0.110	0.864	0.070	0.942	−0.070	0.849	0.005
Sweden	0.895	0.139	1.307	0.191	0.908	0.051	0.880	0.170
UK	0.749	0.046	0.748	0.109	0.697	−0.027	0.781	0.085
Average	0.726	0.101	0.628	0.123	0.690	0.113	0.740	0.110

Note: EU and US represent β_{iR} and β_{iw} respectively.

to achieve exchange rate stability and financial stability through the US dollar. They do not have a regional monetary arrangement, and their monetary policies are often focused on exchange rate stability against the US dollar.[10] This explains the US influence on their financial markets. Also, controls on foreign equity investment were abruptly loosened after the Asian crisis in 1997. To overcome the crisis, the crisis-stricken East Asian countries heavily depended upon IMF financial support and foreign capital. Because the US had a great deal of influence on the IMF support and the capital, the financial integration of East Asian markets with the US market appeared to be strong.

However, the strong ties with the US have led to a mismatch between real and financial integration in East Asia. If the financial integration process has any meaningful implication for the real integration process, East Asian financial markets should be closely integrated with each other and at the same time the regional rather than the global factor should be the main element in the integration process. However, as explained above, the progress of financial integration in East Asia is not due to deepening regionalism but simply to the opening of the market to the world. Thus, while the real sector in East Asia is more regionalized through intra-regional trade and investment, the financial sector is more globalized. This hinders the financial markets from adequately reflecting the movements of the real economy and financial integration from achieving financial efficiency.

6.3   EXPANSION OF REGIONALISM AND CHANGE IN THE INTERNATIONAL MONETARY ORDER

The continued expansion of regional arrangements elsewhere in the world and the change in the international monetary order are other motivations for the East Asian initiative of collective action. Even though the euro is now struggling, its successful launch in 1999 provided a good example (demonstration effect) that various currencies can be fused into one currency through harmonization in domestic policies. This boosted the support for monetary integration that had been lukewarm till then, analogous to the EMU, in many areas over the world.

The launch of the euro, however, stimulated East Asian interest in pursuing regional monetary integration as a defensive reaction as well as providing a demonstration effect. With the introduction of the euro, incentives emerged for East Asian countries to form a countervailing monetary bloc to protect their interests against the polarization of the international monetary order after the EMU. The formation of the EMU and the expansion of the dollar bloc may have damaging effects on East Asian countries, and a countervailing Asian monetary union may be needed to compensate for the loss of welfare.[11] Furthermore, if the ECB becomes inward-looking and adopts the same type of exchange rate policy as the US Federal Reserve has done,[12] as feared by some, the exchange rates of East Asian currencies may become more unstable and many countries will be victims of the benign neglect policy of the two economic superpowers. This motivates East Asian countries to create a zone of monetary and financial stability insulated from these extraneous influences.[13]

As mentioned above, most Asian foreign reserves were invested in US Treasury bonds because most Asian currencies were not internationally accepted. If Asian countries integrate their currencies into one, as European countries did, and if Asian savings are invested in Asian currency denominated assets, it might be helpful in imposing discipline on US economic policy by rendering the international environment less forgiving of its mistakes.

> In that case, US policy errors could cause massive portfolio diversification out of the dollar assets, and sustaining a large currency account deficit may become very costly. The United States may have to reduce imports sharply by fiscal and monetary tightening or maintain very high interest rates to attract capital inflow. (Kwan, 2001, p.7)

The recent global financial crisis vividly demonstrated the heavy price East Asian countries pay because of the mistakes in US monetary policy.

The launch of the euro was not sufficient to impose discipline on the US and stabilize exchange rates in East Asia. When the dollar became unstable and lost value, East Asian countries replaced dollar assets with euro assets only to a small extent. The replacement effect would be sufficient only with a regional common currency. Furthermore, neither the US nor the EU took a cooperative stance in international policy coordination. If Asian countries come together to form monetary integration, it could therefore contribute to a more stable international monetary system.

Disappointment with the reform of the international financial system has also encouraged a regional monetary initiative in East Asia. The progress of the reform was delayed largely because the supply side of international financial markets was reluctant to address the inherent problems of the current international financial system. Moreover, it was unclear whether the discussion on reforming international financial institutions would take into account East Asian countries' interests, because it was mainly led by the US and the EU. The reform undertaken since the Asian crisis has focused on strengthening the financial and corporate sectors of emerging and developing economies instead of rectifying the imperfections of international capital markets.

There is now universal agreement that international financial institutions (IFIs), including the IMF and the World Bank, are in need of reform. The idea of IFIs' reform was reinforced by the painful experience of the global crisis: the IFIs were not equipped to conduct proper surveillance and to provide early warnings on macroeconomic and financial risks, and could not stop the crisis from spreading. Many crisis-hit countries were even reluctant to rely on their rescue, in particular from the IMF, because of a 'stigma effect' and because they regarded it as doctrinaire and responsive mainly to its largest shareholders, in particular the US. At the London G20 Summit held in 2009, 'there was a shared understanding of the key problems facing the IMF such as insufficient resources, stigma among the emerging market economies, and lack of credibility/capacity in surveillance.' Also the G20 members recognized that 'governance reform in the World Bank needs to be accelerated, with merit-based senior management selection processes.'[14] To improve the legitimacy, credibility and effectiveness of IFIs, important actions have been undertaken by the G20. But these actions alone are not sufficient, and additional actions are needed to enhance the governance structure of IFIs to complete the reform.[15]

Faced with the uneven and slow process of the reform, many emerging market economies have begun to develop their own defence mechanisms against future financial crises. Instead of waiting for the G8/G20, whose effectiveness is questionable, to create a new international financial architecture, East Asia would have to work together to create its own system of defence. Moreover, in order to reflect their interests in the new international financial architecture, East Asian countries need regional monetary cooperation through which they can make their voice heard in international monetary affairs.

Finally, it should be noted that until now, the existing international economic institutions have failed to provide East Asia with a role that is consistent with its economic position in the world. The US and the EU always hold the dominant decision-making power in international organizations while Asian countries are under-represented and have little decision-making power. For example, the size of three big East Asian economies, China, Japan and Korea together, is as large as that of the US and far larger than that of the EU in purchasing power terms. But the sum of their quota in the IMF was around one half of the US quota and less than one third of the EU quota. The Toronto G20 Summit held in 2010 recognized this problem and decided to shift the IMF quota share of over 6 per cent from the over-represented countries to the under-represented ones.[16]

What is more important than this quota readjustment is enhancing the governance structure of IFIs through an open, transparent and merit-based selection process for the heads and senior leadership of all the IFIs in the context of a broader reform. Even if Asia's quota increases, for example, 'if the US continues to wield veto power and if the head of the IMF is always selected from Europe', the higher quota shared by Asia may not translate into its changed status.[17] An American scholar pointed this problem out and suggested a rationale for a separate regional monetary arrangement in East Asia:

> The top management situation is even worse. No Asian has even been considered for the top position at either the Fund or the Bank because Europe and the United States allocated these positions to themselves half a century ago and show no signs of relenting. Japan's proposal of a former Vice Minister of Finance to run the IMF, and his immediate endorsement by other Asians, is the latest expression of this frustration. So was the prolonged effort to elect a highly qualified Asian to head the WTO, which ended with the unsatisfactory compromise of a split term in which the Asian had to wait three years to take over. East Asia's desire to create its own institutions is driven importantly by its lack of adequate representation in the global bodies. (Bergsten, 2000, pp.6–7)

NOTES

1. National currencies can be replaced by a common currency through the adoption of another country's currency (dollarization) or the introduction of a new currency.
2. McKinnon (1999, p.2) says that 'a credible peg of 360 yen to the dollar was the monetary anchor in Japan's own great era of high growth and rapid financial transformation in the 1950s and 1960s.'
3. For example, see Bergsten (1997).
4. Krugman (1998) called those internal problems of Asian countries the 'Asian sin'.
5. Rather, there was the perception that the events of 1997–8 had been compounded by the large positions of highly-leveraged institutions in New York and the less than generous assistance and conditionality of multilateral financial institutions in Washington DC (Eichengreen, 2001).
6. Refer to the G20 Summit Declarations at Pittsburgh (2009), Toronto (2010) and Seoul (2010).
7. There have been two motives behind their accumulation of foreign reserves. One is the motive of the war chest (self-insurance) against a potential future crisis, and the other is that of keeping competitive exchange rates to support export-led growth. Empirical studies such as Aizenman and Lee (2005) support precautionary motives rather than mercantilist motives.
8. This section is from Chai and Rhee (2005).
9. A variance decomposition, which is another method to distinguish between the regional and global influences on local individual markets, also provides similar conclusions to this.
10. Bergsten and Park (2002), Wyplosz (2001).
11. Goto and Hamada (1995) show the damaging effect of regional economic integration on outsider countries in a trade model with increasing returns to scale and product differentiation.
12. The benign neglect policy of the US is summarized by the expression 'the dollar is our currency but it's your problem'.
13. Yam (1997, p.9) pointed out that 'It is the greater volatility of G-3 currencies that ultimately contributed to, if not caused, the volatility in smaller regional currencies'. Moon (1999) and Moon and Rhee (1999) also emphasize similar problems.
14. The G20 (2009), Final Communique: The London Summit Declaration, 2 April.
15. For more discussion on this issue, see Bark and Rhee (2010) and S. Kim (2010).
16. The G20 (2010), The G-20 Toronto Summit Declaration, 26–7 June.
17. Rogoff (2010).

7. The beginning of monetary cooperation in East Asia and the Chiang Mai Initiative

The road towards Asian monetary cooperation started with the outbreak of the Asian currency crisis in 1997. Indeed, the Asian currency crisis provided a new opportunity to discuss a permanent monetary institution within Asia; in this context the idea of an Asian Monetary Fund (AMF) was born. Japan proposed it first. Fearing that the yen would drop to a junior international currency status after the dollar and the euro, Japan had already tried to develop the yen as an international currency. The crisis, however, made this Japanese effort redundant. Amid the rapid decline of Japanese influence on monetary and financial matters in Asia, the establishment of an AMF emerged as an urgent issue for Japan. Again, this idea encountered strong opposition from the US and the IMF. Asian countries had to take a long detour. First, they established as the main vehicle for regional economic and monetary cooperation the ASEAN+3 framework, which only included Asian countries; on the basis of this framework, they launched the Chiang Mai Initiative (CMI) for their financial self-help. Through the CMI process, the facility for the emergency provision of funds continued to expand, and the operational procedure improved over time, leading to the development of The Chiang Mai Initiative Mutualisation (CMIM) agreement and an independent surveillance unit. The eruption of the global financial crisis in 2008 was another factor that helped to strengthen this development. Asian countries are now ready to see an AMF become reality.

7.1 PRELIMINARY STEPS FOR CLOSER MONETARY COOPERATION

7.1.1 The Internationalization of the Yen

Interest in the international role of the yen was first sparked in the discussion seeking a new international monetary system in the wake of the collapse of the Bretton Woods system and the adoption of a floating exchange rate system in March 1973. During the 1960s, the US continued to suffer a continual decline in its global economic standing, leading to deteriorating international confidence in the dollar. Simultaneously, Japan emerged as an increasingly important player for the global economy.

With huge trade surpluses and conflicts with the US, the Japanese Minister of Finance considered the internationalization of the yen as one of its major policy objectives. The Yen–Dollar Committee was established in 1984 to discuss the issues concerning the liberalization of Japan's financial and capital markets, the internationalization of the yen, and the lowering of the barriers to access to foreign financial institutions participating in Japan's financial and capital markets. Against this background, the Minister of Finance assigned the task of conducting deliberations on the internationalization of the yen to the Council on Foreign Exchange and Other Transactions, an advisory group to the Japanese Minister of Finance.

In March 1985, the Council submitted its report, which included the following specific measures for promoting the internationalization of the yen: (i) financial liberalization (particularly the continued liberalization of interest rates, and the further development and expansion of open short-term capital markets); (ii) liberalization of the euro–yen market as the first step toward improving the convenience of the yen for non-residents; and (iii) the establishment of a Tokyo offshore market to facilitate euro–yen transactions in Tokyo. Responding to these developments, steady progress was made through the second half of the 1980s and 1990s in the programme for financial liberalization, which included the easing and abolition of euro–yen regulations.

The year 1985 was a critical time because the Plaza Accord was concluded. The dramatic appreciation of the Japanese yen after 1985 led to a veritable explosion of Japanese investment in the region. The flow of aid also continued to increase as Japan recycled its trade surpluses with the region. 'All governments in Southeast Asia became accustomed to bidding for Japanese investment capital, illustrated by the massive deregulation of their economies and the lucrative incentives that they were willing to grant to foreign investors. More importantly, Japan's developmental state became an object of emulation' (Katzenstein, 2000, p.359).

The internationalization of the yen started extensively in 1985. This was also facilitated by the end of the Cold War, which influenced regional arrangements in East Asia. However, there was no further progress after 1990 as Japanese economic growth slowed down.

New momentum arose with the outbreak of the currency crisis in East Asia in 1997. The Council on Foreign Exchange and Other Transactions

(1999), published a report in April 1999, similar to its earlier study, titled 'Internationalization of the yen for the 21st century'. Recognizing that the effort to boost the use of the yen should start in Asia, a region which shares strong economic ties with Japan, the Council recommended several measures to promote the yen as a real international currency. These measures included: achieving exchange rate stability between the dollar, euro and yen; establishing an Asian currency basket composed of the dollar, euro, yen and other currencies, with each currency being assigned a weight in proportion to its trade and economic importance; improving the Japanese financial and capital markets; allowing the Bank of Japan to expand yen-denominated credit facilities to foreign central banks; increasing the use and holding of yen by non-residents and providing official financial aid and assistance in yen and so on.[1] To pursue these goals, the Council also emphasized that Japan should be prepared to accept international responsibilities and rapidly restore its ties with the Asian economies.

7.1.2   Asian Monetary Fund

When the currency crisis broke out in 1997, the crisis-hit East Asian countries had to seek international financial rescue. From the viewpoint of these countries, however, the assistance was neither swift nor sufficient enough to pacify turbulent markets. Moreover, the policy packages imposed by the IMF conditionality caused the economies of these countries to sink into unprecedentedly deep and enormously painful recessions.

The creation of an AMF is a partial answer to this problem. The idea of an AMF occurred in August 1997 to support crisis-hit Thailand. The Japanese government, which took the initiative in leading the creditor country meetings at the time, thought it necessary to create a US$100 billion fund to prevent the recurrence of the crisis. Soon after, Japan proposed this idea on an unofficial basis in a series of finance ministers' meetings of the G7 and ASEAN countries that were held in September 1997. It was argued that an AMF would provide sufficient liquidity that could be quickly mobilized to forestall speculative attacks on the region's currencies. Despite strong support from Malaysia, the idea was turned down at the fifth Asia-Pacific Economic Cooperation meeting in Manila. In particular, Japan was not successful in getting the necessary support from China and Korea, as it encountered strong opposition from the US government, which feared an AMF's potential to undermine US leadership in the region. The US and the IMF argued that an AMF was a duplication of the IMF and would only exacerbate moral hazard behaviour of borrower countries. This might explain why the concrete content of the proposal for an AMF was not made public.

The concrete idea for an AMF came from Shinohara (1999). In fact, according to him, the main functions of an AMF are: (i) to promote policy dialogue; (ii) to provide emergency financial support; and (iii) to prevent possible future crises. However, it is clear that the most important function of an AMF is to provide emergency financial support to the would-be crisis-hit countries. In so doing, the mobilization of funds could be realized by borrowing from member countries (member countries should earmark a significant amount of their foreign exchange reserves to contribute to an AMF), by borrowing from capital markets (member countries should offer another proportion of foreign exchange reserves to an AMF as a lender of last resort), and extending guarantees to member countries.

Soon after its rejection by the IMF and the US, however, there emerged a change of opinion about an AMF. This was essentially due to the following two reasons. First, the attitude of the US became more flexible. In fact, as the Asian currency crisis spread to Latin America and Russia during 1998, the US government had to come to the rescue, contrary to what it did during the Asian currency crisis. Moreover, the interventions of the IMF in the crisis-hit countries were increasingly criticized as inappropriate and discriminatory. For example, Chaipravat (2002) criticized the imposition of the IMF conditionality on the East Asian countries as completely inappropriate, on the grounds that the root cause of the Asian currency crisis was not the traditional long-term current account disequilibria which the IMF conditionality was originally designed to address, but the short-term capital account volatilities.

Faced with these increasing criticisms, the US government and the IMF could no longer oppose the idea of an AMF as strongly as before (Shinohara, 1999). Indeed, these criticisms led Wade and Venoroso (1998) to support the idea of a regional fund. They made a strong case for the creation of an AMF, suggesting that it could build on Asia's saving surpluses, foreign exchange reserves, and net-creditor status (including reserves and Treasury bills). An AMF could also raise the necessary funds for its core financing from subscriptions by member governments. Rose (1999) was also in favour of establishing a regional monetary fund parallel to the IMF. He noted that currency crises would tend to be more regional, spread out along the lines of trade linkages, and thus disrupt regional trade flows. Since currency crises create costs to the region, the region would have an incentive to mitigate these by providing a financial safety net. Compromising between the need for an AMF and the interest of the US to maintain its influence in the region, Bergsten (1998) suggested that Asian countries and the US form an Asia Pacific Monetary Fund (APMF). He pointed out three reasons why such a regional scheme would be necessary. First, no Asian country could lead a regional initiative effectively, because the rest of the region would reject any hint of Japanese domination, while China is not ready yet for such a role. Second, an Asian countries-only group has a higher risk of division than a group that unites the two sides of the Pacific. Third, the US could play a decisive role in making an APMF work. However, underlying this proposal was the idea that the US should take charge of leading such an institution, with Japan's role being limited to providing the necessary funds.[2]

At any rate, the idea of an AMF could not be completely dissipated (Curtis, 1998; Yam, 1997); it re-emerged repeatedly under the name of different initiatives.

7.1.3   Miyazawa Plan

In October 1998, the Japanese Finance Minister Miyazawa (1998) made a proposal at the annual meeting of the IMF and the World Bank. His proposal is known as 'the New Initiative to Overcome the Asian Currency Crisis'. In the proposal, he emphasized the risk of a deflationary spiral of the world economy and criticized the IMF structural adjustment programmes on the grounds that they failed to understand that the economic turmoil in East Asia was largely due to the abrupt flows of short-term capital, and not to fundamental changes in the economies. Then, to overcome the Asian currency crisis, he proposed setting up a financial assistance scheme totalling US$30 billion. In particular, he stated that US$15 billion would be provided as mid- and long-term financial assistance for the recovery of the real economies of Asian countries and that another US$15 billion would be used to provide for the short-term capital needs of the region. Finally, after he pointed out that the 'over-dependence on the US dollar was obviously one of the causes of the currency crisis that erupted in Asia the year before, [which] has led many countries in the region to look to the yen to play a greater role' (Miyazawa, 1998, p.9), he insisted that the increasing use of the yen, together with the dollar and the euro, would contribute to the stability of the international monetary system.

The Miyazawa plan was careful to include the G7 countries, the IMF and the World Bank through a larger aid package. At that time, the IMF was running out of funds and the US Congress was hesitating over the approval of further US funding. The IMF and the US could no longer oppose the Miyazawa Plan as strongly as they did the previous AMF proposal (Narine, 2001).

7.2 POST-CRISIS REGIONAL INITIATIVES: FROM THE MANILA FRAMEWORK GROUP TO ASEAN+3

The Manila Framework Group (MFG) was the first important regional cooperative framework for coping with possible currency and financial crises. It worked through frequent exchanges of information and regional surveillance and through a network of repurchase and swap arrangements to reinforce foreign exchange reserve positions.

The MFG was established on 18–19 November 1997, as deputy finance ministers and central bank governors from 14 countries within and outside the Asia-Pacific region agreed on 'a New Framework for Enhanced Asian Regional Cooperation to Promote Financial Stability' (the Manila Framework). The Manila Framework established a mechanism for regional surveillance, which was complementary to the global surveillance of the IMF. This mechanism provided a basis for a more intensive and high-level process of surveillance and dialogue among participating member countries with support from the IMF, the World Bank, and the ADB (Institute for International Monetary Affairs, 2005). The Manila Framework Group had meetings twice a year from 1997 to 2001, and once a year from 2002 to 2004. However, because it had no formal status (secretariat) and included both Asian and non-Asian countries, it was prevented from functioning as an effective forum for regional surveillance and peer pressure. The Manila Framework Group meeting was eventually terminated in 2004. The role of the MFG as a regional forum was replaced by ASEAN+3 meetings, to which the IMF was not invited.

ASEAN was the driving force which led regionalism in East Asia. While the +3 North-East Asian countries had limited regional cooperation, ASEAN countries had much more experience in regional cooperation. With the onset of the Asian financial crisis in 1997, however, it became clear that ASEAN alone could not cope with such a large-scale economic problem. Total official funds provided by the IMF, other international institutions, regional governments and others to the two ASEAN countries, Thailand and Indonesia, amounted to US$17.2 billion and US$36.1 billion, representing 12 per cent and 17 per cent of their GDP respectively, while Korea alone received $58.4 billion, 12 per cent of its GDP. The regional financial cooperation had to extend beyond ASEAN. Thus, after the proposal for an AMF failed, the heads of states and governments of ASEAN invited the leaders of China, Korea and Japan to combine efforts to strengthen economic cooperation in East Asia. The first ASEAN+3 Summit Meeting was held in Kuala Lumpur, Malaysia, in December 1997. Then, at the third ASEAN+3 Summit Meeting held in Manila, the

Philippines, in November 1999, the leaders of the ASEAN+3 countries released a 'Joint Statement on East Asian Cooperation' covering a wide range of possible areas for regional cooperation and decided to establish the ASEAN+3 framework as a main vehicle for building the regional community. Diverse ministerial meetings were set up to support the Summit Meetings. In the area of monetary and financial cooperation, for instance, an ASEAN+3 Finance Ministers' Meeting was set up, and finance ministers have been convening every year since their first meeting in Manila in 1999 (see Kawai and Houser, 2007). Also, an informal ASEAN+3 Finance and Central Bank Deputies Meeting (AFDM+3) has been held twice every year since its first meeting in Yangon, Myanmar in 2002. The ASEAN+3 framework has broadened and deepened. Consisting of one summit, 16 ministerial, 23 senior official and other numerous meetings, it now covers all important areas of cooperation including political, economic, financial and social cooperation. The ASEAN+3 framework is important, in the sense that it includes the most important +3 countries in East Asia (China, Japan and Korea) and that it excludes countries outside the region.[3]

The activity of ASEAN+3 in the area of monetary and financial cooperation could be divided into two areas: the monitoring and surveillance processes, and the resource provision mechanisms.

First, given that the currency crisis in Asia was caused by the swings of short-term disruptive, portfolio capital flows, monitoring was naturally the first concern for Asian countries. Thus, the primary activity of ASEAN+3 was to develop an effective capital account monitoring system capable of identifying and distinguishing short-term portfolio inflows/outflows from desirable long-term capital flows in the region. In May 2000, ASEAN+3 finance ministers agreed to introduce an ASEAN+3 Economic Review and Policy Dialogue (ERPD), which would become the most important information exchange mechanism on economic conditions and policies in East Asia. The ERPD process is an extension of the ASEAN surveillance process. To follow the ERPD, the ASEAN+3 Finance Ministers have been meeting annually, and the Finance and Central Bank Deputies have met twice a year for policy coordination. The ASEAN Finance Ministers established the ASEAN surveillance process in October 1998 to provide the necessary liquidity as a guard against the recurrence of a currency crisis. Although this process was not effective due to the limited available data and understaffing, it was an important initiative because it would allow ASEAN countries to exchange information on economic developments and policies, and to consider individual and collective responses to events that could negatively impact their regional economic prosperity.

Following the goal of the ASEAN surveillance process, the ASEAN+3 ERPD was intended for the prevention of financial crises through an early detection of financial vulnerabilities and the swift implementation of remedial policy. The ERPD process encompasses: (i) assessing global, regional and national economic conditions; (ii) monitoring regional capital flows and currency markets; (iii) analysing macroeconomic and financial risks; (iv) strengthening banking and financial systems' conditions; and (v) providing an Asian voice in the reform of the international financial system (Kawai and Houser, 2007). Compared to the MFG, which includes countries like the US and Australia, the ASEAN+3 ERPD includes Asian countries only, and in this sense is more appropriate for satisfying the regional monetary and financial interests.

Secondly, the resource provision mechanism was established after the second ASEAN+3 Finance Ministers' Meeting, which was held in Chiang Mai, Thailand, in May 2000. In this meeting, ASEAN+3 Finance Ministers agreed to strengthen the existing financial arrangements in the region to supplement existing international liquidity facilities. 'In order to strengthen our self-help and support mechanisms in East Asia through the ASEAN+3 framework, we recognized a need to establish a regional financial arrangement to supplement the existing international facilities' (Joint Ministerial Statement of the Second ASEAN+3 Finance Ministers' Meeting, 6 May 2000, Chiang Mai, Thailand).

This initiative is known as the Chiang Mai Initiative. In addition to reiterating the need for strengthened policy dialogues and regional cooperation activities, the CMI called for: (i) an expanded ASEAN Swap Arrangement that would include all ASEAN countries and a network of bilateral swap and repurchase agreement facilities between ASEAN countries, the PRC, Japan and Korea; (ii) use of the ASEAN+3 framework to promote the exchange of consistent and timely data and information on capital flows; (iii) the establishment of a regional financing arrangement to supplement existing international facilities; (iv) the establishment of an appropriate mechanism (early warning system) that could enhance the ability to provide sufficient and timely financial stability in the East Asian region.

In 2004, the ASEAN+3 leaders agreed that the establishment of an 'East Asian Community' was their long-term objective and affirmed the role of ASEAN+3 as the 'main vehicle' for the establishment of an East Asian Community. The idea of creating such a community had been proposed by the East Asia Vision Group (2001), whose wide-ranging proposals were considered by the official East Asia Study Group (2002). The ASEAN+3 leaders in 2002 received the Study Group's Final Report, which identified 17 concrete short-term measures and 9 medium- to long-term measures – including regional financial cooperation – to move East Asian cooperation forward. Key medium- and long-term recommendations included, among others, the establishment of a regional financing facility, the pursuit of a more closely coordinated exchange rate mechanism, and the establishment of a regional surveillance process. The CMI was considered to be an initial step towards the establishment of a regional self-help financing facility, and the ERPD became the vehicle for regional economic surveillance (Kawai and Houser, 2007).

Because the CMI was a milestone toward a regional monetary and financial arrangement, its contents warrant detailed examination.

7.3   THE CHIANG MAI INITIATIVE

7.3.1   Institutions

The CMI consists of two regional financial arrangements: an expanded ASEAN swap arrangement (ASA) and a network of bilateral swaps and repurchase agreements between the eight members of ASEAN+3.

In 1977, five ASEAN countries (Indonesia, Malaysia, Philippines, Singapore and Thailand) agreed to establish an ASA to provide liquidity support for the participating countries that experience balance of payments difficulties. The utilization of the ASA, however, remained very limited. Even during the Asian financial crisis, countries did not turn to this swap facility. With the launch of the CMI in 2000, the ASA expanded to cover all 10 ASEAN members and its total amount also increased from US$200 million to US$1 billion. Then the ASA was further enlarged to US$2 billion in 2005. Under the ASA, a member country could request to swap its domestic currency for the US dollar, yen and euro, up to twice its committed amount for up to six months. As a quick disbursement facility, drawdown from the ASA would be made within seven working days upon request to the designated agent bank managing the facility.

Also, the ASEAN Swap Arrangement was enlarged to include the +3 North-East Asian countries, China, Japan and Korea, through a network of bilateral swap arrangements (BSAs). The BSA is a facility designed to provide short-term liquidity assistance in the form of swaps of US dollars with the domestic currencies of a participating country. Participating countries can draw on the BSA for a period of 90 days. The first drawing may be renewed seven times. The interest rate applicable to the drawing is the LIBOR plus a premium of 150 basis points for the first renewal drawings. Thereafter, the premium is increased by an additional 50 basis points for every two renewals, but not exceeding 300 basis points. While the framework paper lays out the basic principles, each bilateral agreement could be slightly different. The BSA is complementary to the IMF's assistance in that countries drawing from the facility are required

to accept an IMF programme for macroeconomic and structural adjustment. The BSA, however, allows an automatic disbursement of up to 10
per cent of the maximum amount of drawing without any linkage to an
IMF programme or conditionality. Initially, some countries like Malaysia
expressed reservations about the linkage of the BSA with the IMF conditionalities and proposed to abolish the IMF linkage after a transition
period. However, because the severance of the IMF linkage required the
creation of a regional surveillance system, there was consensus that the
BSAs should remain complementary and supplementary to the IMF facilities until the establishment of a regional surveillance system (Park and
Wang, 2002). This limitation would have been relaxed as the region developed its own surveillance capacity. Repurchase agreements (repos) were
also to be established to provide short-term liquidity to a participating
member though the sale and buyback of appropriate securities. Securities
eligible under the repo agreements are US Treasury notes or bills with a
remaining life of five years or less and government securities of the coun-
terparty country. However, the repurchase agreement was rarely used, and
since the Chiang Mai initiative no further progress was made.

Together with the bilateral swap arrangement, the Economic Review
and Policy Dialogue was established as the region's economic surveillance
mechanism. As pointed out, the purpose of the ASEAN+3 ERPD process
was to strengthen policy dialogue, coordination and collaboration on
financial, monetary and fiscal issues of common interest. Like the ASEAN
Surveillance Process, however, the ASEAN+3 ERPD Process was not
effective. There were no organizations, either autonomous or professional,
carrying out analyses and assessments and thereby supporting the surveillance and monitoring process, except for the ADB that provided some
data on developing members' economies.

7.3.2 Achievements

Since the ASEAN+3 summit meeting in November 2000, Japan, China
and Korea have been negotiating BSAs with each other and with the
ASEAN countries. In the beginning, Japan was the most active in the negotiations. On the other hand, Singapore and Brunei showed little enthusiasm
for the CMI, largely because they believed the BSAs with their neighbouring countries would be one-way arrangements in which they would be
asked to provide a large amount of liquidity in the event of a crisis affecting
the ASEAN region. However, Japan was successful in bringing Singapore
to the negotiating table by proposing a BSA that would use local currencies
rather than the US dollar. In fact, Japan concluded a similar local currency
BSA with China. Indonesia also had little interest in negotiating BSAs

Table 7.1   The status of the bilateral swap agreements under the CMI

	Support currency	As of May 2004		As of May 2006	
		Amount (Billion US$)	Ways of support	Amount (Billion US$)	Ways of support
China–Japan	Yen/RMB	6	Two way	6	Two way
Japan–Korea	US$/Won	2	One way	21	Two way
Korea–China	Won/RMB	4	Two way	8	Two way
Japan–Thailand	US$/Baht	3	One way	6	Two way
Japan–Philippines	US$/Peso	3	One way	6.5	One way
Japan–Malaysia	US$/Ringgit	1	One way	1	One way
Japan–Indonesia	US$/Rupiah	3	One way	6	One way
Japan–Singapore	US$/Sing.$	1	One way	4	Two way
China–Thailand	US$/Baht	2	One way	2	One way
China–Philippines	RMB/Peso	1	One way	1	One way
China–Malaysia	US$/Ringgit	1.5	One way	1.5	One way
China–Indonesia	Rupiah/RMB	1	One way	2	One way
Korea–Thailand	US$/Won–Baht	2	Two way	2	Two way
Korea–Malaysia	US$/Won–Ringgit	2	Two way	3	Two way
Korea–Philippines	US$/Won–Peso	2	Two way	3	Two way
Korea–Indonesia	US$/Won–Rupiah	2	Two way	2	Two way
Total BSAs		36.5		75	
Total ASAs		1		2	

Source: Ministry of Finance, Japan.

because of its preoccupation with domestic economic issues and management of its huge foreign debts, not to mention escalating political instability. Indonesia concluded a BSA with Japan, although it did not place a high priority on contracting additional BSAs with other members of the CMI.

The first phase of CMI contractual agreements was completed in May 2004 with a total of US$36.5 billion for 16 BSAs. The BSAs included one-way and two-way swaps. It is worth noting that China's and Japan's initial contracts with the ASEAN countries were one-way BSAs from which only the ASEAN countries could draw, while Korea's swaps with the ASEAN countries were two-way BSAs. The status of the BSA network as of May 2004 and 2006 is summarized in Table 7.1.

7.3.3 Limits of and the Expansion of the CMI

Although it was undeniably an important first step in establishing regional monetary cooperation, the Chiang Mai Initiative is far from truly being such a regional arrangement.

First, the total amount of the financial arrangement needs to be increased, since large financial arrangements serve as a deterrent to future financial crises. Second, as pointed out, the agreed swap arrangements are incomplete and insufficient to cope with a currency crisis because of the absence of an independent monitoring and surveillance system and the consequential linkage to IMF facilities. In the initial agreement, surveillance was not required because up to 10 per cent of each BSA swap could be disbursed without the consent of swap-providing countries, and any additional drawing was subject to IMF surveillance. The linkage to IMF conditionality was necessary to 'provide some comfort to lenders as it would limit the moral hazard problem', but it also left open the danger of sufficient swap funds not being available until too late. Thus, a regional surveillance system is crucial to secure regional autonomy and maintain a reasonable balance between global and regional arrangements. Third, the arrangements are bilateral, not multilateral. Thus, to improve the efficiency and effectiveness of the financial arrangement, the network of bilateral swaps should be organized into a multilateral arrangement, which may eventually lead to the establishment of an institution.

In May 2004, the first phase of the CMI was completed and the ASEAN+3 Finance Ministers decided to review the CMI process. Meeting in Istanbul in May 2005, the ASEAN+3 Finance Ministers reached a set of major agreements to improve the effectiveness of the CMI:

- Significant increase in the size of bilateral swap arrangements: to cope with financial crises, ASEAN+3 Finance Ministers agreed to increase the size of swaps by 100 per cent.
- Integration and enhancement of the ASEAN+3 ERPD into the CMI framework and increase in the BSA disbursement unlinked to the IMF programme from 10 per cent to 20 per cent; the implementation of the CMI swap arrangement will depend on the capacity of the ASEAN+3 ERPD to conduct an effective economic review. However, as the ERPD acquires the capability to accurately assess economic and financial conditions of a country in or near crisis and to draft policy conditions associated with its liquidity support to a crisis country, it should be linked to the CMI, both in operation and in evolution, independently of the IMF. There is a mutually reinforcing relationship between the evolution of the ERPD and the CMI. Furthermore, as ASEAN+3 countries continue to move towards developing a regional financial arrangement, they ultimately need a surveillance unit independent of the IMF. In fact, the degree of the CMI's linkage to the IMF programmes was considered too tight,

and hence the CMI swap arrangement could not be effective if the linkage were not to be reduced or eliminated.

- A clear definition of the CMI swap activation process and the adoption of a collective decision-making mechanism as a step towards CMI multilateralization.

The second phase of the CMI process was completed in May 2006 when the ASEAN+3 Finance Ministers met at Hyderabad, India. The total size of the swaps reached US$75 billion (see Table 7.1) and the Finance Ministers adopted a collective decision-making procedure for CMI swap activation as a step toward multilateralizing the CMI. The Finance Ministers also tasked their deputies with studying further the various possible options toward a multilateral CMI or post-CMI arrangement, with the goal of establishing an advanced framework for the regional liquidity support arrangement.

7.3.4   CMIM and Institutionalization

The bilateral nature of the CMI was regarded as an impediment to its quick activation. Hence, the centralization of the facility for prompt joint activation in the event of a crisis was considered and there were continual efforts to convert the network of BSAs frameworks into a common pool where ASEAN+3 countries set aside a modest share of their foreign exchange reserves. In particular, several proposals were put forward on the detailed modality of such reserve pooling schemes. They included a Framework for Regional Monetary Stability (Institute for International Monetary Affairs, 2000), an East Asian Fund (Ito et al., 1999), a Regional Financing Arrangement (Yoshitomi and Shirai, 2000), a Regional Financing Facility (Rana, 2002), and an Asian Currency Fund (Chaipravat, 2002). For instance, ASEAN recommended that each monetary authority set aside a modest percentage, say 5 per cent of its international reserves, and place the funds with the other 12 central banks on a pro rata basis that would be determined by some equitable formula. This multicurrency placement was designed to achieve the dual objective of increasing the role of currencies within the region while decreasing that of outside currencies. The proposal was also to let each country borrow multiples of the placement amount, a concept similar to the much-practised margin loans in the securities business (Rana, 2002). Also, Chaipravat (2002) proposed to place a part (for instance, 40 per cent) of the foreign exchange reserves that would arise from excessive short-term portfolio capital inflows as deposits in the other central banks in the region. These reserves would be used to create a central pool called the Asian Currency

Fund, to administer and manage the deposits. This Asian Currency Fund was to be a supranational institution with surveillance capabilities and decision-making power on behalf of the financial authorities of the ASEAN+3 countries.

In May 2007, the ASEAN+3 Finance Ministers convened at Kobe, Japan, and agreed in principle on a self-managed reserve pooling arrangement governed by a single contractual arrangement. This was considered an appropriate form of CMI multilateralization. The phrase 'self-managed' means that the reserves would not be physically collected in a common fund but would instead be held by national central banks and earmarked for that purpose (Henning, 2009). They then instructed their deputies to carry out further studies on the key elements of 'self-managed reserve pooling' – including surveillance, reserve eligibility, size of commitment, borrowing quota and activation mechanism.

Furthermore, there were attempts to expand the size of the CMIM, as major economies in the region, notably Japan and China, had abundant foreign exchange reserves, In May 2008, there was an agreement made to increase the total size of the CMIM to US$80 billion and to fix the proportion of the contributions coming from ASEAN countries and the +3 North-East Asian countries at 20:80. Then in February 2009, the total size of the CMIM was again extended to US$120 billion due to the realization that US$80 billion was still not enough to cope with the global financial crisis that happened in 2008.

Finally, meeting in Bali, Indonesia in May 2009, ASEAN+3 Finance Ministers reached agreement on all the main components of the CMIM including individual countries' contribution size, borrowing accessibility and surveillance mechanism. First, Table 7.2 summarizes the contribution size, borrowing agreement and voting power of the CMIM.

The broad decision-making mechanism of the CMIM was also defined. Fundamental issues such as the review of the size, contributions, borrowing multipliers, re-admission, membership, terms of lending, and so on, were to be decided through consensus among the ASEAN+3 members, while lending issues such as lending, renewal and default were to be decided through majority vote.

The last important remaining issue concerned the surveillance mechanism. A decision was also made to establish an independent 'surveillance unit' to 'monitor and analyse regional economies and support CMIM decision-making' as well as an 'advisory panel of experts' to 'work closely with the Asian Development Bank and the ASEAN Secretariat to enhance the current surveillance mechanism in order to lay the surveillance groundwork for the CMIM' (Joint Media Statement of the 12th ASEAN+3 Finance Ministers' Meeting, May 2009). In a sense, the CMIM is heading

Table 7.2 *The main features of the CMIM*

	Financial contribution		Borrowing agreements		Total voting power			
	US$ (billion)	(%)	Multipler	Maximum swap	No. of basic vote	No. of votes based on contribution	No. of total vote	(%)
China+HK	38.40	32.00	0.72	19.2	1.60	38.40	40.00	28.41
(China)	(34.2)	(28.50)	(0.5)	(17.1)	(1.60)	(34.20)	(35.8)	(25.43)
(Hong Kong)	(4.2)	(3.50)	(2.5)	(2.1)	(0.0)	(4.20)	(4.2)	(2.98)
Japan	38.40	32.00	0.5	19.2	1.60	38.40	40.00	28.41
Korea	19.20	16.00	1	19.2	1.60	19.20	20.80	14.77
+3	96.00	80.00	0.69	57.6	4.80	96.00	100.80	71.59
Indonesia	4.552	3.793	2.5	11.9	1.60	4.552	6.152	4.369
Thailand	4.552	3.793	2.5	11.9	1.60	4.552	6.152	4.369
Malaysia	4.552	3.793	2.5	11.9	1.60	4.552	6.152	4.369
Singapore	4.552	3.793	2.5	11.9	1.60	4.552	6.152	4.369
Philippines	4.552	3.793	2.5	9.2	1.60	4.552	6.152	4.369
Vietnam	1.00	0.833	5	5.0	1.60	1.00	2.60	1.847
Cambodia	0.12	0.100	5	0.6	1.60	0.12	1.72	1.222
Myanmar	0.06	0.050	5	0.3	1.60	0.06	1.66	1.179
Brunei	0.03	0.025	5	0.2	1.60	0.03	1.63	1.158
Lao PDR	0.03	0.025	5	0.2	1.60	0.03	1.63	1.158
ASEAN	24.00	20.00	2.63	63.1	16.00	24.00	40.00	28.41
Total	120.00	100.00	1.16	120.7	20.80	120.00	140.80	100.0

Sources: The Joint Ministerial Statement of the 13th ASEAN+3 Finance Ministers' Meeting held in Tashkent, Uzbekistan, 2 May 2010, and Kawai (2009a).

toward a more institutionalized structure, operating with the support of a surveillance unit and under the guidance of an advisory panel of experts.

7.4   AMF AGAIN?

Kawai (2009a) proposed to transform the CMIM into an AMF. This would require the improvement of the ERPD such that lending conditionality, independent of IMF programmes, could be formulated in the event of CMIM activation. To this end, Kawai made the following recommendations:

- clarify rules for activating CMIM lending;
- establish a joint forum for finance ministers and central bank governors to intensify policy dialogue between them;
- set up a competent professional secretariat, with the required analytical expertise and policy experience, to enable it to support regional economic surveillance (ERPD), CMIM activation, and independent conditionality formulation;
- improve the quality of economic surveillance by moving beyond the simple 'information sharing' stage to a more rigorous 'peer review and peer pressure' stage, and eventually to a 'due diligence' stage.

Once these conditions have been met, a de facto AMF will emerge, capable of conducting effective surveillance and handling regional financial crises. In May 2010, the ASEAN+3 Finance Ministers agreed to establish an ASEAN+3 Macroeconomic Research Office (AMRO) in Singapore in May 2011, initially with a small number of professional staff, to work with the ASEAN Secretariat. The AMRO was to encourage frank 'peer reviews' of other countries' policies and to strengthen the CMIM as well, as more effective surveillance encouraged governments to undertake necessary policy reforms and, hence, increase their partners' willingness to lend.

It seems that Asian countries are now well prepared to create an Asian Monetary Fund after taking a long and time-consuming detour through the CMI process, and to express their shared views and opinions on global and regional monetary affairs with one voice. Given that the goal of the CMI was achieved to a large extent, it is now important for Asian countries to set up new goals and visions for Asian regionalism. Unless they do this, further institutionalization toward an AMF will be difficult.

Once an AMF is created, it will supplement the role of the IMF and would thereby contribute to global rebalancing through boosting the regional demand of many Asian economies and correcting payments imbalances. After the Asian financial crisis of 1997–8, many economies in the region saw great value in building foreign exchange reserves as protection against currency crises, as they recalled the bitter experience of the unjustly harsh conditionalities imposed by the IMF. These governments had every incentive to accumulate reserves by running large current account surpluses. The region's emerging economies would welcome the rebalancing if an AMF could reduce financial turbulence and act as the region's lender of last resort. However, it is very unlikely that this new AMF will assume the role of the regional lender of last resort fully, at least in the near future. In deciding the future role of an AMF, two points should be considered.

First, the role of an AMF should be considered within the framework of global and regional financial safety nets, and in this respect the role of a global lender of last resort is still very important, separate from an AMF. In fact, no matter how much an AMF is strengthened, it is clear that an AMF will not substitute for the global lender of last resort. The financial resources that could be mobilized through an AMF will not be enough. The appropriate role for an AMF is to supplement the global lender of last resort as much as possible. In Korea, for instance, the maximum fund it could finance through the CMIM is merely US$19.2 billion (or just US$3.84 billion if only the fund, unlinked to the IMF, is considered). This sum of money would be insufficient to contain a crisis. Such a small amount would not be enough to discourage the incentives of accumulating its international reserves and to contribute to balanced growth. Given its current size, an AMF would be more appropriate for handling a crisis in developing ASEAN countries, should it happen.

Second, bilateral swaps between central banks will continue to be of importance and an AMF will not overshadow the bilateral swaps among individual Asian central banks. For instance, when the global financial crisis took place in 2008, independently of the IMF the Federal Reserve System played a key role as the world's central bank in mitigating the impact of the crisis and preventing the crisis from spreading out to other regions and countries. As pointed out by Moon (2010), central bank swaps mobilized much larger sums of money than the IMF did to cope with the financial crisis. For instance, while the IMF provided a mere sum of 33 billion SDRs to dozens of developing countries, the US Federal Reserve Board concluded a total of US$412 billion swaps with 14 developed and developing countries. Although its long-term effect is not certain, this central bank swap proved to be more effective in stabilizing the financial markets. Korea's case is a good example. As seen in Figures 7.1 and 7.2, the Korean government borrowed a total of US$30 billion from the IMF

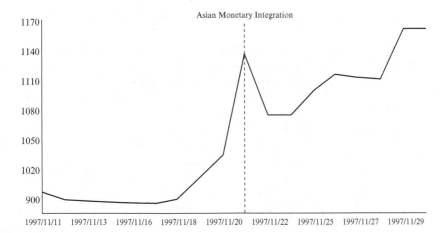

Source: Bank of Korea.

*Figure 7.1   Won–dollar trend around the IMF bailout loan
(US$27 billion) on 21 November 1997*

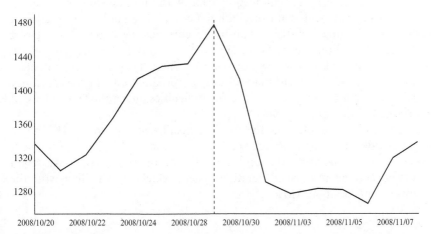

Source: Bank of Korea.

*Figure 7.2   Won–dollar trend around the Korean-US currency swap
(US$30 billion) on 29 October 2008*

during the 1997 currency crisis. However, this announcement did not help
the Korean economy to stabilize its foreign exchange market. In contrast,
in October 2008 the Bank of Korea entered into a US$30 billion currency
swap arrangement with the US Federal Reserve System, which was helpful

in addressing its financial market turbulence caused by the global financial crisis.

In particular, bilateral swaps in local currencies will still be important because the supply of funds is guaranteed on the basis of printing power. Korea had the same types of swap arrangements with the Bank of Japan and the People's Bank of China in December 2008. The situation was not different for other Asian countries. For instance, as pointed out by Kawai (2009a), a country like Indonesia faced a dilemma as it could mobilize smaller funds under the CMIM than under the bilateral swaps of the CMI. As a result, the Japanese Ministry of Finance announced in May 2009 that it would begin to arrange yen-based bilateral currency swap lines with other Asian economies, including Indonesia, of up to a total of 6 trillion yen (equivalent to US$60 billion). These arrangements are unusual in the sense that they are subject to the same conditionality that the CMIM and IMF offer, and that Japan's Ministry of Finance would raise the needed funds through the Foreign Exchange Special Account by borrowing from the market through issuing yen-denominated short-term financing bills. It is reported that Japan's Ministry of Finance will set up a swap line of 1.5 trillion yen (US$15 billion equivalent) with Indonesia and is preparing similar arrangements with the Philippines and Thailand (Kawai, 2009a). Similarly, China arranged yuan-based currency swap lines with Hong Kong (200 billion yuan), Korea (180 billion yuan), Indonesia (100 billion yuan), and Malaysia (80 billion yuan).[4] These swap lines are intended more for trade settlement than for emergency situations, such as currency speculation and balance of payments difficulties, given the yuan's lack of capital account convertibility.

In order to supplement the funding insufficiency of an AMF and to accelerate monetary and financial cooperation in Asia, the permanent swap system between the central banks of the +3 North-East Asian countries may also be a significant step, which goes in line with the establishment of an AMF.

NOTES

1. Especially noteworthy among these measures was the provision of yen-denominated credit facilities to other countries, as it could be interpreted from this that the Japanese government has decided to take greater responsibility in regional monetary cooperation.
2. In theory, an APMF to which the US can supply international liquidity (dollars) without limit may be superior to an AMF. But considering that the contagion of a crisis operates first and most powerfully within regions and that the US took a different attitude towards the recent Asian crisis than from the Mexican crisis in 1994, it is doubtful whether the US would be willing to provide the necessary amount of emergency liquidity if a crisis happens again in Asia.

3. The boundary of ASEAN+3 was already set by the former Prime Minister of Malaysia, Mahatir, who proposed the formation of an East Asian Economic Caucus (EAEC) in 1990. This proposal could not be realized, however, because of the opposition of the US to any ideas of Asia-only regionalism and its support for the APEC framework that would include itself as a member country.
4. China also arranged similar swaps with Argentina (70 billion yuan) and Belarus (20 billion yuan).

8. Financial market integration and Asian bond market initiatives

Despite various attempts and ideas, there has been little significant progress made in East Asian monetary integration apart from the Chiang Mai Initiative. Eichengreen (2002) argues that 'monetary and exchange rate cooperation is the wrong project for Asia', highlighting that Asia lacks the political commitment to deepen integration and to establish supranational institutions with agenda-setting power. This led him to argue in favour of 'cooperation to deepen and strengthen regional financial markets', or more concretely, the establishment of an 'Asian Financial Institute' on the platform of ASEAN+3. Because of East Asian countries' fear of losing their national monetary sovereignty, there is greater potential for financial cooperation than for monetary cooperation in East Asia. Whenever talks about monetary and exchange rate cooperation issues reached a stalemate, financial cooperation issues emerged as an alternative for circumventing the deadlock and continuing regional cooperation. Against this background, initiatives to develop regional bond markets have attracted special interest from many countries in the region. First, the development of regional bond markets was considered helpful in solving the double mismatch problem of short-term bank borrowings by East Asian companies from foreign banks, allied to long-term East Asian investment in foreign assets, and of East Asian loans in foreign currencies from foreign banks being vulnerable to exchange rate fluctuations. Second, the post-crisis accumulation of foreign reserves in US dollars, unprecedented in its magnitude, prompted a discussion on bond market development. The development of regional bond markets has since been at the centre of discussions in many ASEAN+3 and APEC meetings.

8.1   OBJECTIVES

The outbreak of the Asian currency crisis provoked strong interest in monetary and financial cooperation in Asia, with calls for the provision of liquidity to cope with short-term capital outflows. The Chiang

Mai Initiative undertaken by ASEAN+3 finance ministers in May 2000 was a direct response to such calls. At the same time, East Asia's bank-dominated financial system and banks were considered to be one of the main factors behind the extreme volatility of short-run capital which precipitated the Asian financial crisis. It led governments in the region to focus on bond market development. Firms had been dependent for so long on banks for their investment funds, and this dependence aggravated the currency crisis because firms could not find alternative sources of financing. Bond markets were underdeveloped in East Asia. One reason was the presence of development banks which helped to complement the weak bond markets. In order to develop industries rapidly and catch up with advanced countries, East Asian countries needed to set up many industrial or development finance banks. Commercial bank loans were by definition short-term, making client companies financially vulnerable to short-term swings in the economic environment. Hence, they were not suitable for fixed investments, like infrastructure investment. Thus, there was a significant mismatch between the maturity structure of assets and liabilities of firms and banks. To fill the gap and support fixed investment, East Asian governments intervened, setting up development finance institutions, particularly development banks. As a result, these banks were established as special institutions with specific mandates or policy objectives, and they were either wholly-owned by government or jointly-owned by government and the private sector (Moon et al., 2005).

Table 8.1 shows that capital markets in Asia were underdeveloped compared to the bank loan market. The bond and stock markets have developed rapidly in Asia since 1997. However, this change is not yet big enough to transform the East Asian financial system into a market-oriented system such as the US financial system. As Mohanty and Turner (2010) indicated, although direct financing through the bond and stock markets grew rapidly after the currency crisis, bank intermediation is still playing an important role in Asia.

As the 1997 financial crisis made clear, a long-term local currency bond market is useful in avoiding the 'double (maturity and currency) mismatch' problem. First, East Asian countries were borrowing short while investing long. For example, East Asia was traditionally well-known for its high level of savings and investments (about 30–40 per cent of GDP). Because of weak national and regional capital markets, however, these savings were invested in the form of long-term and safe assets in industrialized countries, while their investments were mainly financed in the form of short-term international bank loans from industrialized countries. This led to the growing vulnerability of East Asian countries, and eventually

Table 8.1   Selected indicators on the size of the bank and capital markets in East Asian countries (% of GDP)

	Bank claims		Bonds outstanding		Stocks outstanding	
	1997	2007	1997	2007	1997	2007
Japan	191.3	98.0	97.4	202.2	52.1	101.7
China	94.2	131.4	8.5	49.9	21.7	184.1
Korea	59.8	98.3	29.7	102.6	8.9	107.1
Hong Kong	170.3	139.7	23.3	24.8	234.4	561.4
Indonesia	61.8	26.0	2.0	19.8	13.5	49.0
Malaysia	161.9	112.5	54.4	84.6	93.5	174.4
Philippines	59.6	26.7	20.3	37.6	38.1	71.7
Singapore	101.3	92.5	24.9	58.2	110.9	211.7
Thailand	165.7	89.7	6.9	57.0	15.6	79.3
East Asia total	157.6	105.9	68.9	119.7	48.1	138.8
US	66.1	90.8	139.7	168.5	137.1	145.2

Sources: IMF, International Financial Statistics; Bank for International Settlements, available at http://www.bis.org; World Bank; World Development Indicators, available at www.worldbank.org/data.

precipitated the 1997 crisis. The development of regional capital markets, where regional savings are directly recycled into regional investments, would therefore reduce such vulnerability in the future. A more serious problem than the maturity mismatch is the mismatch between currencies borrowed and invested. Eichengreen (2002), for instance, emphasized the currency mismatch as the structural weakness ('original sin') of emerging economies that experienced financial crises. Because international investors favour bonds denominated in selected international currencies, exchange rate fluctuation of international currencies may weaken the balance sheet of corporations and governments with a high leverage in foreign currencies. The development of Asian bonds denominated in Asian currencies is considered a prerequisite to avoid the risk of future financial crises.

Another important post-crisis development that contributed to the development of a long-term local currency bond market was the rapid swing in current account balances. For instance, East Asian countries, apart from Japan and China, recorded current account deficits in 1996. Since the Asian currency crisis in 1997, however, all East Asian countries started to run current account surpluses. One reason for this current account surplus was the so-called 'twin fears'; the fear of a crisis and the fear of floating, which led many East Asian countries to accumulate

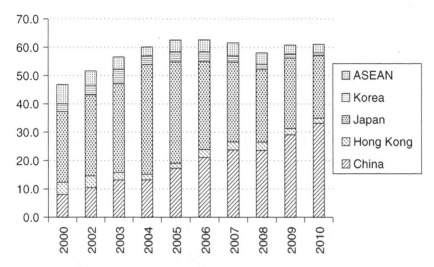

Note: East Asian figures are for the sum of the US Treasury securities held by China, Japan, Korea, ASEAN and Hong Kong.

Source: US Treasury, Report on Foreign Portfolio Holdings of US Securities, available at http://www.treasury.gov/resource-center/.

Figure 8.1   US Treasury securities held by major Asian countries (%)

massive foreign exchange reserves (see Park and Park, 2003). As witnessed in the case of Asian countries that avoided the worst consequences of the 1997 crisis by using their high levels of reserves – namely China, Hong Kong, Singapore and Taiwan – higher levels of official foreign exchange reserves were supposed to serve as a safeguard against financial vulnerability (Aizenman and Marion, 2002). More importantly, the fear of floating contributed to the accumulation of huge current account surpluses, preventing East Asian countries from adjusting the current account imbalance between East Asia and the US by exchange rate appreciation. As indicated in Table 6.5 (Chapter 6), the official foreign exchange reserves of East Asian countries continued to increase, reaching US$3.8 trillion in 2008, which accounts for 55 per cent of the world's total foreign reserves. The accumulation of these huge reserves necessitates the management of exchange rates. As already pointed out, East Asian countries invested these foreign exchanges in safe and liquid assets of the US. Figure 8.1 shows that East Asia is the largest foreign purchaser of US Treasury securities. As of June 2010, the East Asian countries as a whole hold around US$ 2 trillion, accounting for 61 per cent of the total foreign holdings of long-term US Treasury bonds, which are worth US$3.3 trillion. It is

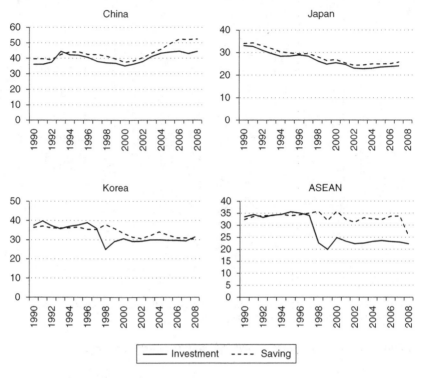

Source: World Bank.

*Figure 8.2   Investment and saving rates for individual East Asian countries
             (% of GDP)*

interesting to note that traditionally Japan was the largest holder of the
US Treasury securities in East Asia but in 2009 China emerged as the
largest holder, overtaking Japan.

  Fundamentally, the rapid decline in investment in many East Asian
countries brought about their current account surpluses. Figure 8.2 shows
the trend of investment and saving rates in East Asian countries. In Korea,
for instance, the fixed investment ratio (relative to GDP) declined by
around 10 per cent during the period 1996–2007, from 38.9 per cent to 29.4
per cent, while the savings rate declined only slightly by 3.5 per cent during
the same period, from 35.4 per cent to 30.9 per cent. Thus the net saving
turned into positive 1.5 per cent from negative 3.5 per cent. A similar
trend is observed for Japan and the ASEAN countries. The investment
rates dropped to 24.1 per cent and 23.0 per cent respectively in Japan and
the ASEAN countries during the period 1996–2007. The case for China

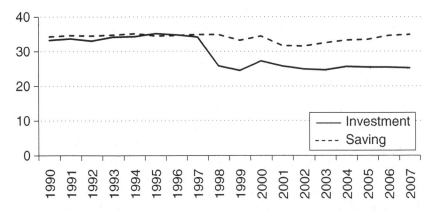

Note: East Asia refers to China, Japan and Korea, the five advanced ASEAN countries and Hong Kong.

Source: World Bank.

Figure 8.3   Investment and saving rates for whole East Asia (% of GDP)

is different, however, because the fixed investment rate did not decline. Although the fixed investment rate in China declined from 40.4 per cent to 37.8 per cent in 2002, it quickly recovered to 43 per cent in 2007. The current account surplus was rather due to the rapid increase in the savings rate. Indeed, the savings rate in China increased from 42.5 per cent in 1996 to 52.1 per cent in 2007 and this widened the gap between investment and saving rates from 2.0 per cent to 9.1 per cent.

Figure 8.3 summarizes this trend for the whole of East Asia. All these new phenomena contributed to the huge accumulation of long-term savings in East Asia and transformed Asian countries from being capital importers to capital exporters, highlighting the potential of the asset management industry and the growing role of pension funds.

Along with the growth of the long-term capital market and the need to manage long-term financial assets, opportunities for cross-border investment will become greater. After witnessing the rapidly growing long-term capital market in Asia, many institutional investors and life insurance companies are now eagerly looking for new long-term investments abroad.

The development of the asset management industry including pension schemes requires large bond allocations. The lack of a deep bond market in East Asian countries, however, means that much of the increased demand for bonds has been satisfied by investments in bonds denominated in major foreign currencies. Indeed, the net portfolio outflows from the nine emerging markets in Asia (including both public and private sectors)

BOX 8.1   ASIA'S SOVEREIGN WEALTH FUNDS AND PENSIONS

The emergence of excess reserves in East Asia has led to wide-spread calls for more active reserve fund management. The sovereign wealth fund (SWF) is the natural framework for shifting the excess FX reserves from a passive liquidity management to an active profit-seeking investment. SWFs have two features: (1) ownership and control by government and (2) pursuit of high-risk-adjusted returns or long-run wealth maximization as the central objective. Thus, unlike central banks, which traditionally managed their reserves for liquidity purposes only, SWFs use FX reserves to pursue commercial profits (Park and Wyplosz, 2010).

Although the term SWF has been coined only recently by Rozanov (2005), the world's oldest SWF is known as the Kuwait Investment Authority (KIA), created in 1953. This fund was an investment vehicle for managing countries' excess revenues from exporting natural resources, especially oil. More famous SWFs were the two Singaporean funds: Temasek and GIC. The commercial success of these SWFs has been a major driving force behind the establishment of SWFs in Asia. In particular, due to their impressive long-term investment track records, Temasek and GIC have attracted the attention of regional policymakers as potential benchmark models. New SWFs have already been established in Asia and may be progressing beyond their planning stages. For instance, Korea set up the Korea Investment Corporation (KIC) in 2005 and the PRC followed suit with the China Investment Corporation (CIC) in 2007. Table 8.2 lists the major SWFs of developing Asia.

Table 8.2   East Asia's main sovereign wealth funds

Country	Fund names	Assets (US$ bn)	Inception	Origin
China	SAFE Investment Company	$347.1	1997	Non-commodity
	China Investment Corporation	$332.40	2007	Non-commodity
	National Social Security Fund	$146.50	2000	Non-commodity
	China-Africa Development Fund	$5.00	2007	Non-commodity
Hong Kong	Hong Kong Monetary Authority Investment Portfolio	$259.30	1993	Non-commodity

Table 8.2   (continued)

Country	Fund names	Assets (US$ bn)	Inception	Origin
Singapore	Government of Singapore Investment Corporation	$247.50	1981	Non-commodity
	Temasek Holdings	$133	1974	Non-commodity
Korea	Korea Investment Corporation	$37	2005	Non-commodity
Malaysia	Khazanah Nasional	$25	1993	Non-commodity
Indonesia	Government Investment Unit	$0.30	2006	Non-commodity

have increased sharply after the 1997 currency crisis, from US$50 billion in 1998 to US$225 billion in 2003. Asia as a whole is now a large net exporter of portfolio capital (Yam, 2004). All these developments explain the recent increasing interest of Asian countries in Asian bond markets.

However, the creation of a sovereign wealth fund is not the only available alternative for more active FX reserve management. Many countries in Asia, for instance, have established large and systemically important state pension funds, with the objective of prefunding at least some future sovereign liabilities with respect to old age provision and insurance. These pension funds are large and still in the phase of accumulation and growth. For example, Japan's Government Pension Investment Fund (GPIF) is the largest pension plan in the world with its US$1.3 trillion assets, and is expected to peak in 2050; Korea's National Pension is the fifth largest pension fund in the world, with US$230 billion in assets and will continue to grow until the mid-2040s; in China, the National Social Security Fund (NSSF) currently has US$100 billion in assets and is growing fast. Other similar pension funds in the region include Hong Kong's Mandatory Provident Fund (MPF), Malaysia's Employee Provident Fund (EPF), Singapore's Central Provident Fund (CPF), Thailand's Government Pension Fund (GPF), and Taiwan's three state pension plans. These funds are investing more and more of their assets abroad, particularly in the East Asian region.

8.2   INITIATIVES

For this reason, the development of a region-wide bond market is essential. In this context, a number of initiatives have been undertaken to develop regional bond markets. These can be grouped into two main initiatives, each falling under the auspices of a major regional multilateral organization.

8.2.1 Asian Bond Funds

The first of these initiatives, the Asian Bond Fund, falls under the auspices of the Executives' Meeting of East Asia-Pacific Central Banks (EMEAP). It is designed to boost the demand for Asian bonds, and to take the form of bond funds. It aimed at channelling a small portion of the very large official reserves held by the Asian economies into the region.

EMEAP is a forum of regional central banks which developed from an initiative by the Bank of Japan. Its first meeting, which was held in 1991, was attended by officials of nine central banks in Asia and the Pacific area (Japan, Korea, the five advanced ASEAN countries, Australia and New Zealand). Later its membership was extended to 11 countries with the participation of China and Hong Kong. Its primary objective is to strengthen the cooperative relationship among its member central banks. In 1996, before the currency crisis, EMEAP was nothing but an informal and deputy-level meeting held twice a year to exchange ideas and information on regional economic and financial developments. However, since 1996, against the background of increasing interdependence between members' economies, the structure of EMEAP has been strengthened and the governors of central banks have been meeting once a year.

The EMEAP central banks established a Working Group on Financial Markets along with those on payment and settlement systems and bank supervision. The working group on financial markets studied the feasibility of establishing an Asian bond fund, which had the objectives of (i) acting as the lead investor and thus serving as a catalyst to attract private investors and boost investment in Asian issues, and (ii) diverting the investment of foreign currency-denominated assets held at central banks and monetary authorities away from US/European securities and towards Asian bonds (Hyun and Jang, 2008, p.6).

Against this background the Hong Kong monetary authorities proposed to establish an Asian Bond Fund at the Working Group Meeting on Financial Markets that was held in June 2002. This proposal obtained the full support of all EMEAP members, and the launch of the first Asian Bond Fund (ABF) was announced on 2 June 2003. The fund was managed by the Bank for International Settlements in a passive style in accordance with a specific benchmark. The fund, which had an initial size of about US$1 billion, invested in a basket of US dollar-denominated bonds issued by Asian sovereign and quasi-sovereign issuers in eight EMEAP countries (other than Japan, Australia and New Zealand). The launch of the US dollar ABF was an important step in regional cooperation in promoting bond markets in the region.

After the successful launch of the US dollar ABF, EMEAP proceeded to extend the ABF concept to include bonds denominated in local currencies, further contributing to the broadening and deepening of bond markets in the region. In December 2004, EMEAP launched the second fund, the ABF2, which would invest in local currency-denominated sovereign and quasi-sovereign bonds issued in the eight Asian countries. The ABF2 consisted of two components, a Pan-Asian Bond Index Fund (PAIF) and a Fund of Bond Funds (FoBF). The PAIF is a single bond index fund which invests in sovereign and quasi-sovereign local currency bonds issued in eight EMEAP countries. The FoBF has a two-tier structure, with a parent fund investing in eight single-market funds, which in turn invest in sovereign and quasi-sovereign bonds in each local currency issued in their respective markets. Both are passively managed by private fund managers against a group of benchmark indexes called the iBoxx ABF Index Family. EMEAP members' investment in the ABF2 will be US$2 billion, with half of it being allocated to the PAIF and the other half to the FoBF. Table 8.3 summarizes the main features of the two Asian Bond Funds.

Asian bond markets are very fragmented due to heterogeneous legal and regulatory frameworks among Asian countries. The EMEAP working group (2006) identified the following as major barriers to regional bond markets: lack of international standards for investor protection; lack of mutual recognition of financial products and institutions; different withholding and capital gains taxes; 'buy and hold' preferences of Asian investors; and lack of transparency in Asian bond markets. In this situation, the Asian Bond Fund initiative could have been an advantageous experiment that could have served as a catalyst to remove these barriers and thereby build a more integrated regional bond market. However, there was no further progress after the ABF2. One possible reason for this was that ASEAN+3 started to overshadow EMEAP as a main vehicle for building the regional community in Asia. In fact, any new initiative of the EMEAP is likely to overlap with the ASEAN+3-led Asian Bond Market Initiative.

8.2.2   Asian Bond Market Initiative

The Asian Bond Market Initiative (ABMI) involves a variety of efforts led by ASEAN+3 countries to create a regional bond market through the creation of new securitized debt instruments, the issuance of debt by international financial institutions, the creation of regional credit guarantees

Table 8.3   Key features of Asian bond funds

	ABF1	ABF2	
		PAIF	Single Market Fund
Initial fund size:	US$ 1.25 billion	US$ 1 billion	US$ 1 billion
Fund structure:	Non-listed open-ended fund	Listed open-ended fund (as of June 2006)	China sub-fund: Exchange Trade Fund or unlisted open-ended fund Hong Kong, Malaysia, Singapore and Thailand sub-funds: ETF Korea, Indonesia and Philippines sub-funds: non-listed open-ended fund
Qualifying assets:	US dollar bonds issued by sovereign and quasi-sovereign issuers in 8 EMEAP countries	Domestic currency bonds issued by sovereign and quasi-sovereign issuers in 8 EMEAP countries	Domestic currency bonds issued by sovereign and quasi-sovereign issuers in 8 EMEAP countries
Currency denomination	US Dollar	US Dollar	Domestic currency
Investment Style:	Passively managed against a designated benchmark index	Passively managed against a designated benchmark index	Passively managed against a designated benchmark index
Benchmark index	JP Morgan Asia Credit Index	Pan-Asian Index of iBoxx Asian Bond Indices provided by International Index Company (formerly known as iBoxx)	Respective market sub-indices of the iBoxx Asian bond indices to be provided by the International Index Company (formerly known as iBoxx)

Table 8.3 (continued)

	ABF1	ABF2	
		PAIF	Single Market Fund
Initial fund size:	US$ 1.25 billion	US$ 1 billion	US$ 1 billion
Fund Manager	BIS	SSgA (State Street Global Advisors Singapore Limited)	National Fund Managers
Custodian	State Street Bank Luxembourg SA or BIS nominated custodian	HSBC (Hong Kong and Shanghai Banking Corporation Limited)	HSBC (Hong Kong and Shanghai Banking Corporation Limited)
Place of Domicile:	–	Singapore	Respective jurisdictions of fund investment
Place of Listing	–	Hong Kong Stock Exchange	Stock exchanges in the respective jurisdictions of fund investment

Sources: EMEAP Working Group on Financial Markets 2006 and Bank of Korea 2008.

and enhancement facilities, and the establishment of local and regional credit rating agencies. This initiative was originally proposed by Thaksin Shinawatra, Prime Minister of Thailand, in October 2002 (Thaksin, 2002). Then it was endorsed at the ASEAN+3 Deputies Meeting in Chiang Mai, Thailand on 17 December 2002 and approved at the ASEAN+3 Finance Ministers' Meeting in August 2003 in Manila. Six working groups were initially established to further the development of Asian bond markets.[1] Then, the six working groups were reorganized in May 2005 into four working groups and an ad hoc support team for the Focal Group, plus a Technical Assistance Coordination Team (TACT).

These working groups have actively promoted the ABMI in order to meet the regional needs for medium and long-term financial resources and to enable further regional economic development to take place. To develop Asian bond markets further, at the 10th ASEAN+3 Finance Ministers' Meeting in May 2007 in Kyoto, Japan, finance ministers endorsed the undertaking of research in the following new areas: (i) exploring new debt instruments for infrastructure financing; (ii) promoting securitization of loan credits and receivables; and (iii) promoting an Asian medium-term note (MTN) programme. The ABMI focused mainly on the following two areas: (i) facilitating access to bond markets for a wider variety of issuers, and (ii) building and enhancing the market infrastructure necessary to foster bond markets in the region.

There was, however, no tangible progress. More specific action plans were needed for the further development of liquid and well-functioning bond markets and an effective channelling of the region's abundant savings to meet increased regional investment needs. In May 2008, the ASEAN+3 finance ministers agreed on the new ABMI roadmap at their Madrid meeting and decided to further the development of the Asian bond market. The new ABMI roadmap stated that countries' voluntary efforts are crucial to developing local currency-denominated bond markets. In this regard, member countries were encouraged to develop 'references for self-assessment', which would serve as their benchmarks. Through the self-assessment process and peer pressure, each country was expected to be more motivated to make voluntary efforts toward the development of its bond market based on the development stage of its financial market and economy.

To implement the new ABMI roadmap, the four working groups changed into four task forces. Specifically, the four task forces are charged with identifying and addressing the major issues in four key areas: (i) promoting the issuance of local currency-denominated bonds (supply side); (ii) facilitating the demand for local currency-denominated bonds (demand side); (iii) improving the regulatory framework; and (iv) improving the related infrastructure. Furthermore, a steering group has been newly established, while TACT continues to exist given the importance of technical assistance in decreasing the disparities in bond market development levels among member countries.

At the ASEAN+3 Finance Ministers' Meeting in Bali in May 2009, the finance ministers stressed again the importance of local currency bond markets in recycling regional savings towards regional bond markets. Following continual calls to establish the necessary infrastructure for the regional bond market, they also agreed to create the Credit Guarantee and Investment Mechanism (CGIM), which was later renamed the Credit Guarantee and Investment Facility (CGIF). As Ho and Wong (2003) and Arner, Lejot and Rhee (2005) had already pointed out, the low credit rating of the underdeveloped Asian economies was the most serious problem, because it prevented the supply of ordinary bonds from increasing. In fact, in many Asian countries, the junk-bond market was absent and only a few Asian companies could get investment grade credit ratings. Table 8.4 summarizes the credit rating situation for long-term East Asian

Table 8.4   Credit ratings for the ASEAN+3 long-term government bonds

		Ratings	Foreign currency denominated	Local currency denominated
Appropriate for investment by S&P ratings	Appropriate for central bank's investment	AAA	Singapore	Singapore
		AA+	–	–
		AA	Japan	Japan
		AA–	–	–
		A+	China	Korea China Malaysia
		A	Korea	–
	Inappropriate for central bank's investment	A–	Malaysia	Thailand
		BBB+	Thailand	–
		BBB	–	–
		BBB–	–	–
Inappropriate for investment by S&P ratings		BB+	–	Indonesia the Philippines Vietnam
		BB	Indonesia, Vietnam	–
		BB–	the Philippines	–
		B+	Cambodia	Cambodia

Source: Park and Rhee (2011).

government bonds according to which only the +3 North-East Asian countries, Malaysia, Thailand and Singapore, meet the appropriate invest-ment grading according to Standard and Poors' ratings.

Thus, the CGIF will provide local currency-denominated bonds with guarantees and promote bond issuance by addressing the following issues:

1. Due to the conservative investment policy of institutional investors in the region, even quality companies rated single-A by local credit rating agencies have difficulty in financing by bond issuance and issu-ance of longer-term bonds, although these options are possible.
2. Finance for SMEs and infrastructure development is easily influenced by the credit crunch since it depends substantially on indirect finance, such as bank loans.

The fund will be established with capital of US$700 million as a trust fund of the Asian Development Bank. For this trust fund, China and

Japan will each contribute US$200 million, Korea US$100 million, ADB US$130 million and ASEAN US$70 million. This initiative will contribute to developing regional bond markets through the issuance of local currency-denominated corporate bonds. Details regarding the establishment of the CGIF such as the business scope, leverage ratio and country limit are to be further discussed at working level by the ASEAN+3 Finance Ministers' Meeting (AFMM+3) in order to make the mechanism effective. The creation of the CGIF is the first step in coping with the absence of a common infrastructure for the development of regional bond markets.

8.3   ACHIEVEMENTS AND ASSESSMENTS

8.3.1   Development of Local Bond Markets

Since the Asian financial crisis, East Asian countries have taken important steps at both national and regional levels to develop local and regional bond markets. In this regard, it is important to note that there has been quite a remarkable growth in local currency bond markets. Driven by continued demand in the market, the number of bonds outstanding in local currencies has grown substantially. Table 8.5 shows that total local currency bonds outstanding in East Asia have doubled to US$15.8 trillion in 2009 from US$9.1 trillion in 2003, when the ABMI was officially launched. Currently, they account for 25 per cent of the world's domestic bond market (see Figure 8.4). Although Japan has the highest level of debt securities outstanding in East Asia, its share in East Asia declined from 85 per cent to 72 per cent over the period 2003–2009. China and Korea

Table 8.5   Size of East Asian local currency bond markets, 2003 and 2009

	2003		2009	
	US$ billion	%	US$ billion	%
Japan	7818	85.13	11 522	72.51
Korea	575	6.26	1067	6.72
China	448	4.88	2565	16.14
Hong Kong	46	0.50	100	0.63
ASEAN	296	3.23	635	4.00
East Asia	9184	100.00	15 890	100.00

Source: BIS, International Financial Statistics, Tables 16A and 16B.

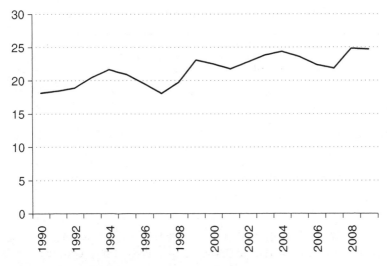

Source: BIS Quarterly Review.

Figure 8.4   *The share of Asian bonds outstanding to the world's bonds stock*

have the next largest bond markets in Asia, with their shares growing continuously.

It is also notable that this rapid growth of local bond markets was largely led by government bonds. This is especially true for Japan, which saw its government bond market overtaking that of the US due to explosive government debt. In fact, a robust development of the bond market in Asia requires a wide variety of issuers and products in addition to the sovereign bond issuances by Asian governments. The development of financial and corporate bonds markets is especially remarkable in Korea and China (see Table 8.6). Corporate bonds are almost non-existent in some underdeveloped Asian countries because few domestic corporations are capable of directly issuing bonds. Moreover, the development of the corporate bond market needs credit ratings, and if necessary, credit enhancement such as the CGIM agreed by ASEAN+3 Finance Ministers' Meeting held in 2009. Thus, the development of corporate and financial bonds has been difficult.

Despite such efforts, however, progress has been slow in developing regional bond markets. Cross-border issuance and investment by foreign entities have been rare. For instance, as Table 8.7 shows, foreign bonds issued by non-resident entities in domestic local currency bond markets of East Asian countries (including India) represent only 0.8 per cent of

Table 8.6   Size of local currency bond markets by issuers (US$ billion)

	2003		2009	
	Government	Corporate	Government	Corporate
Japan	5528.4	904.9	8645.3	963.0
Korea	205.8	308.1	446.3	575.0
China	435.2	13.2	2112.6	454.3
Hong Kong	15.4	56.3	69.5	74.4
ASEAN	226.7	87.5	474.3	198.5
East Asia	6184.9	1282.6	11 274.0	2066.9

Source: Asian bonds online.

the total bonds issued, while the cross-border bond issuance represents only 1.1 per cent of the bonds issued by East Asian countries (ADB, 2010).

As Park and Wyplocz (2010) pointed out, one reason for this slow progress is the failure of the ABMI architects to articulate the structural characteristics and ultimate objectives of the markets that they propose to create. East Asian bond markets are highly fragmented, and each country has its own currency and regulation. Also, most of Asia's bond markets are small and face serious limits to liquidity and efficiency. There are only a few countries in East Asia that are able to issue bonds denominated in their own currencies on global or even regional bond markets. Furthermore, many countries in East Asia have maintained a policy of dividing domestic and foreign markets. Thus, apart from Japan, these countries still do not allow foreign investors to hold large amounts of their currencies for fear that it will erode their control over monetary policy and make them susceptible to currency speculation. This control limits cross-border fund transfers between domestic and foreign markets in East Asian countries. Table 8.8 shows the current state of foreign exchange controls in East Asian countries.

Another barrier is the prominent role of non-Asian institutions in East Asia. The transfer of funds between East Asian countries is largely handled by international financial institutions and international clearing and settlement systems outside the Asian region. For example, non-Asian international financial institutions are dominant as lead managers in the international bond and securities markets, even for Asia-related bond business. Furthermore, they are effectively managing the global custody services, or the international securities depository business in the region (Inukai, 2008). A possible way to remove this barrier is to set up a regional

Table 8.7   Asian currencies bonds issued by Asian issuers (January 2007–September 2009)

Country (currency)	Domestic Bond Market	Foreign Bond Market	Cross-border Bond Market
PRC (RMB)	98.6%		PRC Hong Kong, China 1.4%
Hong Kong, China (HKD)	97.9%		Korea 2.1%
India (INR)	99.9%	Singapore 0.1%	
Indonesia (IDR)	77.7%	Hong Kong, China, Malaysia, Singapore, Japan 22.3%	
Japan (JPY)	97.9%	Korea 0.6%	Japan, Philippines (ADB), India 1.5%
Republic of Korea (KRW)	99.8%	Singapore 0.2%	
Malaysia (MYR)	96.3%	Singapore, Korea, Japan 3.7%	
Singapore (SGD)	98.5%	PRC, Malaysia 1.5%	
Taipei, China (TWD)	100%		
Thailand (THD)	94.4%	Indonesia, Japan 5.6%	
Vietnam (VND)	91.5%		Vietnam 8.5%
East Asia	US$ 1282 bn (98.2%)	US$ 10 bn (0.8%)	US$ 14 bn (1.1%)

Note: Domestic issuance here is defined as local currency bond issuance by resident entities in domestic markets and foreign bond issuance is defined as bond issuance by non-resident entities in domestic markets. Cross-border issuance is defined as the sum of Eurobond and global bond issuance.

Source: ADB (2010).

settlement intermediary in Asia, and there are ongoing discussions about such an institution and its correct form.[2]

For this reason, the emergence of a regionally-integrated bond market in East Asia is a long-term prospect that is, at best, uncertain. One

Table 8.8 *Foreign exchange controls: regulatory frameworks for current and capital transactions in major countries in East Asia (as of December 2007)*

	China	Hong Kong	Indonesia	Korea	Malaysia	Philippines	Singapore	Thailand	Vietnam	Japan
Arrangements for payments and receipts										
Bilateral payments arrangements					o	o			o	
Payment arrears										
Controls on payments for invisible transactions and current transfers	o					o		o	o	
Proceeds from exports and/or invisible transactions										
Repatriation requirements	o			o	o			o	o	
Surrender requirements										
Capital transactions										
Controls on:										
Capital market securities	o		o	o	o	o	o	o	o	o
Money market instruments	o		o	o	o	o		o	o	o

Collective investments	o	o		o	o		o	o	o	o
Derivatives and other instruments	o	o	o	o	o		o	o	o	o
Commercial credits	o		o	o	o		o	o	o	o
Financial credits	o		o o	o o	o o	o	o o	o o	o o	o
Guarantees, sureties and financial back-up facilities	o		o	o	o		o	o	o	o
Direct investment	o		o	o	o	o	o	o	o	o
Liquidation of direct	o				o	o	o	--		o
Real estate transactions	o		o	o	o	o	o	o	o	o
Personal capital transactions	o		o	o	o	o	o	o	o	o
Provisions specific to:										
Commercial banks and other credit institutions	o	o	o	o	o	o	o	o	o	o
Institutional investors	o	o	o	--	o	o	o	o	o	o

Notes:
o   Indicates that the specified practice is a feature of the exchange system
--   Indicates that data were not available at time of publication

Source: Institute for International Monetary Affairs (2010).

145

method of circumventing the foreign exchange controls and developing regional bond markets is to use offshore bond markets. Indeed, a recent study by the ADB (2010) proposes such a solution for corporate bonds. While it focuses on developing the onshore secondary markets for government bonds, this study emphasizes developing the offshore wholesale primary corporate bond market limited to professionals, which Inukai (2008) named the Asian Inter-Regional Professional Securities Market. If created, this market will be similar to the Eurobond market. Bonds issued in these markets will be denominated in major international currencies, and some currencies of East Asian countries with open domestic bond markets. These offshore bond markets will be subject to little regulation from host regulators and be exempt from income tax.

As some countries in East Asia open their bond markets to foreign borrowers and investors, they have plans to develop such regional bond markets. Japan, Korea, China, Hong Kong and Singapore are all competing to be a regional financial hub. It remains to be seen which markets will survive the ongoing competition to become the major trading centres for Asian bonds.

8.3.2   Assessments and the Global Financial Crisis

The nurturing of bond markets has been carried out for the purposes, first, of creating financial systems that achieve balance between banks and capital markets, and second, of solving the double mismatch problem. This led to the creation of the ABMI and, assisted by the efforts of the ABMI, the Asian local currency bond markets have continued to grow. In particular, the development of government bond markets has been spectacular. In comparison, the development of a regional bond market has been slow. Cross-border issuances and investments remain rare. The degree of development varies drastically from country to country. The creation of a regional bond market will thus take time because, at present, the necessary infrastructure for a regional bond market hardly exists. A fully-fledged regional bond market will need a more sophisticated financial infrastructure, such as a clearing and settlement system, a regional credit ratings agency, and guarantee systems. More importantly, countries in East Asia should open their local domestic bond markets to encourage foreign bond issuers to develop regional bond markets and thereby support economic and financial integration in East Asia. The capital markets of many East Asian countries are not sufficiently liberalized and many different kinds of capital controls are still imposed. Nevertheless, there are positive signs for the Asian bond market development. Local currency government bond markets in many East Asian countries are becoming more and more open

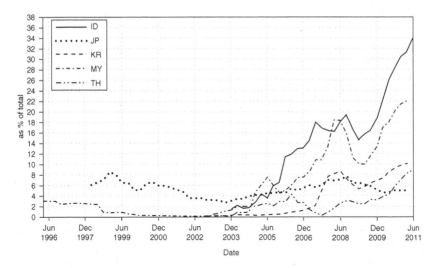

Source: Asian bonds online.

Figure 8.5 Foreign holdings in local currency government bonds

to foreign investors. In fact, as Figure 8.5 shows, foreign holdings in local currency government bond markets started to take off rapidly after 2003. There is no data to tell how many of these foreign investors came from the East Asian region, but it is expected that there will be an increasingly large number of East Asian investors holding East Asian local currency government bonds. This is because East Asian countries are increasingly investing their assets abroad, strengthening financial market linkages between East Asian countries.

The recent breakout of the global financial crisis shed new light on the goal and future of the ABMI. Because funding from capital markets has contracted and lower interest rates have improved the banks' business environments, financial systems depend on banks to an ever greater extent. Under these circumstances, as regards the continuation of the ABMI, there are calls for a greater emphasis on new aims, such as the use of bonds in the financing of intraregional infrastructure development and a greater effort in the development of financial regulations and supervision. In particular, Kawai (2009a) proposes the establishment of an Asian Financial Stability Board (AFSB) to strengthen cross-border financial supervision and regulation at regional level and to further Asia's financial stability. According to him, an AFSB would be a forum comprising finance ministries, central banks, and financial market regulators and supervisors in East Asia and would supplement the role of an AMF.

NOTES

1. These working groups are: new securitized debt instruments chaired by Thailand; credit guarantee and investment mechanisms chaired by Korea and the PRC; foreign exchange transactions and settlement issues chaired by Malaysia; issuance of bonds denominated in local currencies by Multilateral Development Banks (MDBs), foreign government agencies and Asian multinational corporations chaired by the PRC; ratings systems and dissemination of information on Asian bond markets co-chaired by Singapore and Japan; and technical assistance coordination co-chaired by Indonesia, the Philippines and Malaysia.

2. For instance, Hong Kong and Korea have each proposed a regional settlement system owing to the inconvenience and limitation and the low coverage of ICSD, Euroclear and Clearstream. The Hong Kong Monetary Authority (HKMA) has proposed the establishment of 'AsiaClear' as a regional settlement infrastructure for clearing and settling Asian bonds. This would bilaterally connect the existing clearing and settlement systems (NCSD) in the Asian region using IT. Korea has proposed 'AsiaSettle' as a new regional ICSD, pointing out the limits of bilateral linkages. Japan has proposed a dual core approach to cross-border securities settlement using the existing systems, Japan Securities Depository Center and the Korea Security Depository.

9. Exchange rate coordination and regional currency unit

In a meeting of the ADB held at Hyderabad, India on 3 May 2006, finance ministers from Korea, China and Japan announced that they would take steps to coordinate their currencies in a way that would ultimately produce a common regional currency similar to the euro. They also added steps to study all the related issues, including the creation of a regional currency unit (RCU), which was often called an Asian Currency Unit (ACU). Although an Asian monetary union is a distant goal, the idea of an RCU could be an important step towards realizing monetary union in Asia. Indeed, an RCU was strongly supported by Kuroda (2006), President of the ADB, as a way of facilitating regional monetary union in Asia, and following his aspiration, the ADB is promoting the use of an RCU and preparing a regional cooperation and integration strategy.

The idea of a currency basket has been a top policy concern of the Japanese government for a long time, although it has implied that it wanted to include external currencies, such as the dollar and the euro, in the basket. However, Japan changed its proposal so as to include regional currencies such as the Korean won and the Chinese yuan (Moon et al., 2005). Its recent proposal to introduce an RCU reflects this change in Japan's policy regarding a regional currency. Since then, many academics have suggested developing an RCU as a parallel currency in Asia to further monetary integration in Asia. For instance, Ogawa and Shimizu (2005) proposed using an RCU as a deviation indicator for the coordination of exchange rates in East Asia. Eichengreen (2007) argued that the introduction of an RCU would help foster monetary and financial integration in Asia, catalyse Asian bond markets, and serve as an Asian exchange rate arrangement similar to the European Exchange Rate System. Together with the CMI, which ended up with the creation of a multilateral liquidity support system, an RCU would serve as an effective instrument for facilitating regional monetary cooperation and integration. An RCU can be developed into a parallel currency. The introduction of an RCU, however, would pose many unresolved questions, such as which currencies to include in the basket, what weighting to attribute to the component currencies, and which institution to use to publicize an

RCU value. Creating an RCU composed first of the three largest North-East Asian economies, China, Japan and Korea only, and then extending it to other Asian countries would be a more realistic option. China has good reason to support this option because it would help to promote the internationalization of the yuan.

9.1 CHOICE OF EXCHANGE RATE SYSTEM

East Asian countries and many other emerging market economies pursued exchange rate policies that would promote growth, trade and invest-ment. For them, an intermediate exchange rate arrangement like a soft peg or a managed float was naturally attractive because it helped them to minimize the negative impact of possible exchange rate appreciation on their exports, which were the motor of their economic growth. This led East Asian economies to adopt a pegged exchange rate system, generally vis-à-vis the US dollar, without institutional commitments. The de facto US dollar-pegged system, however, triggered the speculative movements which resulted in the 1997 Asian financial crisis. Reflecting on this experi-ence, some East Asian countries opted for a more flexible exchange rate system after the crisis. As a result, the East Asian region currently has diverse exchange regimes (see Table 6.1, Chapter 6). For instance, accord-ing to the official IMF classification, some countries, such as Japan, the Philippines and Korea, are adopting an independent floating system. Countries such as Indonesia and Thailand are also now getting greater exchange rate flexibility under the managed floating system. In com-parison, China adopted a fixed exchange rate system in 1994, although its exchange rate fluctuation margin has tended to widen recently. Malaysia is also adopting a fixed exchange rate system. The case of Malaysia is particularly interesting because Malaysia shifted from a managed float-ing system to a fixed exchange system, moving in the opposite direction to other crisis-hit Asian countries' systems that allowed greater exchange rate flexibility. Hong Kong maintains a currency board system, a hard peg to the US dollar.

This means that there is no single exchange rate system that is always desirable for all countries in East Asia. As Frankel said (Frankel, 1999), 'No single currency is right for all countries or at all times'. Three pos-sible options can be considered as the basis of what is called the 'impos-sible trinity theorem': capital movement, free floating and monetary policy autonomy. What is then the optimal choice among the three options for East Asia as a whole? The answer to this question is by no means clear.

9.1.1   Fixed Exchange Rate System with Capital Controls

The first alternative to consider is re-introducing short-term capital controls. It is now widely recognized that short-run capital controls may sometimes be necessary for small open economies. This is essentially due to two countries' experiences.

First, thanks to its underdevelopment, China was subject to severe capital controls and was unscathed during the Asian currency crisis period. This has led to quite a firm belief that capital controls helped to protect a country like China from the contagion of the Asian currency crisis (for example, Yu, 2001). However, the diagnosis that capital controls alone shielded China from the currency crisis looks unfounded. Foreign direct investment in China started to increase enormously after the early 1990s, and leading up to the crisis there was a relative decline of international bank loans in capital flows, in opposition to what happened in other countries like Korea.[1] Thus, it is questionable whether the capital controls by themselves were the main reason for crisis prevention in China. Nevertheless, this wrong diagnosis was held as unassailable justification for China's traditional policy stance which favoured capital controls. In fact, capital controls do not seem to be an appropriate long-run alternative for a country like China. Considering its economic status, and its ambition to make the yuan a key currency competing with the yen, the liberalization of China's capital market is essential.

Secondly, capital controls were introduced in Malaysia on the grounds that the root cause of the financial instability was the short-term speculative capital flows. Indeed, Malaysia temporarily banned certain types of foreign exchange remittances, such as those arising from sudden and massive sales of listed stocks by foreign portfolio investors.

> Believing that the IMF program with its 'traditional' conditionalities would be not only counterproductive but also destructive to its long-term economic policy and strategy, the Malaysian government decided to do three things simultaneously: (i), pegging the ringgit 100% to the US$ and defending it, (ii), de-internationalizing the ringgit (by banning residents from maintaining excessive foreign currency positions and banning non-residents from holding excessive ringgit assets and liabilities), and (iii), installing an exchange control on the remittance of short-term profits and sales of listed shares by foreign portfolio investors. (Chaipravat, 2002)

This type of short-term capital regulation was not limited to Malaysia. Other ASEAN countries relied on such measures, if necessary. In fact, there is worrying evidence that capital controls were strengthened rather than weakened after the Asian currency crisis. After the 2008 global financial crisis, even the IMF acknowledged the necessity for some short-term capital controls. In particular, prudential regulations and taxes dealing with external borrowing are considered to be helpful in mitigating the downside risk of short-term capital inflows (Ostroy et al., 2010; Aizenman and Pinto, 2011). Until then, the IMF had been a strong proponent of capital liberalization. However, capital controls are not a panacea. They risk putting the whole regional economic integration process (for instance, trade and investment liberalization) in peril.

9.1.2 Currency Board

Capital controls are a difficult option to choose if capital market integration in East Asia is to be maintained. The appropriate choice of an exchange rate system, then, is related to the fundamental question of whether or not a small open economy with liberalized capital accounts can retain an independent monetary policy. This is known as the 'hollowing out' hypothesis. It posits that countries should either allow their currencies to float or peg their currencies permanently, but that intermediate policy regimes between hard pegs and floating are not sustainable.

A currency board system is clearly a complete peg. But this system is unacceptable because of the sovereignty problem. A country with a currency board system no longer has sovereign discretion over monetary policy. Another drawback is that it once and for all fixes a country's terms of trade, irrespective of economic differences between it and its trading partners. These two drawbacks cannot be acceptable to sovereign East Asian countries. Currently in Asia, only Hong Kong is adopting the currency board system.

9.1.3 Floating

After the currency crisis, the free floating system was strongly recommended to East Asian countries by the IMF. The free floating system, however, is a very difficult option for many developing East Asian countries. Calvo and Reinhart (2002) enumerate several reasons why emerging countries fear floating and prefer exchange rate stability. According to them, emerging countries suffer from a lack of credibility in monetary policy setting. Also, when devaluations happen in emerging countries, they tend to be correlated with recessions due to liability dollarization, and current accounts adjustment of these countries is far more acute and abrupt than in advanced countries. Exchange rate volatility is also more damaging to trade in emerging economies because trade is predominantly invoiced in US dollars and hedging opportunities are limited. Finally, the pass-through from the exchange rate swings to inflation is far higher in emerging countries than in advanced countries. It means that the emerging countries concerned with inflation tend to stabilize their exchange rates. Moreover, the recent movements toward a regional free trade agreement contribute to the elimination of some trade obstacles that include tariffs and non-tariff barriers. However, economic agents will regard the exchange rate risk as an important trade obstacle after they conclude free trade agreements within the region. Even though forward contracts can be used to avoid exchange rate risks, there remains a price to pay to avoid those risks. Economic agents in the private sector would face an increasing need to eliminate exchange rate risks and foreign exchange transaction costs, which enhances their willingness to introduce a single common currency in this region in the future. For these reasons, free floating was a short-lived phenomenon even after the currency crisis. Many countries in the East Asian region still maintain a de facto dollar-pegged system, or a system similar to it.

9.2 PROPOSALS FOR A CURRENCY BASKET SYSTEM

Despite the eruption of the currency crisis, East Asian countries did not abandon fixed exchange rate systems completely. As explained, this was not because of the superiority of the fixed exchange rate system but because of the absence of better alternatives. Floating was not an option and neither was the currency board system. Thus, there were continuing calls for fixed exchange rate systems in East Asia.

9.2.1 Return to the US Dollar Pegged Exchange Rate Regime

The unilateral dollar pegged system was considered a prime culprit for triggering the crisis, and many East Asian countries had to move toward more flexible exchange rate regimes. Despite the currency crisis, however, some East Asian countries reverted to US dollar-based regimes, notably Malaysia, which restored a formal US dollar peg.

Several proposals for the adoption of the US dollar standard have been made (for example, McKinnon, 2001; Mundell, 2001). The US dollar standard is simple, transparent and involves no additional costs in ensuring exchange rate stability, both extra- and intra-regionally. As Kawai and many other Japanese scholars argued, however, exchange rate stabilization vis-à-vis the US dollar is not an appropriate exchange rate arrangement from the viewpoint of stabilization of effective exchange rates because the East Asian economies have diverse linkages with Japan and the EU as well as with the US. Given that major tri-polar currency volatility is expected to be high, it is appropriate for emerging East Asian economies to stabilize their exchange rates against not only the US dollar but also the Japanese yen and the euro. Malaysia and China are already adopting such a basket peg system.

9.2.2 Yen Peg

One alternative to the dollar is to use the yen as an anchor, given the economic importance of Japan in the region. However, this option is not realistic, because, putting aside insurmountable political opposition, it would create the same problem as the dollar peg. The 1997 currency crisis showed that the fluctuation of East Asian currencies with respect to the US dollar *and* the Japanese yen was a serious source of instability. Furthermore, the yen's role as regional currency is rapidly diminishing as Japan's economic power continues to decline.

9.2.3 Basket Peg

Thus, the only remaining alternative is to resort to parities against a currency basket rather than a single currency, as numerous Japanese authors have argued. In fact, as Japanese scholars were well aware that the yen peg was not politically feasible, they instead argued for a basket peg including the yen, the US dollar and the euro. They probably thought that the basket peg system would help the internationalization of the Japanese yen. No matter what the Japanese scholars had in mind, they argued that the basket system would help overcome two important flaws of the de facto dollar peg system that caused the currency crisis in East Asia. The first flaw was the misalignment of exchange rates. According to Ito et al. (1998), Hughes (1999) and McKinnon (1998), for example, the depreciation of the dollar and the rapid appreciation of the Japanese yen since 1985 contributed to the increased exports in developing Asian countries and to the Japanese outbound FDI to the region. However, the devaluation of the Chinese yuan in 1994 as well as the rapid appreciation of the US dollar after 1995 suddenly reversed this pattern, causing current account deficits and outflows of foreign capital from these countries. The second flaw was volatility of capital flows associated with the dollar peg (Ito, 1999; Wyplosz, 1998). For many Japanese scholars (Ogawa and Ito, 2000; Ito et al., 1998; Ono, 1998; Kwan, 2001), the multi-currency basket peg system, which consisted of including, among others, the US dollar, the euro and the Japanese yen as the principal currencies, would help East Asian countries overcome the problem of the dollar peg and maintain a stable exchange rate system. In fact, they claimed that the basket system would prevent excessive fluctuations in effective exchange rates while allowing a currency some flexibility to move within a certain range. But this proposal has some flaws.

First, there is no guarantee that a basket peg would help to stabilize the Asian economy more than the dollar peg did. Moreover, the choice of an exchange rate regime for developing Asian countries is a matter of national sovereignty, and therefore Japan has no authority to force the issue.

Second, this proposal does not point out the burden-sharing aspect to maintaining a pegged system, especially the foreign exchange market intervention burden. It is clear that if Asian countries adopt a basket peg system on the basis of the US dollar and the euro, neither the US nor the EU will have any responsibility in shouldering the intervention burden to maintain a stable exchange rate between the basket and their currencies. The dollar and the euro are not regional currencies, and solidarity between Asian countries and the US or the EU will not be strong. This implies that Asian countries will have to rely on unilateral intervention, not bilateral cooperative intervention, for instance, if the value of their currency basket in terms of the US dollar or euro deviates from its target value. It is indeed important to note that in the case of Korea, for instance, unilateral intervention without any support from the US contributed to depleting its foreign reserves, bringing about its currency crisis. Thus, no Asian country is likely to accept a multi-currency basket peg system without a strong commitment from the US and the EU to support it in emergency situations. The only feasible exchange rate system for East Asian countries would be consequently to construct the basket on the basis of solely regional currencies. This was in fact what happened in the case of European monetary integration. The ECU was a basket composed only of regional currencies.

The Korean experience of foreign exchange market intervention and sterilization showed how burdensome it was for an individual country to maintain a stable exchange rate system by unilateral intervention. Nevertheless, exchange rate stabilization was never abandoned as a policy objective and the Korean government could not detach itself from foreign exchange market intervention.

In this respect, the proposal to include the Chinese yuan (or the Korean won) as a basket currency is more advanced. For example, there was a proposal to include the Chinese yuan in the basket, which reflected on how to procure the necessary foreign currencies, for example, to intervene in the related foreign exchange market. This requires both parties, for example

BOX 9.1   FOREIGN EXCHANGE MARKET INTERVENTION COST IN KOREA

Since the Asian financial crisis, East Asian central banks have intervened extensively in foreign exchange markets to limit the movement of their currencies. As pointed out by Mohanty and Turner (2006), such intervention operations are costly. Interest rates tend to be higher in countries with fast-growing emerging markets than in those that are major financial centres. The result is an adverse income or balance sheet effect for the emerging market country's central bank.

This problem has been especially acute in Korea. There have been three recent periods of extensive intervention in the foreign exchange market: during the Asian currency crisis, between 2003 and 2006, and after 2008. The first episode was of course when the authorities were attempting to prevent the won from depreciating excessively; the Bank of Korea therefore sold dollars for won. This intervention ended when the inability of the authorities to control the crisis led to the exhaustion of the Bank's dollar reserves (see Moon and Rhee, 2006). A similar episode took place during the 2008 global financial crisis. Although Korea did not experience a depletion of its reserves, its reserve decrease was the biggest ever since 1997. The episode between 2003 and 2006 was the reverse case. The Korean government tried to prevent the Korean won from appreciating excessively against the dollar, as it was receiving large capital inflows. This time the government sold won for dollars.

There were various types of foreign exchange market intervention in Korea. One type was to use the Foreign Exchange Stabilization Fund established in 1967. The Korean government intervened both in the spot market and in the forward market. Another type was for the government to borrow from the Bank of Korea and to use the funds to buy dollars. The Bank of Korea in turn issued Monetary Stabilization Bonds, sterilizing the impact on the money stock (see Moon and Rhee, 2009).

Table 9.1 shows the balance sheet of the Exchange Stabilization Fund. As of 2007, the liabilities of the Stabilization Fund reached 91 trillion Korean won, while its assets remained only at 64.8 Trillion Korean won. The accumulated loss of the Fund was 26 trillion Korean won, which accounted for 40 per cent of its

Table 9.1   *Size of exchange stabilization fund and its performance (trillion won)*

	Assets	Liabilities	Accumulated losses/profits
2000	14.5	15.0	−0.5
2001	13.8	14.4	−0.6
2002	18.4	20.9	−2.5
2003	31.0	33.9	−3.0
2004	38.7	54.1	−15.4
2005	49.9	68.8	−18.9
2006	54.1	80.1	−26.0
2007	64.8	91.1	−26.4

Source: Moon and Rhee (2009)

assets. This huge loss was essentially due to the massive foreign exchange market intervention conducted by the Korean government since 2004. Indeed, the size of the assets was relatively modest and almost equal to that of liabilities until 2003, but the assets and liabilities together increased enormously from 2004.

In addition, the Korean government used borrowed money from the Bank of Korea to intervene in the foreign exchange market. To absorb the increasing liquidity, the Bank of Korea relied on sterilization, selling Monetary Stabilization Bonds (MSB) and Exchange Stabilization Bonds (ESB). Table 9.2 shows the outstanding amount of MSBs. In 1999, the amount of MSBs was just 51.5 trillion Korean won, but it rapidly increased to 150.3 trillion won in 2007. It is notable that there was a substantial increase in MSBs when there was only a minor increase in ESBs (due to the depletion of funds mobilized through the Exchange Stabilization Fund).

Table 9.2   *Reserve money, MSB and interest cost (trillion won)*

	Reserve money	MSBs outstanding	Interest paid
1999	28.4	51.5	3.8
2000	28.2	66.4	4.7
2001	32.8	79.1	4.9
2002	37.9	84.3	4.8
2003	40.7	105.5	5.0

Table 9.2   (continued)

	Reserve money	MSBs outstanding	Interest paid
2004	38.7	142.8	5.6
2005	43.2	155.2	6.1
2006	51.9	158.4	6.8
2007	56.4	150.3	7.5

Source: Moon and Rhee (2009)

China and Japan, to hold each other's currency, particularly in the form of government bonds, following the example of the Rosa bond which was introduced in 1961 between the US and Germany. Moreover, both parties are required to issue government bonds denominated in the other party's currency, and the fund thus mobilized could be used for foreign exchange market intervention, for example.

9.3   CREATION OF AN RCU

9.3.1   Some Technical Problems

In the meeting of the ADB held at Hyderabad, India on 3 May 2006, the ASEAN+3 finance ministers announced that they would take steps to coordinate their currencies in a way that would ultimately produce a common regional currency similar to the euro. They also announced that they would study all the issues related to the creation of a regional currency unit. Before the introduction of an RCU, however, there are three very sensitive issues which need to be settled: which currencies to include in the basket, what weightings to attribute to the component currencies, and which institution to use to publicize an RCU value (Ogawa, 2006; Ogawa and Shimizu, 2006; Moon et al., 2006).

First, given that ASEAN+3 framework was established as a main vehicle for building a regional community in East Asia, it seemed natural that the currencies of all ASEAN+3 countries be included as appropriate ones to construct the basket. However, ASEAN is a group of 10 countries that are economically and politically very different, and many of them are financially undeveloped. Thus, it will not be realistic to launch an RCU on the basis of all ASEAN+3 currencies. It might be more appropriate to

Table 9.3   Summary of various currency basket weightings

Countries	Central Bank NEER			RIETI AMU	Currency Weightings (per cent) as of 2005				CMIM share
	FRB	ECB	BOE		PPP-GDP	Nom-GDP	Intra-trade	CMI-swap	
China	38.5	26.9	27.6	34.8	53.33	21.80	26.11	16.67	32.0
Japan	28.9	38.7	38.8	27.8	25.51	59.05	26.87	30.86	32.0
Korea	11.7	12.4	10.3	9.8	6.29	9.76	13.87	17.28	16.0
Indonesia	2.5	3.2	–	5.1	5.88	3.29	4.45	11.11	3.98
Malaysia	6.1	5.0	6.0	5.3	1.62	1.48	8.28	4.94	3.98
Philippines	2.4	2.4	–	2.9	2.94	1.10	2.86	6.79	3.07
Singapore	5.9	7.0	11.2	6.4	0.86	1.36	11.13	4.94	3.98
Thailand	4.1	4.5	6.0	5.1	3.55	2.16	6.43	7.41	3.98
Other ASEAN[1]	–	–	–	2.9	–	–	–	–	1.34
ASEAN + 3	100.0	100.0	100.0	100.0	100.0	100.0	100.0	100.0	100.0

Note: 1. This includes Vietnam, Brunei, Cambodia, Laos PDR and Myanmar

Sources: Kawai (2009b) and Moon et al. (2007).

create an RCU first on the basis of the +3 North-East Asian countries and then to extend membership to ASEAN countries.

Second, it is important to determine the appropriate weighting of each national currency in an RCU basket. There are many ways to calculate the potential weightings of the composite currencies of an RCU. Table 9.3 shows possible weightings for the East Asian currencies.

The basic principle is that the weightings should be determined so that an RCU can adequately reflect the values of the Asian currencies in international transactions and so that any one currency is not too dominant in the basket. A popular idea is to define the weightings according to the shares of GDP. However, there are two kinds of GDP, one that is based on the PPP exchange rate, and another based on the market exchange rate. The weightings vary significantly depending on which GDP is used. When the PPP-based GDP is used, China is well ahead of the others as number one, while Japan is well ahead of China when the market-based GDP is used. This variance suggests that the attribution of weightings using GDP cannot reflect the values of Asian currencies appropriately. Another problem of using GDP is that countries like China or Japan are

too dominant in the composition of the basket and thus can cause problems of asymmetry between nations. One proposal is to have each country's weighting represented by the country's importance in international
transactions and its contribution to economic cooperation in the region.
Using the volume of international transactions in trade and finance can
accurately reflect the value of a currency, not only in international transactions but also in economic power. The use of its CMI contribution level
as a weighting can also encourage a country's participation in regional
economic cooperation. The attribution of weightings in consideration
of intraregional transactions and regional economic contribution can be
helpful in avoiding the asymmetry problem because no single currency's
weighting becomes overly dominant. The case of the ECU suggests that
the largest weighting attributed to a currency should not be over one
third.

Third, the institutions to which the responsibility for publishing
the value of an RCU will be delegated should be determined. Since
very recently, the Research Institute of Economy, Trade and Industry
(RIETI), a Japanese policy think-tank, has started to publish the value
of the Asian currency basket called the 'Asian Monetary Unit' on its
website. However, there is no agreement among East Asian countries on
the publication of the value of the RCU. The publication was decided
unilaterally by the institute itself. Furthermore, Asian countries have
not yet agreed on the weightings of Asian currencies used in these calculations. In the long run, the publication should be taken on by central
banks in East Asia. In fact, major central banks such as the Federal
Reserve System, the European Central Bank and the Bank of England
already regularly publish their real effective exchange rates, and in this
regard allocate what they think the most appropriate weightings on
the basis of their trade relations to East Asian currencies. Once Asian
central banks agree on the main points of an RCU, they could publish
the output.

9.3.2   Possible Roles and Development of an RCU

The creation of an RCU can play a pivotal role regarding monetary stability in Asia and speed up the process of creating a monetary union in Asia.
This was exactly what happened with the EMS. In the case of the EMS,
the development of the ECU has benefited from the EMS and the official
recognition of the ECU by member countries as an integral part of the
EMS; the reverse is not true. As indicated by Steinherr (1989, p.60) indeed,
'EMS and ECU were not seen as two juxtaposed and independent innovations but as the two necessary and strongly mutually reinforcing pillars

of the new regional monetary system to fulfil two expectations: creation of a European zone of monetary stability and greater independence from outside disturbances.' Thus, the development of an RCU will certainly be constrained by the development of an exchange rate arrangement in Asia. At the official level of the EMS framework, the ECU was used in the following way:

- as a unit of account for denominating the value of EMS countries' currencies and as a reference unit for the operation of the divergence indicator;
- as a denominator for operations in the intervention and credit mechanisms;
- as a reserve asset (settlement instruments between central banks of the member states).

In East Asia, an RCU, even if its creation is agreed upon, will not be used for all these official purposes. Initially the roles of an RCU will be limited to being a unit of account for denominating the value of Asian currencies and for measuring the divergence of Asian countries. As the least binding of transactions, these will not require intensive political discussion among Asian countries.

Further development of an RCU will not be possible, however, without more intensive discussion on the degree and type of regional monetary and financial integration in East Asia. For instance, the use of an RCU as a settlement currency between central banks will necessitate the introduction of a credit provision facility among them. Also, if an RCU is to be used for foreign exchange market intervention, East Asian countries should agree on establishing a regional exchange rate system. Figure 9.5 summarizes the possible use of an RCU at official level.

The use of an RCU at official level also leads to the private use of an RCU. In particular, it can help to promote an RCU-denominated bond market in Asia, which is indispensable for eliminating the underlying causes of regional financial instability and coping with the global imbalance that originates from the continuing current account deficits of the US and surpluses of the East Asian countries. At the same time, an RCU can be used in private capital markets as a denomination of market transactions such as bond issuance. Issuing bonds on the basis of an RCU is a good way to make use of increasing foreign reserves in East Asian countries. An RCU can become a supplementary framework for the development of regional financial markets in East Asia. However, in the EU's experience, the use of a private ECU could be activated only if the use of an official ECU was guaranteed in the official sector (Moon et al., 2006).

BOX 9.2   STABILITY OF AN RCU

As part of the ASEAN+3 countries' study group's work, the Institute for International Monetary Affairs (IIMA) (2011) calculated the value of an RCU based on the CMIM contributions of the ASEAN+3 countries. This study found that the volatilities of the RCU are lower

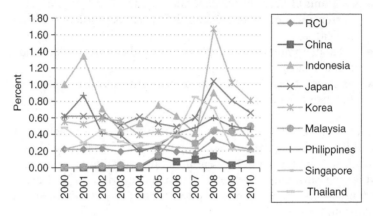

Source: IIMA (2011).

Figure 9.1   Asian exchange rates' standard deviation vis-à-vis the US$

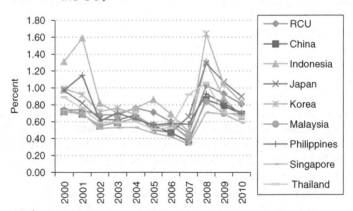

Source: IIMA (2011).

Figure 9.2   Asian exchange rates' standard deviation vis-à-vis the euro

than those of most East Asian currencies. For instance, the RCU turns out to be the second most stable vis-à-vis the external currencies such as the US dollar and euro (see Figures 9.1 and 9.2).

In addition, the exchange volatilities of the RCU vis-à-vis the regional currencies such as the Japanese yen and Chinese yuan turn out to be the second lowest (see Figures 9.3 and 9.4).

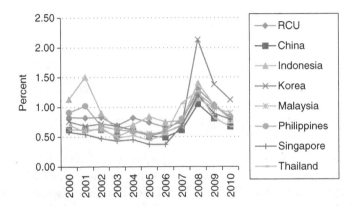

Source: IIMA (2011).

Figure 9.3   Asian exchange rates' standard deviation vis-à-vis the Japanese yen

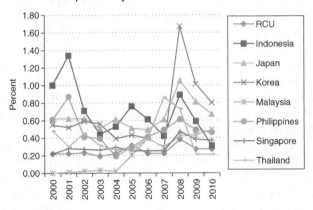

Source: IIMA (2011).

Figure 9.4   Asian exchange rates' standard deviation vis-à-vis the Chinese yuan

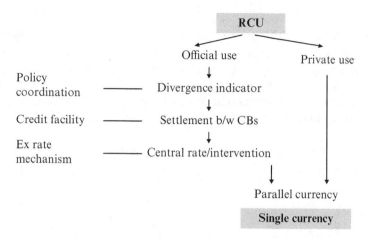

Figure 9.5   RCU's role for monetary integration

Thus, finding a way to develop financial markets linked to an RCU at official level such as the ABMI is important in stimulating private sector interest in the use of an RCU. An RCU can also serve as a useful instrument for the introduction of a regional settlement system to link Asian financial markets as well as that of a swap arrangement and surveillance mechanism to improve the efficiency of the CMI.

In the final stage, an RCU could be developed into a single currency in Asia. If an RCU is given legal tender status for domestic transactions in East Asian countries, it could circulate in parallel with their national currencies and eventually pave the way to a monetary union in Asia. This idea of the so-called parallel currency approach was intensively discussed, even prior to the creation of the EMS, by European scholars (Vaubel, 1978) and was applied to Asia recently by Eichengreen (2007). Given that it is an implausible long-term agenda, however, we address the role of an RCU in three possible areas of monetary cooperation and suggest strategies for further monetary integration in East Asia.

In this regard, however, it is important to cope with the asymmetry problem arising from the difference in weightings attributed to the currencies in the basket. As examined by Moon et al. (2006), the higher the weighting of the currency in the basket, the lower its depreciation (appreciation) against an RCU. In so far as the exchange rate fluctuation is concerned, a country with higher weighting in the basket will have smaller exchange rate fluctuations of its currency in terms of an RCU, while countries with lower weighting will have to face larger fluctuations of their exchange rates in terms of an RCU. If there is an intervention band such

BOX 9.3   FEATURES OF A REGIONAL CURRENCY UNIT

According to the standard basket valuation of the ECU, the official price of the Asian basket in terms of currency *i* can be defined similarly as a weighted sum of the official exchange rates of currency so that

$$RCU^i = \Sigma_j \alpha_j S^i_j, \tag{9.1}$$

where RCU^i = the official price of the basket currency in terms of currency *i*; α_j = the amount of currency *j* in the basket; and S^i_j = the value of currency *j* in terms of currency *i*.

De Grauwe and Peters (1978) and De Grauwe (1997) explain in detail the properties of the currency basket ECU. These properties can be understood easily with a simple example. Imagine a basket composed of the three East Asian currencies, JY, KW and CY, with each currency having the same weight, i.e. 33⅓ per cent in the basket. Assume that the current exchange rates in the market are 1 JY = 2 KW = 3 CY. Then, because 1 unit of Asian currency unit is defined as 1 RCU = 1/3 JY + 2/3 KW + 3/3 CY, the value of the basket in terms of each national currency is 1 RCU = 1 JY = 2 KW = 3 CY. There are a couple of important properties of the currency basket.

First, when a currency depreciates (appreciates) against the other currencies in the basket, the depreciation (appreciation) against an RCU will typically be lower. For instance, suppose that there is an exchange rate fluctuation between national currencies such that the JY revalues 100 per cent against the KW and the CY. Then 1 JY = 4 KW = 6 CY. Then the value of the basket in each national currency changes:

    1 RCU (in JY) = 1 JY + 0.5 JY + 0.5 JY = 2 JY
    1 RCU (in KW) = 4 KW + 2 KW + 2 KW = 8 KW
    1 RCU (in CY) = 6 CY + 3 CY + 3 CY = 12 CY.

Thus, the JY appreciates by 100 per cent against the KW and the CY, while it appreciates only by 33⅓ per cent against an RCU. Inversely, KW and CY depreciate by 100 per cent against the JY but only by 33⅓ per cent against an RCU. This implies that it will be less onerous for countries to keep their exchange rates within a certain margin of a central rate against an RCU than to maintain bilateral exchange rates against other currencies.

There is also the problem of uncertainty about the value of an RCU due to its variable weighting. In fact the share of currency i in the basket decreases (increases) when it depreciates (appreciates) in terms of an RCU. In the example above, the share of the JY in the basket, as it appreciates by 100 per cent against all other currencies, went up from a mere $33^{1}/_{3}$ per cent to 50 per cent, while the shares of the KW and the CY went down to 25 per cent. This feature leads to some problems. If the currency amounts are left unchanged, the strong currencies will continuously increase in importance in the valuation of an RCU. In the extreme case where currency i continues to appreciate against all the currencies, its share will continue to increase such that the value of the currency basket will be determined only by the appreciating currency.

Second, if an RCU is expected to play a role in the future exchange rate arrangement in Asia, there arises the important problem of asymmetry. The reason is that a change in a bilateral exchange rate affects a more weighty currency's RCU rate less than a less weighty one's. In other words, the larger the share of the currency, the lower is its depreciation (appreciation) against an RCU. Suppose that the share of the JY in the basket rises twice to $66^{2}/_{3}$ per cent, while the shares of the KW and the CY decrease by half. Then an RCU will be constructed by 1 RCU = 2 JY + 1 KW + 1.5 CY and its value in national currencies will be 1 RCU = 3 JY = 6 KW = 9 CY. Assume now that, as before, the JY appreciates by 100 per cent against the KW and the CY. Then it yields:

$$1 \text{ RCU (in JY)} = 2 \text{ JY} + (1/4) \text{ JY} + (3/2)(1/6) \text{ JY} = 2.5 \text{ JY}$$
$$1 \text{ RCU (in KW)} = (2)(4) \text{ KW} + 1 \text{ KW} + (3/2)(2/3) \text{ KW} = 10 \text{ KW}$$
$$1 \text{ RCU (in CY)} = (2)(6) \text{ CY} + 3/2 \text{ CY} + 3/2 \text{ CY} = 15 \text{ CY}$$

In so far as the band of exchange rate fluctuation is concerned, a country like Japan, with 66 per cent share in the basket, will see its currency appreciate by $16^{2}/_{3}$ per cent against an RCU, while countries like Korea and China will have see their currencies depreciate by $66^{2}/_{3}$ per cent against an RCU. Thus, if there is an intervention band such as a target zone, there arises the asymmetric case where the country with the smaller share will have to intervene, while the country with a higher share will not need to do so. Thus, in terms of the burden of intervention, the bilateral exchange rate parity system can be considered to be more equitable than an RCU system.

For any given band of margins, however, a basket unit offers more flexibility than a bilateral exchange rate. With margins of x per cent against the basket, it is possible for one member currency to move by more than x per cent against another, provided that this movement is offset, at least to some extent, by movements in the opposite direction against other currencies, without the intervention limits against the basket being breached. Moreover, a regime with a basket unit might be less vulnerable to speculation, since market participants would not know for certain which currency the central bank concerned would intervene in, although they would know when a particular currency reaches its upper or lower intervention limit. Suppose that while the share of the JY remains at $2/3$ of the basket, the shares of the KW and the CY account for $2/9$ and $1/9$ of the basket respectively. Then the value of an RCU in each national currency will be the same as before the change in the shares. Thus, 1 RCU = 3 JY = 6 KW = 9 CY. Suppose now that the CY depreciated 100 per cent vis-à-vis all other currencies such that 1 JY = 2 KW = 6 CY from 1 JY = 2 KW = 3 CY. Then the value of an RCU in each currency would be:

1 RCU (in JY) = 2 JY + (4/3)(1/2) JY + (1/6) JY = $2^{5/6}$ JY
1 RCU (in KW) =(2)(2) KW + 4/3 KW + (1/3) KW = $5^{2/3}$ KW
1 RCU (in CY) = (2)(6) CY + (4/3)(3) CY + 1 CY = 17 CY

The JY appreciates by $1/18$ against the RCU, the KW appreciates by $1/18$ against an RCU and the CY depreciates by $8/9$ against an RCU. Thus, only China will have to intervene to stabilize its exchange rate vis-à-vis an RCU, but it is not clear whether China will intervene in the JY or the KW.

as a target zone, this asymmetry is all the more important because the country with the lower weighting will have to intervene, while the country with a higher weighting will not have to do so. Thus, for the monetary integration process to move forward smoothly, this asymmetry problem needs to be resolved. Indeed, the European experience shows that the development of the EMS since the fall of the Bretton Woods system was a history of coping with asymmetry. In the case of the EMS, for example, there was an upper limit to the weighting of strong currencies. Moreover, for currencies with lower weighting, a larger exchange rate fluctuation band was allowed while a smaller exchange rate fluctuation band was reserved for countries with higher weighting. The fluctuation band in the EMS was actually set to be +/−2.25 per cent (1-basket weighting) around the central rate, where 2.25 per cent was a predetermined exchange rate fluctuation band.

9.4   THE INTERNATIONALIZATION OF THE YUAN AND AN RCU

As Japan suffers from a long economic slowdown, the international role of the yen is receding. In contrast, the Chinese yuan is gaining international importance, given the rise of China as the world's second superpower next to the US. Furthermore, the breakout of the global financial crisis in 2008 revealed the weakness of the current international monetary system based on the dollar. According to the Chinese government, the US dollar as an anchor currency for pegging exchange rates made it possible for the US to continue to finance its current account deficits, making the US the largest debtor country in the world. This continuing global imbalance was one important cause of the financial crisis that erupted in 2008. The US could have chosen to reduce its domestic spending to restore equilibrium. Instead, however, the US Fed resorted to quantitative easing, eroding trust in the ability of the US to manage the dollar. Instead, the US pushed China to revalue its currency vis-à-vis the US dollar and shoulder all the adjustment burden for correcting the global imbalance, which China found to be unacceptable. The revaluations will mean a big loss for countries holding a large share of their foreign reserves in the US dollar, let alone a drop in their exports to the US.

Against this background, the Chinese government decided to increase the use of the Chinese yuan in international transactions. Gao and Yu (2009) summarize the current international use of the Chinese yuan on the basis of the general roles of an international currency.

According to Table 9.4, the yuan is not yet a currency which plays the role of a store of value, nor as an anchor for public and private purposes. However, the yuan has started to be used by resident and non-resident entities as a vehicle and an invoicing currency in trade and financial flows. For instance, the yuan is widely used in border trades with China's

Table 9.4 Summary of international/regional use of the yuan

Function of CNY	Public purpose	Private purpose
Store of value	International reserves None	Currency substitution and investment CNY deposits in Hong Kong CNY loans in Hong Kong CNY bonds in Hong Kong by policy and commercial banks CNY government bonds under ABF2 CNY equities via QFII
Medium of exchange	Vehicle currency BSAs under the CMI Bilateral swap arrangements between central banks	Invoicing currency Trade settlement in CNY
Unit of account	Anchor for pegging None	Denominating currency

Source: Gao and Yu (2009).

neighbouring countries such as Vietnam, Laos, Myanmar, Central Asia, Russia and so on and it was decided at the Chinese Standing Committee of the State Council held in December 2008 that the RMB should be used on a trial basis in trade, (i) between Quang Dong Province and Hong Kong/Macau, and (ii) between Guangxi and Yunnan Provinces and ASEAN countries. Between 2008 and 2009, China concluded Currency Swap Agreements with Korea, Hong Kong, Malaysia, Belarus, Indonesia and Argentina to provide liquidity for trade and direct investment. These agreements are separate from and additional to the Swap Agreements under the Chiang Mai Initiative concluded between the ASEAN+3 countries to prevent the recurrence of a currency crisis in the region.

China's push for international acceptance of the yuan involves three synchronized steps: an offshore yuan market in Hong Kong, currency outflow to overseas investments and backflows of the yuan to China as foreign investment. Hong Kong was quick to develop a yuan market, allowing its local banks to engage in yuan business for individuals in 2004 and then for corporations in 2007, although with limited conditions. In 2005 foreign entities were permitted to issue RMB-denominated bonds in China. These bonds are called RMB-denominated foreign bonds (generally called 'Panda bonds').

At the same time, China challenged the role of the US dollar as a key international reserve currency, calling for the reform of the current international monetary system. In March 2009, Zhou Xiaochuan, the governor of People's Bank of China, proposed an overhaul of the global monetary system, suggesting that a national currency such as the US dollar should eventually be replaced by a super-sovereign reserve currency such as the IMF's Special Drawing Right (SDR) to avoid the Triffin dilemma and reduce pro-cyclicality in the international system. As a necessary precondition for a greater global role for the SDR, he further proposed to set up a settlement system between the SDR and other currencies, to promote its use in international trade, in commodities pricing, in investment and corporate book-keeping, to create SDR denominated securities and to expand the currencies that are used in the SDR's basket to include the currencies of all major economies. Clearly, the Chinese yuan will be included in the calculation of the SDR's value, given its economic weight.

But because the yuan is not yet a fully convertible currency, it was decided in the 2010 review of the SDR valuation that in spite of China's prominent share of global exports, the yuan should not be included in the SDR basket. Chinese yuan did not meet 'freely usable currency' criteria (IMF, 2011).

The development of the SDR as a real international reserve currency, along with the inclusion of the Chinese yuan in the SDR, will be a long-term agenda. The intermediate step is to start the currency basket on an experimental basis. In this sense, the creation of an RCU as explained above could be considered very positively as an intermediary step. If the RCU can be used actively in regional cross-border transactions, there will be no reason why the use of the SDR cannot be activated in global transactions.

It is clear that the use of the Chinese yuan in international transactions will increase, first as a trade settlement currency through investment currency and finally as an international reserve currency. However, it is too early to expect the Chinese yuan to compete directly with the US dollar and euro in its role as an international currency. Indeed, foreign exchange markets and capital markets in China are still undeveloped and immature, making it difficult for non-resident entities to make transactions freely. If non-resident entities are allowed to make these transactions freely, yuan-denominated transactions will expand and 'the economy of scale' thereof will lower the hedging risks and the transaction costs in foreign exchanges, which will further encourage the expansion of yuan-denominated transactions (Institute for International Monetary Affairs, 2010). Thus, it is more realistic to expect that the Chinese yuan will develop first as a regional currency for Asian regions and countries that China shares a border with, and then later become an international currency. In this context, Ranjan and

Prakash (2010) suggest the following three-step approach for the internationalization of the yuan: first, the RMB emerges as a common currency of 'Greater China' including mainland China, Hong Kong and Taiwan; second, it becomes a major component of an Asian Currency Unit; finally, it acquires a global profile.

NOTE

1. For example, in many crisis-hit countries, including Korea, there was a decline in FDI and an increase in the share of bank loans out of total capital inflows.

10. The road towards monetary union

In a world of financial integration, Asian countries will become increasingly vulnerable to capital flows, which can be caused by investors' whims. International economic crises will continue to occur in the future as they have for centuries past. A single country under such circumstances can choose an exchange rate regime from only three possible options: free floating, complete peg or fixed system with capital controls. As examined in previous chapters, none of these systems is satisfactory. This suggests that a collective regional monetary arrangement should be opted for as an alternative to the deadlock of the individual choice of exchange rate regime. In fact, the need to foster a collective regional monetary arrangement in East Asia is very strong, because intraregional exchange rate stability among East Asian countries is essential for their economic prosperity.

However, given that the economies of East Asian countries are very heterogeneous, and that almost all these countries moved to more flexible exchange rate systems after the currency crisis, collective monetary arrangements are still a long-term goal. There has never existed in East Asia what could be called a regional monetary arrangement, and there is a total absence of political solidarity among East Asian countries.

Although the possibility of creating such a regional monetary arrangement in East Asia seems slim at least in the near future, there are some signs of change. Critical was the change in the Chinese policy toward the idea of a regional monetary arrangement. China was initially reluctant to embrace any such idea due to its underdeveloped economy. However, as the Chinese economy is gaining importance in the world economy and the Chinese government is under pressure to appreciate its currency, China has started to show growing interest in such a monetary arrangement as well.

A regional monetary arrangement in East Asia will take time. The road toward a collective monetary arrangement in East Asia is clearly gradual. First, countries in East Asia need to accumulate sufficient experience in coordinating economic policies among themselves. Then they can move to a fully-fledged regional monetary arrangement. The European monetary integration process in this respect can be a lighthouse for future East Asian endeavours, although the Asian experience will never be the same as the European one.

10.1 SOME LESSONS FROM EUROPEAN MONETARY INTEGRATION

Countries in East Asia have achieved sustained economic growth through market-driven global integration. Thus, if economic integration means simply an absence of any barriers for the free flow of goods, capital and people, countries in East Asia could have already attained quite a significant degree of market-driven integration. Unlike the EU and other regions, however, East Asian countries remain behind in formal and institutional arrangements. The experience of European economic and monetary integration can be a useful guide for formal institutionalization. In particular, the process of the three-stage European monetary integration can be a useful template for the sequencing problem of regional integration. These three stages are: macroeconomic policy coordination and cooperation, common exchange rate system, and monetary union.

The first stage was to set up an environment for macroeconomic policy coordination and exchange rate cooperation. Along with the inauguration of the European Community, European countries established the EC Economic and Finance Ministers' meeting (ECOFIN) and the Committee of Governors of the Central Banks (CGCB) to coordinate the issues of exchange rate management and international monetary policy. These institutions have functioned as channels for sharing important macroeconomic information among members, though policy coordination was not very successful due to conflicts of interest.

The second stage was the establishment of a common exchange rate system. The first such system was the so-called 'snake in the tunnel', established after the failure of the Bretton Woods system in the early 1970s. The goal of this system was to limit the exchange rate fluctuation of European currencies with each other ('snake') inside narrow limits against the US dollar ('tunnel'). However, the tunnel collapsed in 1973 when the US floated the US dollar freely. The snake also proved unsustainable because several European countries had to leave this system amidst continuing speculative attacks and monetary turbulence. The second common exchange rate system was the European Monetary System (EMS), which was established in 1979 as a result of the Franco-German alliance between French president Giscard d'Estaing and German chancellor Helmut Schmidt. The EMS set the exchange rates of European currencies relative to each other, while letting European currencies float jointly against the

US dollar. The EMS had three features. The first feature was a common unit of account, and the European Currency Unit (ECU), a currency basket based on a weighted average of the European currencies, was introduced. The second feature was the exchange rate mechanism (ERM), which, like the 'snake', tried to keep the European currencies within a prescribed margin of fluctuations. To this end, a grid of bilateral exchange rates among European currencies was calculated on the basis of the central rates expressed in ECUs, and member states had to contain the fluctuation of their currencies within a margin of 2.25 per cent on either side of the central bilateral rates. The exception was the Italian lira, which was allowed a margin of 6 per cent. The final feature of the EMS was related to its intervention mechanism and financial credit facility. In the event of the maximum fluctuation margin being reached, the related central banks had to intervene by buying or selling their currencies. Strong-currency central banks were obliged to buy weaker currencies whose value fell below the prescribed margin, while weak-currency central banks were obliged to sell the strong currencies and buy their own currencies. European countries also created the European Monetary Cooperation Fund to provide a mutual credit facility for intervention in the foreign exchange market. The key institution in this regard was the 'Very Short Term Financing Facility' through which weak-currency central banks had an automatic access to the credit of strong-currency central banks.

The third stage of European monetary integration started with the transition to an economic and monetary union (EMU), which included the creation of the European Central Bank (ECB) and a single currency, the euro. The first significant decision in this regard was taken in June 1988 at the Hanover European Council, which appointed the Delors Committee to prepare clear and realistic steps for creating an economic and monetary union. The Delors report set out a plan to introduce EMU in three steps. Then, adopting the Treaty on European Union at the Maastricht European Council in 1991, European leaders decided to shift to economic and monetary union according to the recommendations of the Delors report. The first step for the realization of EMU was to strengthen the role of the Committee of Central Banks in monitoring and consulting central banks on monetary policies. In the second step the European Monetary Institute (EMI) was established as a predecessor of the ECB, in the spirit of the US Federal Reserve System. The third step was the creation of the European Central Bank (ECB), to which national central banks would transfer their authority of national monetary policy and the ECB introduced a single regional currency, the euro, on 1 January 1999. The euro replaced 11 European national currencies as the sole legal tender on 1 March 2002.

Table 10.1   Three stages of monetary integration

Stages	Stage I	Stage II	Stage III
Objective	Environment for coordinated policy making	Common exchange rate mechanism	Single currency
Tasks	Multilateralize CMI Institutionalize policy dialogue Create a system for information sharing	Exchange rate cooperation Introduce a regional currency unit Create financing facilities for intervention	Create an Asian central bank Substitute national currencies with a regional currency unit
Institutions to be added	Secretariat	Further inter-governmental negotiation	Supra-national institutions

Sources: Lee and Yoon (2007) and author's work.

Following the European monetary integration process, monetary integration in East Asia can also occur in three stages: the first stage aims at the creation of an environment for coordinated policymaking and exchange rate cooperation. The second stage targets the establishment of a common exchange rate mechanism to stabilize intraregional exchange rates. It is precisely here that the proposal for an Asian Monetary System (AMS), which could be modelled after the EMS system, comes in (Moon, Rhee and Yoon, 2000). The final stage will be the introduction of a single regional currency, along with the creation of an Asian central bank. Table 10.1 summarizes these processes.

10.2   POLICY COORDINATION AND EXCHANGE RATE COOPERATION

Countries in East Asia are so heterogeneous that gradual monetary integration seems more desirable (from the viewpoint of OCA theory). In this regard, the first important step is for the East Asian countries to strengthen their policy coordination[1]. Basically, the policy dialogue among East Asian countries could constitute an internal monetary policy coordination as well as an external monetary coordination, such as the stabilization of intraregional exchange rates. The reason is that pursuing closer cooperation in monetary and financial affairs necessitates prior consultation on the economic and monetary policies of their respective countries. Furthermore, political as well as economic considerations will be important. For example, in the face of a bipolarizing global monetary order dominated by the dollar and euro, East Asian countries need more concerted action to maximize their voices in international monetary affairs. This suggests a fundamental need for an Asia-only policy forum.

Coordination of policies leads in turn to the establishment of an appropriate organization or an institution. The simple way is of course to set up a secretariat for the forum. Once this is done, then the next step is to set up a monetary and financial committee that will help facilitate policy coordination and cooperation. In the case of Europe, long before monetary integration was pursued, an institution called the Monetary Committee was established. This committee comprised one representative from the central bank and one from the finance ministry of each member country plus two representatives from the EC Commission. This group provided a useful forum for the exchange of information and for the preparation of the Council of Ministers of Economics and Finance (ECOFIN) meetings. As the importance of the intra-European exchange rate stability increased, the role of the Monetary Committee was continuously strengthened such that a prior consultation with the committee was obligatory when it came to member states' decisions on international monetary and financial issues. In 1964, another institution called the Committee of Governors of the Central Banks of the Member Countries of the European Communities was established (Gros and Thygesen, 1998, p.10).

In this regard, the establishment of the AMRO and the development of the CMIM into a future Asian Monetary Fund may be a good opportunity to help East Asian countries mobilize both governmental and central bank officials for policy coordination and information sharing.

There is also some debate on the appropriateness of the targets for policy coordination. For example, Genberg (2006) and Eichengreen (2007) argue for harmonized inflation targeting. According to Genberg, exchange rate targeting might turn out to be disastrous due to the risk of currency speculation. Thus, he proposes the creation of a region of monetary stability in Asia based on the common objective of an inflation target. Eichengreen provides a more comprehensive account of why harmonized inflation targeting is the best approach to encourage monetary integration in Asia. He compares the three different systems (exchange rate coordination, harmonized inflation targeting and the parallel approach) relative to three criteria: robustness with respect to capital mobility, compatibility with prevailing political circumstances, and congruence with modern ideas about the conduct of monetary policy. He argues that exchange rate targeting in East Asia does not satisfy these criteria mainly because of high capital mobility and the absence of political solidarity. For these reasons, he prefers inflation targeting and maintains that such an arrangement, if properly established, might even limit exchange rate instability. According to him, harmonized inflation targeting is less prone to speculative attacks in a world of capital mobility, and is compatible with the current political situation in Asia. However, given that economic conditions, policy preferences and understandings of these factors are very diverse in East Asia, it is almost impossible to calculate appropriate common inflation targets. Even if it is possible, it will be extremely difficult to have all members agree on a common inflation target. It is difficult to say that harmonized inflation targeting is better than exchange rate targeting. Exchange rate targeting might be as necessary as inflation targeting.

Exchange rate targeting has been a policy priority in East Asia for a long time. However, because of increasing financial integration in East Asia, exchange rate targeting is becoming more and more difficult to implement. In fact, the 'Impossibility Trinity Theorem' says that individual efforts to stabilize exchange rates are bound to fail. Collective action for self-protection will be the only possible alternative in the current world of financial integration. Kawai (2009a) suggests that there are two possible collective actions regarding exchange rate coordination. The first one is for each country in Asia to stabilize its currency through a joint reference to a common key currency or a common basket of key currencies, such as an RCU. The second one is for each country in Asia to jointly create a tightly coordinated regional exchange rate system similar to the European Monetary System. However, given that the economic convergence among East Asian countries is not adequate and that the political commitment is insufficient to support the creation of a tightly coordinated exchange rate system, the first approach is regarded to be more realistic in the short run.

10.3   ASIAN MONETARY SYSTEM

The current exchange rate systems in East Asia create, by all measurements, a considerable exchange rate variability vis-à-vis each other, the dollar or a weighted average of major intraregional currencies. This variability makes exchange rate coordination among Asian countries extremely difficult. The exchange rate variability is also harmful for stable economic growth of the region and evokes the need for a greater element of intraregional and interregional exchange rate stability of East Asian currencies.

The recognition of this problem leads to the proposal of a target zone regime, such as the ERM in Europe. This target zone is a voluntary guideline for exchange rates, defined in terms of a band of permissible exchange rate movement. Its objective is to stabilize intraregional exchange rates between Asian currencies, but to let them float collectively against the dollar and the euro. The Asian exchange rate system is a common exchange rate mechanism that needs stronger engagement from participating countries and an institutional infrastructure. Intensive intergovernmental cooperation at all levels between East Asian countries is a prerequisite for the successful operation of an Asian monetary system. The exchange rate mechanism of this Asian monetary system consists of three pillars, namely, an exchange rate mechanism, an anchor currency and a financing system.

10.3.1   Exchange Rate Mechanism

First of all, East Asian countries should adopt a wide band regarding their exchange rate mechanism. Because the economies of East Asian countries are very heterogeneous and many of them have moved to the floating system after the currency crisis, the wide band system seems more pertinent for an East Asian monetary integration. In East Asia there never has been what could be called an economic union and there is little political solidarity among East Asian countries. Therefore, it may be necessary for them to have a psychological buffer period in which coordination and cooperation in economic policies could develop naturally into a fully-fledged integration. If this is the case, what appears to be the most appropriate initial form is a target zone à la Williamson, that is, a wide band basket system (Williamson, 2000).

10.3.2   Anchor Currency

In order to understand exchange rate targeting, it will be helpful to develop an RCU-based divergence indicator and to monitor and coordinate monetary and economic policies in East Asia on this basis. In particular, an RCU could be used to monitor exchange market developments. Indeed, an RCU could be an appropriate tool in identifying misalignment and excess volatility of an Asian currency vis-à-vis other regional currencies. An RCU can also be used as an indicator to monitor how Asian currencies are moving collectively vis-à-vis key external currencies such as the US dollar and the euro.

10.3.3   Emergency Loan Facility

An essential precondition for the use of an RCU is that it must be accompanied by an emergency liquidity provision system that a country can

---

BOX 10.1 VSTFF

In the case of the EMS, the facility for the provision of liquidity was the Very Short Term Financing Facility (VSTFF). It was one of the cornerstones of European monetary cooperation. Indeed, throughout the history of monetary cooperation in Europe, the facility for the provision of liquidity has been constantly strengthened. The European Monetary Cooperation Fund (EMCF) was scheduled to manage the VSTFF. One important point here is that under the VSTFF, the central banks of countries with strong currencies had an obligation to provide unlimited amounts of their own currencies to defend the existing exchange rate margin. This obligation came about because the official reserve holdings that one country can use to intervene in the foreign exchange market are not sufficient to cope with the unprecedented magnitude of private capital movements.

In the case of European countries, the German Bundesbank took this role as the lender of last resort. For example, during the EMS crisis in September 1992, the credit that the Bundesbank had supplied reached around DM93 billion. Because weak currency countries could repay the liabilities they incurred in ECU, the value of German credits decreased after the devaluation of some European currencies. The loss by the Bundesbank was estimated to be in excess of DM1 billion in its VSTFF lending facility (Collignon, 1994). In addition, the ERM crisis in 1992–3 shows that even these EMS institutional frameworks were not sufficient to fend off speculative attacks. Defending the parities would have required a recycling mechanism to counteract destabilizing speculative capital movements. The mechanism should have provided a temporary accommodation of the demand for currency diversification. One such proposal was to remove the asset settlement rule of the ERM. In this case, the central banks that received intervention credit would no longer be obliged to repay the intervention balances in third currencies (Collignon, 1994).

---

dispose of if its currency is under speculative attack. In fact, in order for Asian countries under the pressure of a crisis to be provided with sufficient liquidity, an emergency liquidity facility which lends without limit should be set up. As Eichengreen (1997) pointed out, this need for international cooperation is growing faster than ever, given the magnitude of current capital movements. In this regard, once again European monetary cooperation experiences regarding the Very Short Term Financing Facility (VSTFF) could provide good instructive examples.

This facility is in sharp contrast to the facility available within the framework of the CMIM, which is intended to provide a limited amount of dollar funding as emergency loans. As pointed out (Chapter 6), the simple provision of dollar funds, the total amount of which will be limited to several tens of billions of dollars, cannot be sufficient for East Asian countries to cope with currency crises. Nor will it be easy for East Asian countries to allocate a continuously extended amount of dollar reserves for such a purpose. What is worse is that the dollar, which is not a regional currency in the system, is swapped. This implies that unlike the EMS, the participating central banks cannot rely on printing power to provide intervention currencies, and will be forced to deplete their reserves (Eichengreen, 2001, pp.62–3). The CMIM is thus insufficient as a regional lender of last resort. An institution such as an Asian Monetary Stabilization Fund (AMSF) needs to be developed further. The main function of an AMSF is to address the question of exchange rate cooperation among East Asian countries, unlike the CMIM's function, which is to provide emergency financial support and thereby prevent a possible financial crisis. The function of an AMSF could be compared to that of the European Monetary Cooperation Fund (EMCF), which was to monitor monetary policies, oversee the operation of credit facilities, and authorize realignments among European countries. According to article 3 of its statute 3, the EMCF was responsible for:

- concerted action necessary for the proper functioning of the Community exchange system;
- the multilateralization of positions resulting from interventions by Central Banks in Community currencies and the multilateralization of intra-Community settlements;
- the administration of the very short-term financing and of the short-term monetary support.

Of course, an AMSF cannot institutionally be the same as the EMCF, because of the absence of political solidarity among the East Asian governments. Thus, until the establishment of a regional exchange rate arrangement, it will just assume its function of facilitating a concertation of exchange rate policies and settlements of intraregional debts and credits. There is no risk of this institution excessively constraining the exercise of monetary sovereignty by East Asian national governments. As Eichengreen

(1997) mentioned, even the EMCF possessed little authority, because national central banks were unwilling to delegate their prerogatives.

Once an AMSF is established, there are several ways to extend the use of an RCU. First, as in the case of Europe, central banks in Asia could transfer a certain amount (say, 20 per cent of their dollar reserves) to an AMSF in exchange for RCUs. In Europe, the ECU thus created was to be used as the settlement currency for 50 per cent of the net claims between any two central banks. The second way is to issue RCUs against national currencies. For example, each national government in East Asia could transfer a given amount of its currency to an AMSF and receive RCU deposits in return. In fact, each national central bank would have its RCU account in an AMSF. An AMSF would have the RCU deposits of each national central bank on its liability side and the constituent national currencies on its asset side. If an RCU could be issued against national currencies, exchange rate targeting could be conducted in a centralized manner through an AMSF.[2]

It remains, however, unresolved as to whether a future AMF will assume such a task inside its functions separately from an AMSF. Everything depends on the Asian leadership being able to achieve an Asian monetary union.

10.3.4 North-East Asian Monetary System

It is clear that not all East Asian countries can proceed to the Asian Monetary System at the same speed because of their heterogeneous economic and political conditions. For instance, the economic disparities between the three North-East Asian countries (China, Japan and Korea) and ASEAN countries are too large to form a single monetary zone. Furthermore, ASEAN countries have some concerns about the hegemonic positions of China and Japan, and some of them even want the US dollar to continue to play a dominant role as an anchor currency. Whether they even have a strong interest in creating a regional monetary arrangement is thus uncertain. It is thus wiser to adopt a multi-track approach, whereby only the countries that fulfil the necessary preconditions go forward to the next stage, before the others do. For instance China, Japan and Korea could cooperate first and then extend the cooperation to include the ASEAN countries. The European countries have adopted a similar multi-track approach as well.

There are several reasons why an exchange rate arrangement between China, Japan and Korea is more plausible than an exchange rate arrangement that includes all Asian countries.

First, the industrial structure of China, Japan and Korea overlaps to a great extent. These three countries are competing fiercely in almost all

Table 10.2   Industrial competition between Korea, Japan and China

Industry	Korea ranking	Japan ranking	China ranking
Shipbuilding	1	8	12
Petrochemical	2	5	18
Automobile	3	1	15
Telecom	4	10	3
Semiconductor	5	3	6
LCD	6	20	13
Steel	7	4	8
Basic machine	8	2	5
Computer	9		1
Industrial machine	10	6	10
Fine chemistry	11	7	7
Textile	12		9
Home electronics	13	19	4
Non-ferrous metal	14	14	19
Heavy electric equipment	15	9	19
Plastic	16	13	11
Mechanical elements & tools	17	12	16
Rubber	18	16	14
Batteries	19		
Machine parts & components	20	17	20
Precision machine		11	
Video & audio equipment		15	
Measuring instrument		18	
Furniture			17
Apparel			2

Sources: Jang (2011) and author's calculation.

important export sectors. For instance, Korea and Japan overlap in 17 of their top 20 export industries, while Korea and China overlap in 19 industries (Table 10.2).

China, Japan and Korea are thus more sensitive to their intraregional exchange rate variability. For instance, widening exchange rate divergence between the Korean won and the Japanese yen is one important factor that helped Korean companies to outperform Japanese counterparts in major markets. It also explains why even if a country like Korea adopted a floating exchange rate system, it could not leave the movement of exchange rate only to market forces. In a similar context, the Japanese government decided to intervene to devalue its currency in 2011, after the long abstinence of foreign exchange market intervention. Given that there is a real possibility of conflicts regarding the appropriate level of intraregional exchange rates between China, Japan and Korea, it is likely that the three countries may seek joint action to stabilize their intraregional exchange rates.

Second, although the creation of an RCU is an important step for measuring exchange rate divergences, the inclusion of all the currencies of ASEAN+3 countries in the basket may not be a realistic option. For instance, as IMF (2011) indicates, including all 13 nations' currencies in the basket could enhance the attractiveness of an RCU by increasing its diversity and representativeness. However, this could mean at the same time adding currencies with low weightings, which would increase the complexity and transaction costs tremendously. In particular, given that the economic and political disparities among ASEAN countries are so large, the conditions for the wide use of an RCU are not mature enough. Coherent exchange coordination will be extremely difficult due to the existing gaps in economic and trade structure, labour productivity, capital mobility, and so on. Furthermore, ASEAN countries are wary of their northern partners. Thus, the three largest North-East Asian economies, China, Japan and Korea, may first create a regional currency basket composed of the JY, the KRW and the CY only, and then extend it to ASEAN countries.

Third, independently of the CMIM, Korea concluded bilateral swap arrangements with Japan and China on two occasions. As indicated in Chapter 7, for example, Korea and Japan had a US$30 billion currency swap arrangement during the period of the 2008 global financial crisis, and Korea and China did the same for almost the same amount (180 billion Chinese yuan). In October 2011, Korea and Japan again agreed to extend their currency swap arrangement to more than $70 billion in the face of the escalating eurozone crisis. Then in the same month, Korea and China agreed to double their won–yuan swap arrangement from the existing US$26 billion to US$56 billion (see Table 10.3).

The perpetuation of these extended swaps between Korea, Japan and China will certainly facilitate the creation of the AMSF and concerted foreign exchange market intervention between the three countries to stabilize their intraregional exchange rates.

10.4   MONETARY UNION

The monetary authorities in East Asian countries could develop a common exchange rate system like the EMS, linking their own home currencies to

Table 10.3   Korea–Japan and Korea–China swap arrangements

	Swaps	After the 1997 Asian crisis	After the 2008 global financial crisis	After the 2011 eurozone crisis
Korea–Japan	Won/yen (Extended)	US$3 billion	US$20 billion	US$30 billion
	Dollar/won (New)	0	0	US$30 billion
	Dollar/yen (Existing bilateral CMI)	US$10 billion	US$10 billion	US$10 billion
	Total	US$13 billion	US$30 billion	US$70 billion
Korea–China	RMB/won		180 billion RMB /38 trillion won (US26$ billion)	expired
	RMB/won (New)			360 billion RMB/64 trillion won (US56$ billion)
	Bilateral CMI	US$8 billion	US$8 billion	US$8 billion
	Total	US$8 billion	US$34 billion	US$64 billion

Source: Ministry of Budget and Finance, Korea.

an RCU. This implies that monetary authorities can choose whether or not to realign the exchange rates of the home currencies vis-à-vis an RCU. The existence of this choice might induce speculators to attack weaker currencies. Such a possibility means that the monetary authorities would be advised to make a strong commitment to linking their home currencies to an RCU.

The strongest commitment is to proceed to monetary integration. Once committed, the monetary authorities of the participating countries would not have the option of leaving the monetary union. Such a commitment would contribute to the stability of the exchange rate system because private economic agents would build up their confidence in the coordinated exchange rate policy of East Asian countries. This increase in confidence would decrease the likelihood of an exchange rate collapse, which would, in turn, lower the domestic interest rates of the home currencies because of the reduction in expected depreciation and risk premium. Thus, monetary integration would contribute to a decrease in domestic interest rates.

At a lecture delivered at the ADB, Robert Mundell (2001) argued that Asia would eventually need a common currency like the euro. An Asian Monetary Union is undoubtedly a more advanced form of monetary integration than an Asian Monetary System. If the Impossible Trinity Theorem holds even for an Asian Monetary System, an Asian Monetary Union is the only sustainable system to achieve both the free movement of capital and stability of exchange rates. However, its realization raises some important problems.

The first problem regarding an Asian Monetary Union is related to the loss of monetary sovereignty. One of the reasons why East Asian countries were so sensitive to the loss of sovereignty was that their states had been functioning as developmental states, intervening heavily in the economy so as to industrialize and develop their countries. With the start of the liberalization process, however, the effectiveness of government intervention decreased. In particular, with the liberalization of capital markets that started at the beginning of the 1990s, East Asian countries found it very difficult to conduct an independent monetary policy as European countries had done in the 1980s. The European experience testifies that in this case, countries can benefit more by giving up their sovereignties. This is especially true for countries like France and Italy, because they were already de facto losers of monetary sovereignty in the face of free capital movement. They could regain their monetary sovereignties by sharing decision-making power with other European countries, especially with Germany (Wyplosz, 1997). The same will be true for the smaller countries in East Asia. The burden will be far greater for large countries such as Japan and China.

The second problem is the loss of privilege derived from formal monetary monopoly, that is, the power of seigniorage. In fact, the tighter a currency is pegged, the less room policymakers will have to create the money and augment public expenditure. Thus, the larger a sovereign government's seigniorage, the higher the cost of joining a monetary union. For East Asian countries, however, the cost of giving up the benefit of seigniorage is no longer an insurmountable obstacle.

Table 10.4 shows the ratio of seigniorage revenue to GDP per year in East Asia. In the table, column (1) defines seigniorage as inflation tax, MB/P, where MB is the monetary base and P is the price level, while column (2) shows the opportunity cost of holding money, rMB/P, where r is the interest rate. Column (3) represents the seigniorage from domestic credit only. The table shows that seigniorage revenue is large for some East Asian countries. In China, for instance, seigniorage revenue from MB is 6.10 per cent of GDP (or 2.82 per cent in the opportunity cost concept) and even the revenue from domestic credit is 4.00 per cent. Although it is lower

Table 10.4　Seigniorage flow in East Asia (%)

	1973–79			1980–2000		
	(1)	(2)	(3)	(1)	(2)	(3)
China	---	---	---	6.10	2.82	4.00
Hong Kong	---	---	---	1.55	0.52	−4.56
Indonesia	1.84	0.94	0.25	1.21	1.21	−0.31
Japan	1.15	0.77	1.34	0.59	0.40	0.28
Korea	2.89	2.14	1.76	0.63	0.86	−0.76
Malaysia	1.78	0.43	−1.25	2.13	1.02	−0.81
Philippines	1.12	0.72	0.38	1.67	1.97	1.74
Singapore	2.48	1.17	−4.74	1.20	0.84	−6.49
Thailand	1.12	0.95	−0.13	1.09	0.92	−0.48

Note:　China's data are for 1986–2000 and Hong Kong's data are for 1991–2001.

Source:　IFS.

than in China, seigniorage revenue is often over 1 per cent in many East Asian countries. A reason for these relatively high seigniorage ratios is that East Asian countries have not yet developed advanced banking sectors and payment habits. But two things are noteworthy: first, seigniorage declined rapidly in the 1990s. In particular, seigniorage from domestic credit became very low as East Asian countries continued to accumulate foreign reserves and to liberalize their domestic financial markets. In fact, most countries' seigniorage from domestic credit turned negative in the 1990s. Second, although seigniorage in East Asia is still high compared to the European level of the 1990s, it is as low as that of Europe in the late 1970s, just before EMS. This is especially so for seigniorage from domestic credit. Now, seigniorage revenue in many East Asian countries is not as important a source of government revenue as it was before. Under these circumstances, seigniorage itself may not be such a critical hindrance to monetary integration.

The third problem regarding an Asian Monetary Union is the regional cohesion and solidarity. As can be seen from the case of the yen bloc in Chapter 3, monetary union can make the already large income differences among Asian countries larger, putting the integration process itself in danger. The wide income differences, if they are maintained, can generate political tensions, leading to the separation of economically depressed regions or countries from a given federation or union. Thus, a regional monetary union presupposes a strong regional solidarity. In the existing federations, for example, federal transfers and taxes are needed to narrow inter-regional income gaps and to maintain the unity of member states.

BOX 10.2   DISTRIBUTION OF SEIGNIORAGE
            BETWEEN MEMBER COUNTRIES

Another big issue relating to seigniorage is the distribution of seigniorage revenue from the pooled monetary stock after forming a
monetary integration. To the countries participating in a monetary
union, not only the amount of benefit created from the union but
also the way that the benefit is distributed among the participants
is of concern. A monetary union may have a significant impact on
the distribution of seigniorage revenues among member countries, depending on how the arrangement for the disposition of
seigniorage revenue is agreed. Although there is no perfect rule
for this, the issue can be examined using the rule adopted in the
EMU, where seigniorage from the pooled monetary base is distributed by the average of a country's population and GDP shares
rather than by the contribution to the pooled monetary base. Sinn
and Feist (2000) show that in this regard France is the big winner
while Germany is the big loser.

Replicating the work of Sinn and Feist (2000), Moon and Rhee
(1999) calculated the seigniorage distribution for nine East Asian
countries. Table 10.5 summarizes these results. This table shows
how much each country in East Asia contributes (columns 2
and 3)[3] and how much it receives (columns 4 and 6). Columns
7–9 compare the gains and losses of the different countries.
Assuming that nine East Asian countries join a monetary union,
the total amount of pooled *MB* will be US$1145.80 billion. Two
rival countries, Japan and China, account for the lion's share of
contributions, at 54.93 per cent and 36.01 per cent respectively.
But China receives the largest share of the seigniorage revenue
with 42.91 per cent, while Japan receives the second largest with
37.21 per cent, followed by Indonesia (6.79 per cent) and Korea
(4.39 per cent). According to the table, China and Indonesia
are the big winners while Japan is the big loser. In per capita
terms, Japan (–US$2108.30) is still the largest loser followed by
Hong Kong (–US$813.77) and Singapore (–US$552.91), while
Korea (US$852.15) is the largest gainer followed by Indonesia
(US$426.98) and the Philippines (US$383.86).

Combining these results with the work of Sinn and Feist shows
that both in Europe and in East Asia, the country whose currency
is an important international transaction currency in the region

Table 10.5 *Seigniorage contribution and redistribution in East Asia*

	MB		GDP+Population			Seigniorage Gain/Loss		
	Amount ($billion)	Share (1) (%)	GDP ($billion)	Population (million)	Share (2) (%)	(1)-(2) (%)	Total ($bill)	Per capita ($)
						6.90		
CH	412.61	36.01	1081.02	1266.84	42.91		104.14	82.21
						−0.37		
HK	20.45	1.78	162.64	6.80	1.42		−5.53	−813.77
						5.95		
IN	9.56	0.83	134.52	210.49	6.79		89.87	426.98
JA	629.40	54.93	4454.31	126.87	37.21	−17.72	−267.48	−2108.30
KO	19.77	1.73	409.10	47.27	4.39	2.67	40.28	852.15
MA	21.16	1.85	89.21	23.26	1.31	−0.53	−8.05	−346.15
PH	7.41	0.65	66.17	76.32	2.59	1.95	29.37	383.86
SI	10.92	0.95	91.91	4.02	0.81	−0.15	−2.22	−552.91
TH	14.52	1.27	113.43	62.32	2.57	1.30	19.62	314.79
Total	1145.80	100	6602.30	1824.19	100	---	---	---
SD	229.74	20.05	1432.29	404.37	16.57	7.16	108.07	890.91

Note: Each country's *MB* is the average of 1994–97. SD denotes standard deviation.

Source: Adapted from Moon and Rhee (1999).

(Germany in Europe or Japan in East Asia) is the biggest loser. In contrast, the second largest economy (France in Europe or China in East Asia) is the largest beneficiary. Although the imbalance between seigniorage contribution and seigniorage receipt is not unique in East Asia, the imbalance is still larger in East Asia than in Europe. This larger imbalance suggests that distributional considerations should be more carefully addressed by a prior agreement of monetary integration in East Asia.

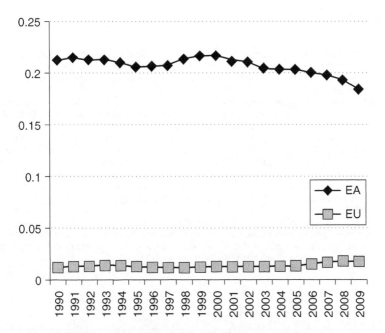

Note: The income convergence is measured by σ-convergence, calculated by the sample standard deviation of the log of the per capita income. The σ-convergences for the EA and the EU are calculated for 10 East Asian countries (China, Japan, Korea, advanced 5 ASEAN countries, Hong Kong and Taiwan) and for the original EU15 member states.

Source: PENN World Table, version 7.

Figure 10.1   Patterns of income convergence in East Asia and Europe

In the case of Europe, although the European Union has no power over the tax systems of the member countries, the goal of regional solidarity is handled through the EU budget and European Investment Bank. Contrary to these cases, however, there is no such mechanism in East Asia. Indeed, this is the main reason why a pessimistic view has prevailed so far regarding the future of regional monetary integration in East Asia (for instance, Eichengreen, 2002).

Figure 10.1 shows the trend of the income disparity between East Asian and European countries. Although the income disparity among East Asian countries is much larger than that among European countries, suggesting a stronger need for regional solidarity in East Asia, the prospect for income convergence is brighter in East Asia. The large income gap in East Asia has tended to decline since 1990.

NOTES

1. In the case of Europe, for example, the Treaty of Rome devotes two chapters to economic policy coordination and balance of payment problems. In particular, Paragraphs 103–107 say explicitly that each member country should consider its conjunctural policy and its exchange rate policy a matter of 'common concern'.
2. Chai et al. (2008) explains this process in detail: suppose that the Korean won reached the lower limit of fluctuation and the Japanese yen the upper limit. Then the Bank of Korea would have to buy the Korean won from an AMSF, decreasing its deposit at an AMSF, while the Bank of Japan would have to sell the Japanese yen to an AMSF and increase its RCU deposit. The end result would leave the total amount of RCU issued by an AMSF unchanged with the composition of constituent assets (currencies) being changed. It is very likely that the central bank with a weaker currency would need RCU deposits or a strong currency country to buy its own currency from an AMSF. This implies that a short-term financing facility is essential for the smooth operation of an AMSF.
3. To calculate a country's future seigniorage revenue yielded to the pooled monetary base, the opportunity concept of seigniorage is used. Since the present value of future revenue is equal to today's market value of the asset, a country's outstanding stock of monetary base is here defined as its contribution to the pool.

11. Hurdles and challenges

When East Asia and Europe are compared, their suitability for regional integration may initially not seem so different from each other. For instance, as Willet emphasized, 'post World War II developments in Asia were quite similar to those in Europe with Japan playing the role of Germany' (Willett, 2005, p.6). However, unlike in the EU, where the economic bloc was formed by mutual agreement at government level for the purpose of integrating the market, economic cooperation in East Asia was a natural consequence of increasing globalization and interdependence. What are the factors that prevent East Asian countries from emulating Europe's institution-led regionalization? Why do they simply accept market-driven regionalization? There are in fact important differences between the two regions. For instance, according to Katzenstein (1996), 'the US encouraged bilateralism in East Asia, but multilateralism in Europe because it had more power in the former region than in the latter'. Also in East Asia 'the relations between the state and society were governed by social rather than legal norms and East Asian governments inherited the colonial tradition of "rule by law" rather than the West European tradition of the "rule of law".' (p.146). No matter how important these differences may be, many obstacles prevent East Asian countries from establishing regional institutions. In particular, economic, political, and social obstacles are noteworthy.

The first obstacle is that East Asia's real regionalization remains institutionally underdeveloped. Monetary integration and real integration go hand in hand in such a way that stronger trade integration leads to deepened monetary integration, and monetary integration facilitates more trade integration. Thus, East Asian countries should strengthen regional trade arrangements further, in particular pan-Asian trade arrangements.

The second and the most serious obstacle that will stand in the way of Asian monetary cooperation is the lack of political leadership. In fact, the vision and the desire of political leaders were an essential ingredient in unifying Europe. In comparison, political leadership is very weak in East Asia. The result is the absence of common rules and institutions, and in this respect the prospect of an East Asian monetary union seems dim (Eichengreen, 1997).

The third potentially big obstacle is the absence of solidarity and cohesion in the region. Economic partnerships presuppose economic solidarity because economic solidarity reduces the probability of economic and political conflicts. Given the large economic disparity in East Asia, it is imperative for East Asia to reduce this gap and nurture regional solidarity, which will contribute to its regional identity.

11.1 INCOMPLETE ECONOMIC COMMUNITY BUILDING

The end goal of any regional integration is the co-prosperity of the region as a whole and thereby to establish and maintain peace in the region. The instrument for achieving this goal is, as it was for Europe, free markets – in particular, the free movement of goods, capital and people. One big problem in this regard is that there was no programme for community-building in East Asia. Therefore, the attempts to achieve free markets in the area of goods, capital and people are so far fragmented and uncoordinated. In particular, the link between trade and monetary integration was weak and fragile. Free trade, however, is a catalyst for closer monetary integration, and inversely, closer monetary cooperation facilitates free trade. Trade and monetary integrations are mutually reinforcing. To enable agreement to be reached on the establishment of some community institutions, therefore, trade integration is essential.

East Asian countries traditionally relied on multilateralism and the WTO for trade liberalization and therefore were latecomers in the move towards regional trade arrangements. During the first decade of this century, however, East Asian countries have been rapidly catching up with the global trend of regional trade arrangements and a proliferation of bilateral and plurilateral free trade agreements (FTAs) took place. By the end of May 2010, there were 45 FTAs completed, and another 84 in various stages of preparation in East Asia (Kawai and Wignaraja, 2010).[1] Although there are now many bilateral and sub-regional FTAs in East Asia, there is no regional FTA unified under the name of an East Asian Free Trade Area. There have been continuing calls for the establishment of an East Asian Free Trade Area (EAFTA), ever since the Prime Minister of Malaysia, Mahatir, proposed the formation of an East Asian Economic Caucus (EAEC) in 1990. As pointed out by the EAFTA expert group, the formation of an EAFTA would increase the awareness of East Asian citizens of their common destiny, institutionalize dialogue and contacts, and increase mutual understanding and cooperation. Furthermore, a growing number of current bilateral and plurilateral FTAs between East Asian countries with their differing rules of origin and tariff reduction schedules will create a spaghetti bowl phenomenon, increasing transaction costs for intraregional trade and raising production costs for production networks in East Asia (Joint Expert Group on EAFTA Phase II Study, 2009). The formation of an EAFTA would certainly be an effective way to reduce these costs and sustain regional economic growth.

Another important regional trade arrangement is an FTA between the three North-East Asian countries (CJK FTA), because their trade accounts for the biggest trade flows in the region. Furthermore, given that there are already the ASEAN Free Trade Area (AFTA) and three ASEAN+1 FTAs, forming a sub-regional CJK FTA will be to remove the last barricade for the realization of an EAFTA. In fact, once a CJK FTA is realized, an EAFTA can be formed by the simple consolidation of the existing AFTA, a CJK FTA and the three ASEAN+1 FTAs. Although discussions about a CJK FTA are underway, however, its formation is by no means certain, which in turn will negatively impact on the prospects of an EAFTA.

In this regard it is worthwhile noting one important feature of current East Asian trade arrangements. The FTAs in East Asia are more extraregional oriented than intraregional. For instance, among the 102 FTAs concluded, negotiated and proposed in East Asia, the number of intraregional FTAs is just 21, while the number of extraregional FTAs reaches 80 (see Kawai and Wignaraja, 2007). This trend is particularly so for Korea, Japan and China, which have seen their FTA activities increasing at an unprecedented speed. Table 11.1 summarizes the status of the FTAs of Korea, Japan and China.

This suggests that East Asian trade arrangements are global rather than regional. As the recent Korea–EU and Korea–US FTAs testify, regional trade arrangements do not have any priority over inter-regional arrangements. Inter-regional arrangements of forums are as active as regional ones (see Box 11.1). This might be due to the absence of necessary political leadership in East Asia and the political rivalry between Japan and China.

11.2 LACK OF POLITICAL LEADERSHIP

While East Asian monetary integration is underdeveloped, there are many cases which succeeded, as we already have seen. However, the lack of political will poses a most serious obstacle to the road of monetary integration. Compared to the EU, political leadership in East Asia is weak and fragmented. Furthermore, the political geometry of East Asia is more complicated. This is because of the continuous involvement of the

Table 11.1   *Status of the FTAs of Korea, Japan and China (as of July, 2009)*

		Within the region	Outside the region
Korea	Concluded		
	(entered into force)	Korea–Singapore	Korea–Chile
		Korea–ASEAN (Goods)	Korea–EFTA
		Korea–ASEAN (Services)	
		Korea–ASEAN (Investment)	
	(Not in effect)		Korea–US
			Korea–EU
	Under negotiation	Japan	Canada
			India
			Mexico
			GCC
			Australia
			Peru
			New Zealand
	In preparation	China	MERCOSUR
		ASEAN+3	Turkey
		ASEAN+6	Russia
Japan	Concluded		
	(entered into force)	Japan–Malaysia	Japan–Mexico
		Japan–Singapore	Japan–Chile
		Japan–Thailand	
		Japan–Indonesia	
		Japan–Brunei	
		Japan–ASEAN	
		Japan–Philippines	
		Japan–Vietnam	
	(Not in effect)		Japan–Switzerland
	Under negotiation	Korea	GCC
			India
			Australia
			Peru
	In preparation	ASEAN+3	Canada
		ASEAN+6	
China	Concluded		
	(entered into force)	China–ASEAN (Goods)	
		China–Hong Kong	
		China–Macau	
		China–ASEAN (Services)	
		China–Singapore	

Table 11.1   (continued)

	Within the region	Outside the region
Under negotiation		Australia
		GCC
		Iceland
		Norway
		South Africa
In preparation	Korea	India
	Peru	Costa Rica
	ASEAN+3	
	ASEAN+6	

Sources: Ministry of Foreign Affairs and Trade; Korea, Ministry of Economy, Trade and Industry, Japan; and WTO RTA Database.

US in East Asian affairs and the power rivalry between Japan and China. ASEAN is leading the integration process politically.

11.2.1   United States

In East Asia, the US has been the sole hegemon for a long time and has tended to be continuously involved in East Asian matters. Whenever its leadership was challenged by Asian regionalism, the US strongly opposed Asia-only initiatives and supported alternatives that enabled continuing US involvement. When the Malaysian Prime Minister, Mahatir, proposed the East Asian Economic Group, the US blocked it because it would lead to an Asia-only grouping. To counter this movement, the US tried to strengthen its control over the region through the institutionalization of APEC, that is, through the elevation of the APEC forum to a summit level.[4] Also, when an AMF was proposed, Bergsten (1998) countered that proposal by an APMF (Asia Pacific Monetary Fund), to include the US and several other countries.

However, the US has shown an inconsistent and ambiguous interest in Asia-Pacific cooperation. While participating in APEC, the US formed an exclusive bloc in NAFTA. The US is now considering promoting a Trans-Pacific Partnership (TPP). Such simultaneous involvement in several regional arrangements, whose particularities are different from each other and whose interests often conflict with each other, has resulted in policy drift in the US and has caused APEC to lapse into ineffectiveness. Although it rhetorically coined the phrase a 'new Pacific community', the US was becoming increasingly more inward-looking in the post Cold-War era, giving priority to domestic problems and becoming less enthusiastic

BOX 11.1   REGIONAL AND TRANS-REGIONAL FORUMS IN EAST ASIA

In East Asia, ASEAN is so far the sole 'Asia-only' regional institution. ASEAN, established in 1967 by five founding members, is the oldest among the regional forums in East Asia. ASEAN was initially set up as a political institution preoccupied with security matters in defence of democracy during the Cold War. Economic considerations later grew to predominate in many respects, in response to which the Group of ASEAN Economic Ministers was eventually established. Since its birth, ASEAN has nurtured regional cooperation, while maintaining the principle of non-interference in national affairs. It took steps to admit the remaining five countries in South-East Asia, making it a ten-member association. In 1992, the ASEAN Free Trade Area (AFTA) was established, and in 1998, ASEAN established a regional surveillance mechanism to promote collaboration in macroeconomic policy. It now constitutes a large group of economies, consisting of 525 million people and a total GDP of US$580 billion.

In contrast, both APEC (Asia-Pacific Economic Cooperation) and ASEM (Asia–Europe Meeting) are trans-regional forums. APEC was founded in 1989, incorporating 18 economies in the Asia and Pacific region under the idea of open regionalism. Even though the objectives of APEC cover comprehensive cooperation in general, financial cooperation was not a main agenda item even during the Asian financial crisis. In fact, the original aim of the APEC was to promote cooperation on trade and investment issues. Consequently, regional monetary and financial arrangements were never a theme of major interest for the APEC Finance Ministers' Meetings. It was in November 1997 that APEC touched on regional surveillance for the first time, strongly endorsing the Manila framework as a constructive step towards enhancing cooperation to promote financial stability. In September 1999, it reaffirmed the value of peer surveillance within APEC economies and the benefits to be derived from greater cooperative efforts at micro-level, particularly in financial and capital markets. However, the agenda of the APEC Finance Ministers' Meetings was confined up to that point to financial market development issues, such as enhancing financial supervision, developing bond markets and strengthening corporate governance. This might be due to the scepticism levied by the US against Asia-only regional arrangements. Indeed, there has been antagonism between East Asian (South-East Asians, China and Japan), and Anglo-Saxon member states (Australia, Canada and the US) within APEC.[2] While East Asian countries had been emphasizing economic cooperation, Anglo-Saxon countries focused on economic liberalization.

In contrast, ASEM, a European version of APEC, was originally designed to provide a gathering place for strengthening the partnership between Asia and Europe. The ASEM Finance Ministers' Meeting was established in September 1997, just after the Thai crisis. Starting in 2002, the meeting is held annually. Although the main goal of ASEM is to promote inter-regional cooperation between East Asia and Europe, it has the potential to provide a value-added contribution to monetary integration in East Asia. Indeed, ASEM addresses East Asian monetary and financial integration issues more liberally than APEC. For instance, at their meeting in January 2001, the ASEM Finance Ministers discussed many cooperative activities in economic and financial areas, such as sharing experiences and lessons in fostering regional economic and monetary cooperation, exchange rate regimes and public debt management.[3]

about working with East Asian countries. When the US was preoccupied with NAFTA while supposedly attending to APEC and 'when the US opted out of the initial support package for Thailand, thereby weakening its credibility and enhancing the prospect of subsequent contagion' (Bergsten, 2000), East Asian countries' suspicion of US commitment to Asia-Pacific cooperation was validated.[5] While an associated element in Europe's integration has strong support from the US, it is not likely that the US will support East Asian regionalism.

Nevertheless, ASEAN+3 was established as the basic framework for any regional institutional arrangements and community-building in East Asia, and after the 1997 crisis there has been continuing debate over the appropriate membership of the region-wide arrangement. Given the nature of the open regionalism in East Asia, however, there is little reason why the US should continue to be so censorious. A regional framework would not be harmful to the US either, especially if it could successfully engage China in regional cooperation (Martin, 2007). For these reasons there seems to be some change in the recent attitude of the US.

11.2.2   Japan and China

The most serious challenge to East Asian regionalism comes from the Asian side arising from the competition for leadership between Japan and China. Japan led the Asian miracle and set the stage for economic expansion in East Asia. Japan was the primary source of capital, technology, aid and markets for the regional economy, replacing the US as the dominant financial power in the 1980s. Even though it has been a major player, however, Japan has neither played the leadership role in presiding over the institutionalization of regional monetary cooperation nor has it been accepted as the leader by the rest of East Asia. Japan's lack of success in converting economic clout into political leadership is attributed to two features of Japan's attitude towards regional (monetary) cooperation: its bewildering Asian–Western dual national identity and its unwillingness to bear the leader's burden.

First, since the mid-nineteenth century, Japan's identity has been predicated upon the perplexing dilemma posed by its often conflicting orientations towards the West and the East. The Japanese attempt to construct a new sense of national identity was centred on reinterpreting its position between Asia and the West and rendered Asia as something to be dissociated from. On the one hand, this effort succeeded, in that Japan became the only Asian country among the world-leading economic powers and challenged China's long hegemony in East Asia. On the other hand, this Janus identity has created problematic legacies in Japan. One legacy is that Japan has always wanted the involvement of Western countries such as the US in East Asian regional matters. It may be because Japan has thought that its main role is a mediator between the West and Asia or because it thought that overcoming China's dominance in the region would be difficult without Western countries' (US) presence. Another legacy is that Japan's attitude has made East Asian countries suspect that it is more concerned with relations with countries outside the region than with regional members: when there is conflict between the two relations, Japan has consistently declined an involvement in regional initiatives.

Second, with the expansion of economic power, Japan has made efforts to have the yen play a more important role in the international monetary arena. An example of this is the drive for the internationalization of the yen in the 1980s, which failed in spite of the fact that the Japanese economy was at its peak at that time and many observers predicted Japan would be the next hegemon challenging the US.[6] Among others, two main fears were behind the failure. One is that Japan feared that internationalization of the yen could lead domestic monetary policy to be influenced by external matters. Japan was loath to have internal matters interfered with by external matters. The other fear was that internationalization of the yen might require Japan to import more from East Asian countries in order to supply yen to the region, which would reduce current account surpluses on a large scale. Japan was not yet ready to accept this burden as a leader.

These features of Japan's attitude have often been reflected in Japan's proposals on regional monetary cooperation. The Asian currency crisis of 1997 provided a great opportunity for discussing a permanent monetary institution within Asia and in this context Japan proposed an AMF. But after the idea was shot down by strong opposition from the IMF and the US out of their fears that it could undermine their leadership roles in the region, Japanese Finance Minister Miyazawa made a variant of the proposal, known as 'the Miyazawa Plan' in 1998. But this proposal was limited in that it was meant to do nothing but provide a limited amount of dollar funds to Asian countries. It did not require Japan to play the role of lender of last resort as Germany did within the EMS. The simple provision of dollar funds, the total amount of which was limited to $30 billion, was totally insufficient for other Asian countries to cope with the currency crisis. If Japan is genuinely interested in taking a leadership role in regional monetary cooperation, it must use the yen as an intervention currency to be ready to provide whatever amount of emergency yen is needed, and not solely a fixed amount of dollars, to defend against speculative attacks on neighbouring Asian countries' currencies. Only if this happens can Japan assume full responsibility as the key currency country in Asia and play the same kind of role that Germany did in Europe.[7]

The action that Japan took in the recent Asian crisis also made its willingness to take leadership responsibility doubtful. Japan did not play the part that it was expected to play but in fact exacerbated the turmoil in the region. Japanese banks were blamed for prompting the Korean crisis by withdrawing their funds altogether and not rolling over short-term debts. Also, it is believed that if Japan had provided Thailand with US$10 billion rather than US$4 billion initially, investors might have viewed Japan as a strong regional leader capable of altering outcomes in the region (Hale, 1998).[8] At the EMEAP, it was agreed that the Bank of Japan would provide emergency loans in yen to neighbouring Asian central banks with Japanese government bonds as collateral if they came under heavy speculative attacks. If they held a large amount of Japanese government bonds, then emergency loans with the bond collaterals would be effective. It is uncertain, however, if this agreement would be really effective given other countries' current meagre holdings of Japanese government bonds. The holding of Japanese bonds is limited because the Japanese financial market is regulated and underdeveloped,[9] and, as was seen in the Asian crisis, such a measure did not work at all.

The Chiang Mai Initiative also tried to provide a defence against attacks through swap arrangements between East Asian countries. However, the amounts to be swapped are limited, and hence are unlikely to be commensurate with the amounts that markets can mobilize; no one plays the lender of last resort. What is worse is that two (the dollar and the euro) of the three currencies against which the participating countries will seek to stabilize are not in the arrangement. The participating central banks cannot print those currencies, and to prevent weak regional currencies from depreciating against them, they will be forced to deplete their reserves. This contrasts with the EMS, where the German Bundesbank took the role of lender of last resort and the parity grid was defined exclusively in terms of participating currencies (Eichengreen, 2001, pp.62–3).

It is clear that the economic problems of East Asian countries will not be resolved unless Japan takes a more active role in the region. But Japan has been reluctant to take responsibility for the growth and stability of the East Asian region. Leadership is often assigned to the benevolent hegemon that bears the disproportionate costs of sustaining a liberal international economic order and providing the public goods of monetary stability and free trade (Deng, 1997, p.51). Japan's ambivalence towards regional monetary cooperation and its avoidance of bearing any burden of providing public goods deligitimizes the leadership that many observers have assigned to Japan on the basis of its economic power.

Consequently, it now seems that Japan's opportunity to provide leadership may have passed and that China's turn is coming. But the time for China's leadership in the region has not yet arrived. After the PRC's creation in 1949, China held a negative attitude towards regional economic cooperation. On the one hand, it was because the Chinese had been locked into the Maoist ideology, and on the other hand it was because proposals for regional economic cooperation, almost all of which limited membership to capitalist countries, seemed to have an underlying strategic purpose to strengthen the regional economic basis against communism.[10] Even after the start of the 'Reform and Opening-up' programme under Deng Xiaoping, China maintained a lukewarm attitude towards regional economic and monetary cooperation. Although the fear of a 'pretext for and façade of imperialist domination and exploitation' disappeared, the primary concern of the reformist Chinese government was economic development through exports and resolution of domestic problems, such as unemployment and economic disparity between urban and rural areas – side-effects of China's rapid economic growth. Thus, China paid more attention individually to the US as a main market and to Japan as a main capital provider rather than to the regional economy.

China's attitude towards regional economic and monetary cooperation began to change in the late 1980s. Since the 1990s, China has shown great interest in and support for regional economic cooperation. For example, China positively supported the idea of the EAEG (later the EAEC) from the beginning, hosted the Pacific Economic Cooperation Council (PECC) in 1993 and APEC in 2001, and is now supportive of the AMF idea, which China initially rejected in 1997. The most fundamental reason behind this change is that as East Asian economies have expanded quickly, regional trade and investment have accounted for a larger share of Chinese international trade and investment and have become more important for the continuing growth of its economy. Another reason is that as its economy has grown to be the second largest in the world (in purchasing power terms) and the Japanese economy has continuously declined, China seems to be convinced that it can be the main actor in the regional economy.

Although the Chinese economy is certain to keep growing in the future and its political clout is the strongest among East Asian countries, there are still constraints to China's leadership role in regional monetary integration for several reasons. First, China is not yet developed enough to undertake the burden of sustaining and providing stable international economic and monetary order. China has much interest in regional economic and monetary cooperation, mainly because cooperation is helpful for its own economic expansion, which is pivotal for resolving its domestic problems. If China behaving as a regional leader is detrimental to its domestic economy, it is not certain that it will still be willing to bear the disproportionate costs accompanying the maintenance of stable regional economic and monetary order.

Second, although China has been transformed into a more market-oriented economy, it is still a highly authoritarian communist regime. International cooperation takes place when the policies actually followed by one government are regarded by its partners as facilitating realization of their own objectives as a result of policy coordination (Keohane, 1984, pp.51–2). It is not certain, however, that the Chinese economic system would provide policies that would lead to mutual benefits. For example, China's avoidance of the Asian crisis is attributed to its capital controls policy, and it has been suggested that following this policy would prevent or overcome a potential crisis. However, capital mobility is now naturally taken as the world's destiny, and capital controls as tight as China's could put the regional economic integration process in peril. Furthermore, it seems unfounded that capital controls protected China from the crisis: since the 1990s, a large share of capital inflow to China has been from foreign direct investment, which is not as mobile as hot money. Meanwhile, international bank loans, which can easily be withdrawn, accounted for much less capital inflow compared to other crisis-stricken countries, including Korea. Thus, it is questionable whether following China's policy would enhance mutual benefits to the countries in the region.

Third, although China has taken pains to allay fears of the Chinese threat, suspicions of China's intentions are growing rather than shrinking, as it steadily expands its economic and military strength, for instance, as witnessed in the South China Sea dispute. Perennial resurrection of such conflicts may lead East Asian countries to outside countries, in particular the US, to resolve internal conflicts (Bergsten, 2000).

No leadership by either Japan or China would suggest a co-leadership or a group leadership in the region. Yet Japan and China are competing for leadership and view each other as rivals more than potential partners. Thus, it will be quite difficult for the two to create the leadership needed to convert the region's desires into reality. Furthermore, their relations with countries outside the region, notably with the US, add further complications to regional monetary integration efforts (Eichengreen, 1997; Bergsten, 2000).

11.2.3 ASEAN

Another potentially big obstacle to integration is the absence of core groups that are really eager to strengthen Asian regionalism. Currently ASEAN has been and is still the central core of Asian regionalism, bringing in neighbouring countries. Inviting the leaders of China, Japan and Korea to their informal Leaders' Meeting in December 1997 for instance, the ASEAN leaders helped to establish the ASEAN+3 framework as the main vehicle for building the regional community. This framework is important in the sense that unlike APEC, it is an Asia-only regional framework including the most important +3 countries. ASEAN is playing a leading role in this regional framework. Although there is a summit meeting for the +3 countries, it is held on the sidelines of the ASEAN+3 annual meeting and it is nothing but an 'annual informal breakfast' (Rathus, 2010). The ASEAN member countries will endeavour to maintain this so-called ASEAN centrality. Nevertheless, there are limits to ASEAN taking a leadership position in developing a true East Asian institution or community.

First of all, ASEAN does not speak with a single voice nor is it a homogeneous entity. Given that it is a group of 10 economically and politically different countries, there can be no strong central leadership. ASEAN is rather a forum, and so far, although there have been many ritualized statements on regional integration issued by ASEAN, action for realizing them has been slow and delayed.

Second and more importantly, ASEAN is an economic dwarf compared to the +3 countries in North-East Asia. ASEAN accounts for only 10 per cent of the region's GDP and 20 per cent of the quota for the CMIM, while the +3 represents 90 per cent of the region's GDP and 80 per cent of the CMIM quota. Most of the ASEAN members except for Singapore are also receiving official development assistance from the +3 countries.

It is needless to say that successful regionalization in East Asia necessitates closer cooperation between the +3 countries, China, Japan and Korea. Rivalry and competition between China and Japan was one reason for slow cooperation among the +3 countries. Obviously, China and Japan have different interests and hence different strategies for economic integration in East Asia. As far as China is concerned, economic integration with the ASEAN members, South Asian and central Asian countries might be more important both economically and geopolitically than financial cooperation or free trade with either Japan or South Korea. While China is a military superpower in the world, it is still a developing economy and has a huge gap to narrow with Japan in terms of technological and industrial development. These differences in the economic and military status of the two countries suggest that, even if they manage to reconcile their troubled memories of the past, they may find it difficult to work together as equal partners for regional integration in East Asia. In fact, ASEAN centrality itself was the result of the coordination failure among the +3 countries.

In that respect, cooperation between the three North-East Asian countries, Japan, Korea and China, will be essential. In fact, without the participation of Japan, China and Korea, any initiative for a regional monetary agreement will not survive. Their economic importance, common cultural heritage and geographical proximity highlight the importance of their cooperation. Moreover, there is an increasing awareness among the three countries about the importance of the stability of the exchange rate between their currencies. China is very sensitive to exchange rate movements between the yuan and the Japanese yen. Korea has always kept a close eye on the exchange rate between the Korean won and the Japanese yen because its industrial structure competes with the Japanese one.

It can be said that the need for regional trade and monetary cooperation at the level of these three countries is greater than at the level of the ASEAN+3 countries. Then why do they show so much interest in ASEAN countries, which are peripheral countries? The main reason might be that direct cooperation between Japan and China is considered implausible, not only by people in the region but also by outside Western observers. No matter what the reason may be, it is clear that Japan will not successfully achieve regional monetary arrangements without the participation of China, and, inversely, China will not do without the collaboration of Japan. Economically speaking, Japan is the natural initiator of such an arrangement but because of past hostility and because of Japan's ambiguous attitude itself, it does not enjoy the necessary trust from possible partner countries. For example, Japan is not clear about its own position, as Yu (2001, p.338) remarked: 'Finally, the Japanese government's attitude toward its own initiation did not help in convincing China of the virtue of the proposed AMF. The Japanese government is not very firm on its own proposal. Whenever the US government raises an objection or reservation, the Japanese government backtracks.' In that respect, Korea might hold the strategic key to helping this idea be realized and can be a natural mediator, given the current rivalry between Japan and China, its geographical location, its economic development stage, and close economic linkage with China and Japan.

Fortunately, in December 2008, Japan held the first trilateral summit meeting between China, Japan and Korea, separate from the ASEAN+3 process, enabling it to acquire its own identity. Then on its third trilateral summit meeting held in Jeju, Korea in 2010, the leaders of the +3 countries agreed to establish a secretariat for the efficient promotion and management of trilateral cooperative projects in Korea. This was the first crucial step towards the institutionalization of the partnership between the +3 countries, which few believed possible. And once this secretariat is in operation, the ASEAN secretariat and CJK secretariat are likely to compete and cooperate to further regional integration in East Asia.

The establishment of the CJK secretariat will contribute to building up a sub-regionalism for North-East Asia in parallel with ASEAN for South-East Asia. More importantly it will serve as a stepping stone for East Asian regionalism given the economic and political importance of the +3 countries in ASEAN+3.

11.3 MISSING IDENTITY

Another important barrier to the successful formation of East Asian monetary cooperation is that East Asian countries do not have a common regional identity. In fact, unlike in Europe, where traditional ideological warfare no longer exists, significant ideological barriers and other barriers to regional integration remain in East Asia. The legacies of colonialism and the Cold War are strong and have a strong negative impact on regional identity. For instance, in South-East Asia, ASEAN has expanded to encompass all ten countries of the sub-region. Nonetheless, the inclusion of Myanmar, Cambodia and Vietnam have scarcely made it a stronger and more united body. In East Asia, China and North Korea remain committed to authoritarianism (if not to communism as such) while the countries around them have embraced more democratic institutions. There are also significant tensions remaining as a legacy of other aspects of twentieth-century history, especially in relation to Japan's record of colonialism and warfare.

In this context it is difficult for East Asia to form a regional identity. Countries in Asia have tended to stick to national sovereignty, reluctant to delegate matters to supranational institutions as is the case in Europe. Thus, as Lawson rightly pointed out, 'whatever form integration will take, it will continue to be mediated by this commitment to sovereignty and its corollary, non-interference in the domestic affairs of a state, for the foreseeable future' (Lawson, 2005).

In the recent past there was a new movement in East Asia to assert common Asian values and cultures. While pre-war pan-Asianism focused on the idea of a struggle for political liberation from Western imperialism and on the hierarchical order of dominance and domination, this new Asianism is based on equal partnership and on the concept of an underlying set of shared cultural values. As in the case of Europe, the values are supposed to give a distinctive character to both the political and the economic destiny (Lawson, 2005).

In this regard it is essential that East Asian countries should have similar standards of living. Wide income differences among East Asian countries prevent them from nurturing necessary regional solidarity and thereby strengthening regional identity. The first step required seems to be to encourage voluntary efforts toward reducing regional economic and social disparities, especially the differences in per capita income in the region. On the theoretical and empirical level, there is no proof that economic integration necessarily leads to the convergence of economic performances across member nations. Some studies suggest rather that the opposite is true (for example, Krugman, 1993; Hanson, 1998).

It is then natural that the economic convergence must be the final goal of economic integration. This is especially true in the case of Europe. It was initially considered that through the removal of barriers to trade of commodities and capital, the factors of production would be redistributed to the different regions and used in their most efficient way, stimulating a convergence of incomes. Nevertheless, there was strong evidence that even the founders of the EU did not believe that the free market alone would bring about such a convergence.[11] In addition, the implementation of common policies (agricultural, regional and social) by the EU right after its successful launch in 1958 suggests already the need for common action in favour of solidarity, that is, correcting disparities across regions. In fact, in the case of Europe, even the idea of a 'Community', let alone a 'Union' already implied some kind of solidarity (Pelkmans, 1997).

BOX 11.2   ADB'S ROLE AND LIMIT

As the only regional development bank, the Asian Development Bank (ADB) comprises 61 member governments and was founded in 1966. It extends loans and equity investments for economic and social development, provides technical assistance to development projects and promotes the investment of public and private capital for development. The idea of establishing the ADB began in Japan in the early 1960s. The US was initially reluctant to accept the proposal on the grounds that the new development bank would unnecessarily duplicate efforts and compete with the World Bank. However, the aspirations of the countries in Asia after the colonial period towards greater regional cooperation and the US geopolitical strategy during the Cold War enabled the ADB to become a reality (Culpeper, 1994). The ADB began operation in December 1966 after three years of discussions initiated by the UN Economic Commission for Asia and the Far East, with 31 member countries including 14 non-regional members.

ADB's primary role is to reduce poverty in the Asia-Pacific region. It aims to improve the quality of people's lives by providing loans and technical assistance for a broad range of economic and social development activities. ADB focuses on poverty reduction, emphasizing the promotion of poorer regions, sustainable economic growth, social development, and good governance. Initially, the functions of the ADB were more narrowly focused on economic issues, such as fostering economic growth and cooperation. It lends to governments and to public and private enterprises in its developing member countries. ADB's principal tools are loans and technical assistance, which are provided to governments for specific, high-priority development projects and programmes. ADB's lending both supports and promotes investment for development based on a country's priorities. However, it seems that the specific goal of building solidarity by reducing the inter-regional income gap was never given proper recognition by the ADB. Rather, the focus of the ADB was put on general philanthropic purposes such as helping poor people and regions.[12]

As explained, East Asia is currently too diverse and underdeveloped for integration. Considering this, can the ADB cope with the widening income disparity? If some Asian countries want to form some kind of regional arrangement and thereby to accelerate regional integration, is the ADB capable of helping the possible member countries reduce the income gap between them?

The ADB is not likely to be capable of fulfilling this task because its functions are too widely defined and its membership too broad. First, the current objective of the ADB is not to directly reduce inter-regional income disparities but rather to help poor people and regions. Even though the two objectives are related, it is clear that balancing out living conditions across the region cannot be considered the final objective of the ADB. Also, the ADB is now accumulating different tasks, including short-term crisis prevention, as well as proper long-term development financing, although these are quite distinct tasks. It seems that even the founding fathers of the Bretton Woods System were well aware of their distinctive roles because the IBRD was conceived as an essential sister institution of the IMF. In so far as the IMF was charged solely with providing short-term credit facilities in temporary illiquid situations, it was clear that this goal must be supplemented by an institution providing long-term development loans and assistance to address structural and development issues.

Second, the member countries are too numerous and too different to form a unified regional identity. ADB assistance is destined for 43 Asia-Pacific countries overlapping with different cultures (Indian, Chinese and Muslim). It means that there are limits to its ability to strengthen solidarity among members. It will be very difficult to bring all these countries together for regional cooperation.

Thirdly, the ADB is restricted in its ability to support sub-regional cooperation when non-ADB member countries are involved, since it is barred from providing direct assistance to non-member countries. Furthermore, a commitment to ensuring a balanced distribution of financial resources among members also hinders the ADB from fully addressing the interests of any one particular sub-region.

This suggests that there is a need to further divide the functions assumed by the current ADB and, if possible, to set up sub-regional or other institutions that focus on more specific goals. There should be no problem of institutional duplication between any new future institutions and the ADB here, as was the case with an AMF vis-à-vis the IMF. In the case of Europe, there was also no duplication of roles between institutions. Different institutions can coexist. For instance, in addition to the Structural and Cohesion Funds managed through the EU budget, there are several institutions with different goals. The European Investment Bank (EIB) was established under the European Community Law to further European integration by reducing the development gap across different regions. It nourishes economic and social cohesion within the European Union, channelling its lending towards those areas lagging behind in development. Also, there is a sub-regional Nordic investment bank with the role of supporting economic cooperation among the Nordic countries, and the Council of Europe Development Bank with an exclusively social goal. Thus, the case of Europe suggests that in East Asia, functionally specific or sub-regional development institutions can be created apart from and in addition to the ADB.

Since wide income divergences may cause tensions, it is necessary to achieve a minimum equity standard across the region. Currently, there is only one multilateral development bank in Asia. The existing ADB has played a role in helping poor regions and countries, thereby reducing poverty. However, its role is very limited in achieving the necessary income convergence among East Asian countries.

NOTES

1. For more details, see the ADB FTA Database at the Asian regional integration center (ARIC) at www.aric.adb.org.
2. This explains why the EAEC proposed by Malaysian Prime Minister Mahathir Mohammad in 1990 to form a regional bloc involving ASEAN, Japan, China and South Korea is as yet only on paper. The US strongly opposes this Asia-only idea and Japan is reluctant to give it much support.
3. A large number of studies under the Kobe project were undertaken by institutions/individuals in Asia and Europe to further enhance monetary and financial cooperation in the Asian region.
4. While many East Asian countries preferred APEC to be a loose, consultative forum based on consensus, the US preferred a more structured and contractual approach. Deng (1997, pp.41–3).
5. It is well known that the US showed a different attitude towards the Mexican crisis in 1995 than towards the Asian crisis in 1997.
6. Lester Thurow (1992) even predicted that the 'producer economics' of Japan would defeat the 'consumer economics' of the United States.
7. In this vein, Japan's proposals for regional monetary cooperation after the crisis such as the creation of an AMF, the Miyazawa and Obuchi plans, were not much appreciated

but were regarded as serving Japan's own interests: first, Japan wanted to keep its hegemonic position in the region by diluting criticism that it triggered and extended the Asian currency crisis; second, as the world economy was polarized into the dollar and euro blocs, Japan felt increasingly isolated and feared that the yen would lose its international currency role in the international monetary scene (Eichengreen, 2002).

8. In contrast, China indicated that it was concerned with the regional economy during the crisis period, regardless of her real intention. During the crisis, the Chinese government openly said that it would not devalue the yuan for the sake of the regional economy. At that time, China's external balance was in good shape and devaluation of the yuan was not needed. Also, if other East Asian countries had depreciated their currencies following China, it would certainly have had negative repercussions for China. Although the Chinese government refrained from devaluing the yuan, it was not because it cared about the regional economy but because it would have received little benefit and would have hurt the reputation of Premier Zhu Rongi, both at home and abroad (Kwan, 1998, p.20). China's abstaining from devaluing the yuan was welcomed by many as an effort to prevent the crisis from spreading further.

9. Yoon (1999) also said that 'considering the importance of Japan, it is particularly urgent for that country to liberalize its economy. . . The liberalization process will also provide Japan with a foundation to lead Asian monetary and financial relations.'

10. In fact, Japan's proposals such as a Pacific Free Trade Area, and a Pacific Basic Economic Council all limited membership only to the capitalist economies and Western industrialized countries at that time.

11. The preamble of the Treaty of Rome, for instance, mentions 'harmonious development' as one of its economic objectives.

12. The Charter establishing the Asian Development Bank (ADB) mandates the ADB to foster economic growth and cooperation in the Asia and Pacific region, and to accelerate the economic development of the developing member countries in the region, collectively and individually.

Bibliography

Aizenman, Joshua and Jaewoo Lee (2005), 'International reserves: pre-cautionary vs. mercantilist views, theory and evidence', IMF working paper no. 05/198.

Aizenman, Joshua and Nancy Marion (2002), 'The high demand for international reserves in the Far East: what's going on?', NBER working paper no. 9266.

Aizenman, Joshua and Brian Pinto (2011), 'Managing financial integration and capital mobility: policy lessons from the past two decades', World Bank Policy research working paper no. 5786.

Akamatsu, Kaname (1962), 'A historical pattern of economic growth in developing countries', *Journal of Developing Economies*, **1**(1), 3–25.

Amyx, Jennifer A. (2004), 'A regional bond market for East Asia? The evolving political dynamics of regional financial cooperation', Australia-Japan Research Centre Pacific Economic Papers, no. 342.

Ando, Mitsuyo and Fukunari Kimura (2003), 'The formation of international production and distribution networks in East Asia', NBER working paper no. 10167, December.

Arner, Douglas, Paul Lejot and S. Ghon Rhee (2005), *Impediments to Cross-Border Investments in Asian Bonds*, Singapore: PECC Finance Forum.

Asia Development Bank (2010), *Institutions for Asian Integration: Toward an Asian Community*, Manila: ADB.

Bae, Yeung Mok (1990), 'A study on money and banking during the colonial period in Korea', PhD thesis, Seoul National University, in Korean.

Baek, Seung-Gwan and Chi-Young Song (2002), 'Is currency union a feasible option in East Asia?', in Han-Kwang Chu and Yungjong Wang (eds), *Currency Union in East Asia*, Seoul: KIEP, pp.107–46.

Bank of Japan (1970), *Nihonkinyushisiryo, Showa Period*, vol. 27, in Japanese.

Banyai, Richard A. (1974), *Money and Banking in China and Southeast Asia During the Japanese Military Occupation, 1937–1945*, Taipei: Taiwan Enterprise Co.

Bark, T. and Y.S. Rhee (2010), 'The G20: from Seoul to Paris and beyond', paper presented at the GSIS-GEM conference on Korea and Europe: at the crossroads, Sciences Po, GEM Policy Brief, 18–19 October, Paris.

Barrett, Ward (1990), 'World bullion flows, 1450–1800', in J. Tracy (ed.), *The Rise of Merchant Empires: Long-Distance Trade in the Early Modern World 1350–1750*, Cambridge, UK: Cambridge University Press.

Barro, Robert (2001), 'Currency unions', mimeo, Harvard University.

Barro, Robert and David B. Gordon (1984), 'Rules, discretion and reputation in a model of monetary policy', NBER working paper no. 1079.

Bayoumi, T., Barry Eichengreen and P. Mauro (2000), 'On regional monetary arrangements for ASEAN', *Journal of the Japanese and International Economies*, **14**, 121–48.

Bergsten, C. Fred (1997), 'The impact of the Euro on exchange rates and international policy cooperation', paper presented at the IMF–Camille Gutt Conference on EMU and the International Monetary System, 17–18 March, Washington, DC.

Bergsten, C. Fred (1998), 'Reviving the "Asian Monetary Fund"', Policy brief no. 98-8, November, Peterson Institute for International Economics.

Bergsten, C. Fred (2000), 'The new Asian challenge', Institute for International Economics policy brief no. 00-4.

Bergsten, C. Fred and Yung Chul Park (2002), 'Toward creating a regional monetary arrangement in East Asia', ADB Institute research paper no. 50.

Boxer, Charles R. (1969), *The Portuguese Seaborne Empire, 1415–1825*, New York: Alfred A. Knopf.

Calvo, Guillermo A. and Carmen M. Reinhart (2002), 'Fear of floating', *Quarterly Journal of Economics*, **117**(2).

Capannelli, Giovanni, Jong-Wha Lee and Peter Petri (2009), *Developing Indicators for Regional Economic Integration and Cooperation*, Manila: ADB.

Chai, Hee-Yul and Yeongseop Rhee (2003a), 'Financial and monetary cooperation in East Asia in light of the European experience', *Asia-Pacific Journal of EU Studies*, **3**(1), Winter.

Chai, Hee-Yul and Yeongseop Rhee (2003b), 'Financial integration in East Asia: a comparison with Europe', in H. Kim (ed.), *European Integration and the Asia-Pacific Region*, Seoul: KIEP.

Chai, Hee-Yul and Yeongseop Rhee (2005), 'Financial integration and financial efficiency in East Asia', paper presented at the 3rd Korea-Italy Conference, Turin University, June.

Chai, Hee-Yul, Woosik Moon, Yeongseop Rhee and Deok-Ryong Yoon (2008), 'Measures for possible use of regional monetary units for surveillance and transaction', paper presented at the ASEAN+3 Research Group Meeting, Vietnam, accessed at www.asean.org/22633-6.pdf.

Chaipravat, Olarn (2002), 'Regional resource provision arrangements for enhanced monetary and financial cooperation in East Asia', prepared for Kobe Research Project based on technical assistance on 'Study on Monetary and Financial Cooperation in East Asia'.

Choi, Dong-Soo (2004), 'Developing bond markets in Asia, the role of credit enhancement and lessons from Korea's experience', paper presented at the ABAC/PECC Conference on Developing Bond Markets in APEC: Moving Forward through Public–Private Sector Partnership, 10–11 May, Taipei.

Chow, H.K. and Y. Kim (2003), 'A common currency peg in East Asia? Perspectives from Western Europe', *Journal of Macroeconomics*, **25**, 331–50.

CIA (Central Intelligence Agency), (various issues), *World Factbook*.

Cohen, Benjamin J. (2000), 'Monetary governance in a world of regional currencies', mimeo, University of California, Santa Barbara.

Collignon, Stefan (1994), *Europe's Monetary Future (Volume I)*, London: Pinter Publishers.

Council on Foreign Exchange and Other Transactions (1999), 'Internationalization of the Yen for the 21st century', Minister of Finance, Japan, 20 April, accessed at: http://www.mof.go.jp/english/about_mof/councils/customs_foreign_exchange/e1b064a.htm.

Culpeper, R. (1994), 'The regional development banks: exploiting their specificity', *Third World Quarterly*, **15**(3), 459–82.

Curtis, Bronwyn (1998), 'Now more than ever: the case for an Asian Yen zone', *The International Economy*, January/February.

Daiwa Institute of Research (2005), 'Trade, investment and financial integration in East Asia', accessed at: www.aseansec.org/17898.pdf.

Davis, Glyn (2002), *A History of Money from Ancient Times to the Present Day*, 3rd edn, Cardiff: University of Wales Press.

De Brouwer, Gordon (1999), *Financial Integration in East Asia*, Cambridge: Cambridge University Press.

De Grauwe, Paul (1997), *The Economics of Monetary Integration*, Oxford: Oxford University Press.

De Grauwe, Paul and Theo Peters (1978), 'The European monetary system after Bremen: technical and conceptual problems', International Economics Research Paper, 17, September, Centrum voor Economische Studien, Katholieke Universiteit Leuven.

Deng, Yong (1997), *Promoting Asia-Pacific Economic Cooperation: Perspectives from East Asia*, New York: St. Martin's Press.

Drake, Peter J. (2004), *Currency, Credit and Commerce: Early Growth in Southeast Asia*, Aldershot: Ashgate.

ESCAP (1998), *Economic and Social Survey of Asia and the Pacific 1998*, UN-ESCAP.

Eichengreen, Barry (1997), 'International monetary arrangements: is there a monetary union in Asia's future?', *Brookings Review*, **15**, March, 33–5.

Eichengreen, Barry (2001), 'Hanging together? On monetary and financial cooperation in Asia', mimeo, University of California, Berkeley.

Eichengreen, Barry (2002), 'Whither monetary and financial coopera-tion in East Asia', paper presented at the 2002 PECC Finance Forum Meeting, 11–13 August, Honolulu.

Eichengreen, Barry (2005), 'Real and pseudo preconditions for an Asian monetary union', in ADB (ed.), *Asian Economic Cooperation and Integration: Progress, Prospects, and Challenges*, Ch.8, Manila: ADB.

Eichengreen, Barry (2007), 'Fostering monetary and exchange rate coop-eration in East Asia', paper presented at the conference on Options for Monetary Exchange Rate Cooperation in Asia, organized by the North-East Asia Research Foundation (EAMC Forum), 23 August, Seoul.

Eichengreen, Barry and Tamim A. Bayoumi (1999), 'Is Asia an optimum currency area? Can it become one? Regional, global and historical perspectives on Asian monetary relations', in S. Collignon and J. Pisani-Ferry (eds), *Exchange Rate Policies in Emerging Asian Countries: Domestic and International Aspects*, London: Routledge.

Eichengreen, Barry and Ricardo Hausmann (1999), 'Exchange rates and financial fragility', NBER working paper no. 7418.

Eichengreen, Barry and Yung Chul Park (2003), 'Why has there been less financial integration in Asia than in Europe?', mimeo, University of California, Berkeley, Institute of European Studies.

Eichengreen, Barry and Yung Chul Park (2006), 'Global imbalances: implications for emerging Asia and Latin America', University of California, Berkeley, accessed at www.econ.berkeley.edu/~eichengr/policy/global_imbalances.pdf.

Eichengreen, Barry, Ricardo Hausmann and Ugo Panizza (2002), 'Original sin: the pain, the mystery, and the road to redemption', paper presented at the conference on Currency and Maturity Matchmaking: Redeeming Debt from Original Sin, Inter-American Development Bank, November, Washington, DC.

EMEAP (2006), 'Review of the Asian bond fund 2 initiative, working group on financial markets', June, accessed at www.emeap.org/emeapdb/upload/WGMeeting/ABF2ReviewReport.pdf.

Emerson, Michael, Daniel Gros, Alexander Italianer, Jean Pisani-Ferry and Horst Reichenbach (1992), *One Market, One Money: An Evaluation of the Potential Benefits and Costs of Forming an Economic and Monetary Union*, New York: Oxford University Press.

Feldstein, Martin (1997), 'The political economy of the European economic and monetary union: political sources of an economic liability', *Journal of Economic Perspectives*, **11**(4), 23–42.

Feldstein, Martin (1998), 'Refocusing the IMF', *Foreign Affairs*, **77** (March/April), 20–33.

Feldstein, Martin (1999), 'Self-protection for emerging market economies', NBER working paper no. 6907.

Findlay, Ronald E. (1996), 'The emergence of the world economy: towards a historical perspective 1000–1750', Columbia University economics discussion paper no. 9596-08.

Findlay, Ronald E. and Kevin H. O'Rourke (2001), 'Commodity market integration, 1500–2000', NBER working paper no. 8579.

Flynn, Dennis O. and Arturo Giráldez (1995), 'Born with a silver spoon: the origin of world trade in 1571', *Journal of World History*, **6**, 201–21.

Flynn, Dennis O. and Arturo Giráldez (2002), 'Cycles of silver: global economic unity through the mid-eighteenth century', *Journal of World History*, **13**(2), 391–427.

Flynn, Dennis O., Arturo Giráldez and Richard von Glahn (2003), *Global Connections and Monetary History, 1470–1800*, Aldershot: Ashgate.

Frank, Andre Gunder (1998), *ReOrient: Global Economy in the Asian Age*, Berkeley, CA: University of California Press.

Frankel, Jeffrey A. (1999), 'No single currency regime is right for all countries or at all times', NBER working paper no. 7338.

Frankel, Jeffrey A. and Andrew K. Rose (1998), 'The endogeneity of the optimum currency area criteria', *Economic Journal*, **108**, 1009–25.

Frankel, Jeffrey A. and Shang-Jin Wei (1994), 'Yen bloc or dollar bloc? Exchange rate policies of the East Asian economies', in Takatoshi Ito and Anne O. Krueger (eds), *Macroeconomic Linkage: Savings, Exchange Rates and Capital Flows*, Chicago, IL: University of Chicago Press.

Frankel, Jeffrey A., Sergio L. Schumukler and Luis Serven (2002), 'Global transmission of interest rates: monetary independence and currency regime', NBER working paper no. 8828.

Fukuda, Hiromasa (2002), 'The theory of optimum currency area: an introductory survey', mimeo, Keio University.

G20 London Summit Committee (2009), *The G20 Final Communique: The London Summit Declaration*, 2 April.

G20 Toronto Summit Committee (2010), *The G-20 Toronto Summit Declaration*, 26–27 June.

Gao, Haihong and Yongding Yu (2009), 'Internationalization of the Renminbi', paper presented at the Bank of Korea-BIS Seminar, 19–20 March, Seoul.

García-Herrero, Alicia, Sergio Gavilá and Daniel Santabárbara (2009), 'What explains the low profitability of Chinese banks?', Banco de España working paper no. 0910.

Gartzke, Erik (2000), 'Preferences and the democratic peace', *International Studies Quarterly*, **44**(2), 191–210.

Gavin, Michael and Ricardo Hausmann (1996), 'The roots of banking crises: the macroeconomic context', Inter-American Development Bank Office of the Chief Economist working paper no. 318.

Genberg, Hans (2006), 'Exchange-rate arrangements and financial integration in East Asia: on a collision course?', *International Economics and Economic Policy*, **3**(3–4), December, 359–77.

Girardin, E. (2005), 'Regime-dependent synchronization of growth cycles between Japan and East Asia', *Asian Economic Papers*, **3**, 147–76.

Goto, Junichi and Koichi Hamada (1994), 'Economic preconditions for Asian regional integration', in Takatoshi Ito and Anne O. Krueger (eds), *Macroeconomic Linkage: Savings, Exchange Rates and Capital Flows*, Chicago, IL: University of Chicago Press.

Goto, Junichi and Koichi Hamada (1995), 'Economic integration and the welfare of those who are left behind: an Asian perspective', RIEB discussion paper series no. 47, Kobe University.

Gros, Daniel and Niels Thygesen (1998), *European Monetary Integration. From the European Monetary System to Economic and Monetary Union*, Harlow and New York: Longman.

Hale, David (1998), 'Hot money debate', *International Economy*, November/December.

Hanson, G.H. (1998), 'North American economic integration and industry location', *Oxford Review of Economic Policy*, **14**(2).

Hao, Yen-P'ing (1986), *The Commercial Revolution in Nineteenth-Century China*, Berkeley, CA: University of California Press.

Hausmann, Ricardo, Ugo Panizza and Ernesto Stein (2001), 'Why do countries float the way they float?', *Journal of Development Economics*, **66**(2), 387–414.

Henning, C. Randall (2002), 'Political economy of East Asian financial cooperation', paper presented at the conference Deepening Financial Arrangements in East Asia, organized by the Japan-Australia Research Centre, Australian National University and China Center for Economic Research, Beijing University, 24 March, Beijing.

Henning, C. Randall (2009), 'The future of the Chiang Mai Initiative:

an Asian monetary fund?', Peterson Institute policy brief no. PB09-5, Washington, DC.

Hiwatari, Nobuhiro (2003), 'Embedded policy preferences and the formation of international arrangements after the Asian financial crisis', *The Pacific Review*, **16**(3), 331–59.

Ho, R.Y.K. and C.S.M. Wong (2003), 'Road map for building the institutional foundation for regional bond market in East Asia', paper presented at the Second Finance Forum of Pacific Economic Cooperation Council, 8–9 July, Hua Hin, Thailand, accessed at www.hkcpec.org/files/f14.pdf.

Hocha, Tobias C. (2005a), 'Developing the market for local currency bonds by foreign issuers: lessons from Asia', Asian Development Bank ERD working paper no. 63.

Hocha, Tobias C. (2005b), 'Local currency financing – the next frontier for MDBs', Asian Development Bank ERD working paper no. 68.

Huff, W. Gregg (2003), 'Monetization and financial development in Southeast Asia before the Second World War', *The Economic History Review*, **56**(2), 300–345.

Huang, Y. and F. Guo (2006), 'Is currency union a feasible option in East Asia? A multivariate structual VAR approach', *Research in International Business and Finance*, **20**, 77–94.

Hughes, Christopher W. (1999), 'Japanese policy and the East Asian currency crisis: abject defeat or quiet victory?', CSGR working paper no. 24/99, February, accessed at http://wrap.warwick.ac.uk/2101/1/WRAP_hughes_wp2499.pdf.

Hyun, Suk and Hong Bum Jang (2008), 'Bond market development in Asia', ESCAP and Bank of Korea.

IMF (2008), 'US financial crisis: IMF head urges greater regulation of financial sector', IMF Survey Online Magazine, 29 September, accessed at www.imf.org/external/pubs/ft/survey/so/2008/new092908a.htm.

IMF (2010), *Regional Economic Outlook: Asia and Pacific*, Washington, DC: IMF.

IMF (2011), 'Enhancing international monetary stability – a role for the SDR?', paper prepared by the Strategy, Policy, and Review Department, January, accessed at www.imf.org/external/np/pp/eng/2011/010711.pdf.

IMF, various issues, *Annual Report*.

IMF, various issues, *Direction of Trade Statistics*.

IMF, various issues, *International Financial Statistics*.

Ingram, James C. (1971), *Economic Change in Thailand, 1850–1970*, Stanford, CA: Stanford University Press.

Institute for International Monetary Affairs (2000), 'Workshop on the framework for regional monetary stabilisation in East Asia',

IIMA Newsletter no. 6, September, accessed at www.iima.or.jp/pdf/NEWSLETTER2000NO6.pdf.

Institute for International Monetary Affairs (2004), 'Towards a regional financial architecture for East Asia', research papers and policy recommendations commissioned by ASEAN Secretariat, March, accessed at www.mof.go.jp/english/international_policy/convention/asean_plus_3/ASEAN_plus_3research-1-3.pdf.

Institute for International Monetary Affairs (2005), 'Economic surveillance and policy dialogue in East Asia', research papers and policy recommendations commissioned by ASEAN Secretariat, March, accessed at www.asean.org/17890.pdf.

Institute for International Monetary Affairs (2010), 'Ways to promote foreign trade settlements denominated in local currencies in East Asia', research papers and policy recommendations commissioned by ASEAN Secretariat, February, accessed at www.aseansec.org/documents/ASEAN+3RG/0910/FR/16a.pdf.

Institute for International Monetary Affairs (2011), 'Possible use of regional monetary units – identification of issues for practical use', research papers and policy recommendations commissioned by ASEAN Secretariat, February, accessed at www.asean.org/documents/ASEAN+3RG/1011/FR/18a.pdf.

Institute of International Finance (1998), 'Capital flows to emerging market economies', IIF Research Note.

Inukai, Shigehito (2008), *Grand Design for an Asian Inter-regional Professional Securities Market*, Tokyo: LexisNexis.

Ito, Takatoshi (1999), 'Capital flows in Asia', NBER working paper no. 7134, Cambridge, MA.

Ito, Takatoshi (2009), 'Global crisis and exchange rates in East Asia', paper presented at the Weatherhead East Asian Institute, 5 November, Columbia University.

Ito, Takatoshi, Eiji Ogawa and Yuri Nagataki-Sasaki (1998), 'How did the dollar peg fail in Asia?', *Journal of the Japanese and International Economies*, **12**(December), 256–304.

Ito, Takatoshi, Eiji Ogawa and Yuri Nagataki-Sasaki (1999), 'Establishment of the "East Asian Fund"', in Institute for International Monetary Affairs, *Stabilization of Currencies and Financial Systems in East Asia and International Financial Cooperation*, March, Tokyo: Institute for International Monetary Affairs.

Iwao, Seiichi (1976), 'Japanese foreign trade in the 16th and 17th centuries', *Acta Asiatica*, **30**, 1–18.

Jang, Wonchang (2003), 'The present status and future agenda of the Asian bond markets', *Korea Financial Review*, Winter.

Jang, Y. (2011), 'Industrial cooperation in the high technology sector between China, Japan and Korea: current status and challenges', paper presented at China–Japan–Korea Economic and Trade Forum, 29 October, Dailian, China, in Korean.

Japan Ministry of Economy, Trade and Industry (2001), *White Paper on International Trade*, Tokyo.

Japan Ministry of Treasury (1970), *History of Showa Public Finance*, Tokyo in Japanese.

Japan Ministry of Finance, various issues, *Annual Report of the International Finance*, Tokyo.

JETRO (2002), *White Paper on International Trade and Investment*, Tokyo: JETRO.

Jiang, Guorong and Robert Neil McCauley (2004), 'Asian local currency bond markets', *BIS Quarterly Review* (June), 67–79.

Joint Expert Group on EAFTA Phase II Study (2009), 'Desirable and feasible option for an East Asia FTA', June.

Kaplan, Edward (1997), 'Chinese economic history from stone age to Mao's age', mimeo, Bellingham, WA: Western Washington University.

Katzenstein, Peter J. (1996), *The Culture of National Security: Norms and Identity in World Politics*, New York: Columbia University Press.

Katzenstein, Peter J. (2000), 'Regionalism and Asia', *New Political Economy*, **5**(3), November, 353–70.

Kawai, Masahiro (2002), 'Exchange rate arrangements in East Asia: lessons from the 1997–98 currency crisis', Bank of Japan, *Monetary and Economic Studies*, December.

Kawai, Masahiro (2009a), 'Reform of the international financial architecture: an Asian perspective', Asian Development Bank Institute working paper no. 167, Tokyo.

Kawai, Masahiro (2009b), 'An Asian currency unit for regional exchange rate policy coordination', in D.K. Chung and B. Eichengreen (eds), *Fostering Monetary and Financial Cooperation in East Asia*, Singapore: World Scientific.

Kawai, Masahiro and T. Motonishi (2004), 'Is East Asia an optimum currency area?', Policy Research Institute, Ministry of Finance, Japan.

Kawai, Masahiro and Shujiro Urata (1998), 'Are trade and direct investment substitutes or complements? An empirical analysis of Japanese manufacturing industries', in Hiro Lee and David W. Roland-Holst (eds), *Economic Development and Cooperation in the Pacific Basin: Trade, Investment, and Environmental Issues*, Cambridge: Cambridge University Press, pp.251–93.

Kawai, Masahiro and Shujiro Urata (2004), 'Trade and foreign direct investment in East Asia', in Gordon de Brouwer and Masahiro Kawai (eds), *Economic Linkages and Implications for Exchange Rate Regimes in East Asia*, London and New York: Routledge Curzon, pp.15–102.

Kawai, Masahiro and Cindy Houser (2007), 'Evolving ASEAN+3 ERPD: towards peer reviews or due diligence?', Asian Development Bank Institute discussion paper no. 79, September, Tokyo.

Kawai, Masahiro and Ganeshan Wignaraja (2007), 'ASEAN+3 or ASEAN+6: which way forward?', Asian Development Bank Institute discussion paper no. 77, September, Tokyo.

Kawai, Masahiro and Ganeshan Wignaraja (2010), 'Asian FTAs: trends, prospects and challenges', ADB Economics working paper series no. 226, Mandaluyong City, Philippines.

Kenen, Peter (1969), 'The theory of optimum currency areas: an eclectic view', in Robert A. Mundell and Alexander K. Swoboda (eds), *Monetary Problems in the International Economy*, Chicago, IL: University of Chicago Press, pp.41–60.

Keohane, Robert O. (1984), *After Hegemony: Cooperation and Discord in the World Political Economy*, Princeton, NJ: Princeton University Press.

Kim, In June and Yeongseop Rhee (2009), 'Global financial crisis and the Korean economy', *Seoul Journal of Economics*, **22**(2), 1–36.

Kim, In June and Yeongseop Rhee (2010), 'Global financial crisis and East Asian monetary cooperation revisited', in Toyo Keizai, *Frontiers of Modern Economics*, Tokyo: Japanese Economic Association.

Kim, J.H. (1998), 'A study on the currency war during the Sino-Japanese war', PhD thesis, Yonsei University, Seoul, in Korean.

Kim, S.M. (2010), 'IMF reform: immediate agenda and remaining challenges', paper presented at the Korea–Canada–France G20 Seminar, 17–18 September, Seoul.

Kim, Soyoung, Jong-wha Lee and Kwanho Shin (2005), 'Regional and global financial integration in East Asia', mimeo.

King, Frank H.H. (1957), *Money in British East Asia*, London: HM Stationery Office.

Kobata, Atsushi (1965), 'The production and uses of gold and silver in sixteenth- and seventeenth-century Japan', *The Economic History Review*, **18**(2), 245–66.

Kobayashi, Keiko (1975), *The Formation of East Asian Co-prosperity Zone and its Collapse*, Tokyo: Ochanomizushobo, in Japanese.

Kojima, Kiyoshi (1970), 'A Pacific currency area: a new approach to international monetary reform', *Hitotsubashi Journal of Economics*, February, 1–17.

Kojima, Kiyoshi (2000), 'The flying geese model of Asian economic development: origin, theoretical extensions, and regional policy implications', *Journal of Asian Economics*, **11**, 375–401.

Korhonen, Pekka (1994), 'The theory of the flying geese pattern of development and its interpretations', *Journal of Peace Research*, **31**(1), 93–108.

Krugman, Paul (1993), 'Lessons of Massachusetts for EMU', in Francisco Torres and Francesco Giavazzi (eds), *Adjustment and Growth in the European Monetary Union*, London: CEPR.

Krugman, Paul (1998), 'Will Asia bounce back?', mimeo, accessed at http://web.mit.edu/krugman/www/suisse.html.

Krugman, Paul and Maurice Obstfeld (2009), *International Economics*, 8th edn, New York: Addison-Wesley.

Kuroda, Haruhiko (2010), keynote speech, 43rd annual meeting of ADB, Tashkent, Uzbekistan.

Kwak, S.Y. (2004), 'An optimum currency area in East Asia: feasibility, coordination, and leadership role', *Journal of Asian Economics*, **15**, 153–69.

Kwan, Chi Hung (1998), 'The theory of optimum currency areas and the possibility of forming a yen bloc in Asia', *Journal of Asian Economics*, **9**(4).

Kwan, Chi Hung (2001), *Yen Bloc: Toward Economic Integration in Asia*, Washington, DC: Brookings Institution.

Lawson, Stephanie (2005), 'Culture, values and regional integration in Asia: critical reflections on the politics of regional identity', in Woosik Moon and Bernadette Andreosso-O'Callaghan (eds), *Regional Integration: Europe and Asia Compared*, Aldershot: Ashgate.

Lee, John (1999), 'Trade and economy in preindustrial East Asia, c.1500–c.1800: East Asia in the age of global integration', *The Journal of Asian Studies*, **58**(1), 2–26.

Lee, J.W., Y.C. Park and K. Shin (2003), 'A currency union in East Asia', The Institute of Social and Economic Research discussion paper no. 571, Osaka University.

Lee, Kyung Tae and Deok Ryong Yoon (2007), 'A roadmap for East Asian monetary integration: the necessary first step', KIEP working paper no. 07-04, 27–8.

Lee, Sheng-Yi (1990), *The Monetary and Banking Development of Singapore and Malaysia*, 3rd edn, Singapore: Singapore University Press.

Lee, Warren (2003), 'Future applications of securitization in Asia', paper presented at Asian Bond Market Forum organized by The Milken Institute and Asian Institute of International Financial Law, 11–14 November, Hong Kong.

Loayza, N., H. Lopez and A. Ubide (2001), 'Comovements and sectoral interdependence: evidence for Latin America, East Asia, and Europe', IMF staff papers no. 48, 367–96.

Maddison, Angus (1995), *Monitoring the World Economy 1820–1992*, Paris: OECD Development Center.

Martin, Christopher (2007), 'Crafting a US response to the emerging east Asia free trade area', *Whitehead Journal of Diplomacy and International Relations*, **8**(2), Summer/Fall, 73–84.

McCauley, Robert Neil (2003), 'Capital flows in East Asia since the 1997 crisis', *BIS Quarterly Review*, June, 41–55.

McKinnon, Ronald (1963), 'Optimum currency areas', *American Economic Review*, **53**, 717–25.

McKinnon, Ronald (1998), 'Exchange rate coordination for surmounting the East Asian crises', paper presented at the 6th Convention of the East Asian Economic Association, 4–5 September, Kitakyushu, Japan.

McKinnon, Ronald (1999), 'The East Asian dollar standard, life after death?', mimeo, Stanford University.

McKinnon, Ronald (2001), 'After the crisis, the East Asian dollar standard resurrected', paper presented at the international conference on Monetary Outlook on East Asia in an Integrating World Economy, Chulalongkorn University, 5–6 September, Bangkok.

McKinnon, Ronald and Gunther Schnabl (2003), 'The East Asian dollar standard, fear of floating, and original sin', Stanford University Department of Economics working paper no. 03-001.

Miyazawa, Kiichi (1998), speech at the Joint Annual Meeting of the IMF and the World Bank, 6–8 October, Washington DC.

Mohanty, Madhusudan and Philip Turner (2006), 'Foreign exchange reserve accumulation in emerging markets: what are the domestic implications?', *BIS Quarterly Review*, September, 39–52.

Mohanty, Madhusudan and Philip Turner (2010), 'Banks and financial intermediation in emerging Asia: reforms and new risks', Bank for International Settlements working paper no. 313.

Mongelli, Francesco Paolo (2002), 'New views on the optimum currency area theory: what is EMU telling us?', ECB working paper no. 138.

Moon, Woosik (1999), 'Euro–dollar–yen exchange rates and international monetary cooperation', in Cae-One Kim (ed.), *Euro: Changes in International Economic Order and Options for Korea*, Seoul: Parkyoungsa, in Korean.

Moon, Woosik (2001), 'Currency crisis and stock market integration: a comparison of East Asian and European experiences', *Korean Journal of EU Studies*, **8**(1), 41–56.

Moon, Woosik (2009a), 'Financial market integration in East Asia: status and options', Seoul National University, mimeo, July, Seoul.

Moon, Woosik (2009b), 'International synchronization of business cycles', in Deok Ryong Yoon et al. (eds), *Macroeconomic Structure for Stable Economic Growth in Korea*, Ch.3, Seoul: KIEP, in Korean.

Moon, Woosik (2010), 'Whither economic integration in East Asia?', Sciences Po, GEM Policy Brief, 18–19 October, Paris.

Moon, Woosik and Yeongseop Rhee (1999), 'Asian monetary cooperation: lessons from the European monetary integration', *Journal of International and Area Studies*, **6**(1), 33–49.

Moon, Woosik and Yeongseop Rhee (2003), 'Seignorage and sovereignty in monetary union: comparing EMU with AMU', *Journal of International and Area Studies*, **10**(2).

Moon, Woosik and Yeongseop Rhee (2006), 'Spot and forward market intervention operations during the 1997 Korean currency crisis', *Banca Nazionale del Lavaro Quarterly Review*, September, pp.243–68.

Moon, Woosik and Yeongseop Rhee (2007), 'Regional currency unit and exchange rate coordination in East Asia', *Kyoto Economic Review*, **76**(1), June.

Moon, Woosik and Yeongseop Rhee (2009), 'Financial integration and exchange rate coordination in Asia', in B. Eichengreen and D. Chung (eds), *Fostering Monetary and Economic Cooperation in East Asia*, Singapore: World Scientific Publishing Company.

Moon, Woosik, Yeongseop Rhee and Deok Ryong Yoon (2000), 'Asian monetary cooperation: a search for regional monetary stability in the post Euro and the post Asian crisis era', Bank of Korea, *Economic Review*, **3**(1).

Moon, Woosik, Yeongseop Rhee and Deok Ryong Yoon (2005), 'Monetary cooperation in East Asia', in Woosik Moon and Bernadette Andreosso (eds), *Regional Integration: Europe and Asia Compared*, Aldershot: Ashgate.

Moon, Woosik, Yeongseop Rhee and Deok Ryong Yoon (2006), 'Regional currency unit in Asia: property and perspective', KIEP working paper.

Mundell, Robert (1961), 'A theory of optimum currency areas', *American Economic Review*, **51**, 657–65.

Mundell, Robert (2001), 'Currency area formation and the Asian region', paper presented to the international conference on Monetary Outlook on East Asia in an Integrating World Economy, 5–6 September, Chulalongkorn University, Bangkok.

Narine, Suresh S. (2001), 'ASEAN and the idea of an "Asian monetary fund", institutional uncertainty in the Asia-Pacific', in Andrew Tan and J.D. Kenneth Boutin (eds), *Non-Traditional Security Issues in Southeast Asia*, Singapore: Select Publishing, pp.227–56.

Officer, Lawrence H. and Samuel H. Williamson (2011), 'The price of gold, 1257–2011', *Measuring Worth*, accessed at www.measuringworth. com/gold/.

Ogawa, Eiji (2006), 'AMU and AMU deviation indicators', Research Institute of Economy, Trade and Industry, Tokyo.

Ogawa, E. and T. Ito (2000), 'On the desirability of a regional basket currency arrangements', NBER working paper no. w8002.

Ogawa, E. and K. Kawasaki (2006), 'Adopting a common currency basket arrangement into the ASEAN Plus Three', RIETI discussion paper series, 06-E-028.

Ogawa, Eiji and Junko Shimizu (2005), 'A deviation measurement for coordinated exchange rate policies in East Asia', RIETI discussion paper series 05-E-017.

Ogawa, Eiji and Junko Shimizu (2006), 'Progress toward a common currency basket system in East Asia', paper prepared for the 5th Asia Pacific Economic Forum, Kangwon National University, 12 June, Chuncheon, Korea.

Oh, Gyutaeg, Daekeun Park, Jaeha Park and Doo Yong Yang (2003), 'How to mobilize the Asian savings within the region: securitization and credit enhancement for the development of East Asia's bond market', KIEP working paper no. 03-02.

Okita, Sabro (1985), 'Special presentation: prospect of Pacific economies', Korea Development Institute, *Pacific Cooperation: Issues and Opportunities* report of the Fourth Pacific Economic Cooperation Conference, pp.18–29, 29 April–1 May, Seoul, p.21.

Oriental Economist (1942), 'Money and banking', September.

O'Rourke, Kevin H. and Jeffrey G. Williamson (2000), 'When did globalization begin?', NBER working paper no. 7632.

O'Rourke, Kevin H. and Jeffrey G. Williamson (2001), 'After Columbus: explaining the global trade boom 1500–1800', NBER working paper no. 8186.

Ostroy, Jonathan D., Atish R. Ghosh, Karl Habermeier, Marcos Chamon, Mahvash S. Qureshi and Dennis B.S. Reinhardt (2010), 'Capital inflows: the role of controls', IMF staff position note, 19 February.

Park, Young-Joon and Dong-Eun Rhee (2011), 'A quantitative assessment of credit guarantee schemes in Asian bond markets', Korea Institute for International Economic Policy working paper no. 11-07.

Park, Yung-Chul and Daekeun Park (2003), 'Creating regional bond markets in East Asia: rationale and strategy', paper presented at the Second Finance Forum of PECC Issues and Challenges for Regional Financial Cooperation in the Asia-Pacific, 7–10 July, Thailand.

Park, Yung Chul and Yunjong Wang (2002), 'Can East Asia emulate

European economic integration?', Korea Institute for International Economic Policy discussion paper no. 02-09.

Park, Yung-Chul and Charles Wyplosz (2010), *Monetary and Financial Integration in East Asia: The Relevance of European Experience*, Oxford: Oxford University Press.

Pelkmans, Jacques (1997), *European Integration: Methods and Economic Analysis*, Netherlands Open University, Harlow: Longman.

Piatt, Andrew A. (1904), 'The end of the Mexican dollar', *The Quarterly Journal of Economics*, **18**(3), 321–56.

Pond, Shepard (1941), 'The Spanish dollar: the world's most famous silver coin', *Bulletin of the Business Historical Society*, **15**(1), 12–16.

Rana, Pradumna B. (2002), 'Monetary and financial cooperation in East Asia: the Chiang Mai Initiative and beyond', ERD working paper no. 6, February, Asian Development Bank.

Ranjan, Rajiv and Anand Prakash (2010), 'Internationalisation of currency: the case of the Indian rupee and Chinese renminbi', *Reserve Bank of India Staff Studies*, 18 May.

Rathus, Joel (2010), 'Next generation on Asia', *East Asia Forum Quarterly*, **2**(3).

Reid, Anthony (1990), *Southeast Asia in the Age of Commerce, 1450–1680*, New Haven, CT: Yale University Press.

Rhee, S. Ghon (2005), 'Cross-border investment in Asian bonds', paper presented at the ADB Conference on Developing Bond Market in APEC: Toward Greater Public–Private Sector Regional Partnership, Tokyo, June.

Rhee, Yeongseop (2004), 'East Asian economic integration: destined to fail?', *Social Science Japan Journal*, **7**(1), 83–102.

Rogoff, Kenneth (2010), 'G20 needs to reform global governance', *Korea Herald*, 7 April.

Rose, Andrew K. (1999), 'Is there a case for an Asian monetary fund?', FRBSF Economic Letter no. 99-37.

Rose, Andrew K. (2000), 'One money, one market: the effect of common currencies on trade', *Economic Policy*, **5**(30), April.

Rothkopf, David (2008), 'The fund faces up to competition', *Financial Times*, 21 October.

Rozanov, Andrew (2005), 'Who holds the wealth of nations', *Central Banking Journal*, **15**(4).

Sánchez, M. (2005), 'Is Time ripe for a currency union in emerging East Asia: the role of monetary stabilization', European Central Bank working paper series no. 567.

Shimazaki, Hisaya (1989), *The History of the Invasion of the Yen*, Tokyo: Nihonkeizaihyoronsha, in Japanese.

Shin, Gwanho (2008), 'Global and regional shocks: challenges to Asian economies', ADBI working paper no. 120.

Shinohara, Hajime (1999), 'On the Asian monetary fund', *Institute for International Monetary Affairs Newsletter*, 4.

Shinjo, H. (1962), 'History of the Yen – 100 Years of Japanese Money-economy', Kobe University.

Siebert, Horst (2008), 'Preventing financial instability and currency crises', Kiel working paper no. 1401, February.

Sinn, Hans-Werner and Holger Feist (2000), 'Seignorage wealth in the Eurosystem: Eurowinners and Eurolosers revisited', CESifo working paper no. 353.

Steinherr, Alfred (1989), 'EMS and ECU: proposals for developing their synergy', in Paul De Grauwe et al. (eds), *The ECU and European Monetary Integration*, Macmillan.

Taguchi, Hiroo (1994), 'On the internationalization of the Japanese yen', in Takatoshi Ito and Anne O. Krueger (eds), *Macroeconomic Linkage: Savings, Exchange Rates and Capital Flows*, Chicago, IL: University of Chicago Press.

Takagi, Shinji (2008), 'Regional cooperation toward greater global stability: a medium-term agenda', mimeo, Osaka University.

Tang, H.C. (2006), 'An Asian monetary union?', CAMA working paper no. 13/2006.

Thaksin, Shinawatra (2002), 'Asia cooperation dialogue – the new Asian realism' keynote address by Thaksin Shinawatra, Prime Minister of Thailand at the East Asia Economic Summit, 6 October, Kuala Lumpur, accessed at www.asean.org/13965.htm.

Thurow, Lester (1992), *Head to Head: The Coming Economic Battle among Japan, Europe and America*, New York: William Morrow.

Twitchett, Denis Crispin and John King Fairbank (1980), *The Cambridge History of China*, Vol. 2, Cambridge, UK: Cambridge University Press.

Vaubel, Roland (1978), 'Real exchange rate changes in the European community: a new approach to the determination of optimum currency areas', *Journal of International Economics*, **8**, 319–39.

Von Glahn, Richard (1996), *Fountain of Fortune: Money and Monetary Policy in China 1000–1700*, Berkeley, CA: University of California Press.

Wade, Robert and Frank Venoroso (1998), 'The resources lie within', *The Economist*, 7 November, pp.19–21.

Watanabe, Shingo and Masanobu Ogura (2006), 'How far apart are the two ACUs from each other?: Asian currency unit and Asian currency union', Bank of Japan Working Paper Series, November.

Willett, Tom (2005), 'Some not entirely random thoughts on the political economy of regional integration', background paper for the Claremont-KIEP Conference, available at: http://www.cgu.edu/include/1118_TW1.pdf.

Williamson, John (2000), 'Exchange rate regimes for emerging markets: reviving the intermediate option', *Policy Analyses in International Economics*, no. 60, Institute for International Economics.

World Bank (1993), *The East Asian Miracle: Economic Growth and Public Policy*, World Bank Policy Research Report, Oxford University Press.

World Bank, various issues, *World Development Indicators*.

Wyplosz, Charles (1997), 'EMU: why and how it might happen', *Journal of Economic Perspectives*, **11**(Fall), 3–22.

Wyplosz, Charles (1998), 'The culture of economic policy advice: an international comparison with special emphasis on Europe', paper presented at the Research Colloquium on the State and Development of the Transfer Process of Economic Knowledge, St. Gallen, Switzerland, 17–19 June.

Wyplosz, Charles (2001), 'A monetary union in Asia? Some European lessons', mimeo, accessed at www.rba.gov.au/publications/confs/2001/wyplosz.pdf.

Yam, Joseph (1997), 'Asian monetary cooperation', The Jacobsson Lecture, September, Hong Kong.

Yam, Joseph (2004), 'The case for an Asian bond market', opening speech at the Asia Pacific Bond Market Congress, 8–9 July, Hong Kong.

Yoon, Deok Ryong, Yeongseop Rhee, Jonghwa Lee and Hee-Yul Chai (2005), *Evaluation of Conditions and Possibility for East Asian Monetary Integration*, Seoul: Ministry of Finance and Economy, in Korean.

Yoon, Young Kwan (1999), 'The political economy of regional integration process: Europe and East Asia', paper presented at the seminar on Models of Integration in Asia and Europe: Generating a Global Space for a Common Future, 19–21 October, Kyoto, Japan.

Yoshitomi, Masaru and Sayuri Shirai (2000), 'Technical background paper for policy recommendations for preventing another capital account crisis', Asian Development Bank Institute, Tokyo.

Young, Arthur N. (1965), *China's Wartime Finance and Inflation, 1937–1945*, Cambridge, MA: Harvard University Press.

Young, Arthur N. (1971), *China's Nation Building Effort, 1927–1937: The Financial and Economic Record*, Stanford: Hoover Press.

Yu, Yongding (2001), 'Lessons from Asian financial crisis', Research Center for International Finance working paper series no. 1, Chinese Academy of Social Sciences.

Yuen, H. (2001), 'Optimum currency areas in East Asia', *ASEAN Economic Bulletin*, **18**(2), 206–17.

Zhang, Z., K. Sato and M. McAleer (2004), 'Is a monetary union feasible for East Asia?', *Applied Economics*, **36**, 1031–43.

Index

surveillance mechanism 164
sustained economic growth 1
swap arrangement 164
symmetry of shocks 67

tael 7, 11, 17
target zone 167, 177
Technical Assistance Coordination
    Team (TACT) 137
Temasek 132
Thygesen, Niels 176
trade interdependence 67–70
transaction costs 89
Trans-Pacific Partnership (TPP) 195
Treaty of Peace and Amity 14
Treaty on European Union 174
Triffin dilemma 170
trilateral cooperative projects 204
trilateral summit meeting 204
Turner, Philip 127, 156
twin fears 128

unilateral intervention 155

Vaubel, Roland 164
vehicle currency 168

Very Short Term Financing Facility
    (VSTFF) 179, 180
volatility of capital flows 154

Watanabe, Shingo 65, 82
Wei, Shang-Jin 89
Willet, Tom 191
Williamson, John 178
Working Group on Financial Markets
    134
World Bank 103
Wyplosz, Charles 86, 132, 142, 154,
    185

Yam, Joseph 97, 110, 133
yang 16, 17
yen bloc 7, 22, 29–33
Yen-Dollar Committee 107
yen peg 154
ying-yang (eagle dollars) 12
Yoon, DeokRyong 81, 175
Yoshitomi, Masaru 118
Yu, Yongding 151, 168, 204
yuan 12

Zhou, Xiaochuan 170